T0390156

Contemporary Bali

Agung Wardana

Contemporary Bali

Contested Space and Governance

Agung Wardana
Universitas Gadjah Mada
Yogyakarta, Indonesia

ISBN 978-981-13-2477-2 ISBN 978-981-13-2478-9 (eBook)
https://doi.org/10.1007/978-981-13-2478-9

Library of Congress Control Number: 2018964261

Cover illustration: Bruno Guerreiro

This Palgrave Macmillan imprint is published by the registered company Springer Nature Singapore Pte Ltd.
The registered company address is: 152 Beach Road, #21-01/04 Gateway East, Singapore 189721, Singapore

To: My Mentor, Dr. Carol Warren

Acknowledgements

I have taken up research on this topic not only out of intellectual curiosity, but also from a sense of personal responsibility. As a Balinese trained as a lawyer, I have been involved in environmental and spatial governance issues in Bali for some years. At first, I should admit that as a lawyer, I used to believe that in order to transform society we have to have laws in the first place. I naively assumed law, which is referred exclusively to state law, as the engine of change and the answer to all societal problems. In 2009, I had the privilege of becoming directly involved as an NGO representative on a legal drafting team to formulate the 2009 Provincial Regulation on Spatial Planning (Perda RTRW Bali No. 16/2009). With other NGO representatives on the team, we proposed including the *Bhisama* religious rulings, provincial strategic areas, and other measures, which we assumed would be able to address Bali's current challenges. However, the outcomes from these efforts at regulation were not what had been expected. Hence, this research in which this book is derived was basically to understand why Bali's spatial governance regime fails to achieve its objectives in addressing the current environmental crisis.

My encounter with socio-legal research and legal anthropology has enriched my perspectives to understand how the law is actually conceived and practiced in a given society. While Margaret Mead is fascinated by anthropology as "something of revelation", my turn to anthropology is actually a search for possibilities, a possibility for social transformation.

In this light, I am indebted to my former PhD principle supervisor Dr. Carol Warren for introducing me to the anthropological lens in understanding better the complexities of the society where I live in and to be sensible towards them. Her patience and encouragement have been very important for the completion of my thesis that is further transformed into this book. I also owe my former co-supervisors, Dr. Jaqui Baker and Dr. Jo Goodie, for their guidance in completing my thesis.

I was very pleased to receive comments on my research project at the Asia Research Centre, Murdoch University, Australia, at an early stage from Prof. Jim Warren, Prof. Vedi R. Hadiz, Prof. Kevin Hewison, Prof. Garry Rodan, Prof. David Hill, Dr. Jane Hutchison, Dr. Ian Wilson, Dr. Shahar Hameiri, and Prof. Benjamin Reilly. I am also indebted to Prof. Keebet von Benda-Beckmann, Dr. Graeme MacRae, and Prof. Adriaan Bedner, Dr. Mary Zurbuchen, and Dr. Anette Fagertun, whose comments and feedback help me to shape and refine my arguments.

During my PhD at the Asia Research Centre, Murdoch University, I was delighted to have very supportive colleagues. They are Dr. Yanti Muchtar (RIP), Dr. Dirk Steenbergen, Dr. Charanpal Bal, Dr. Fabio Scarpello, Rebecca Mackelburg, Lian Sinclair, Dr. Charlotte Pham, Dr. Muninggar Saraswati, Dr. Melissa Johnston, Dr. Airlangga Pribadi Kusman, Dr. Asep Iqbal, Dr. Diswandi, Nurul Aini, Dr. Faris Al Fadhat, Dr. Sait Abdulah, Hikmawan Saefullah, Irwansyah, Rod, Dr. Patricia Dacudao, Lisa Woodward, and Jely Galang. In the fieldwork, I would like to thank Nyoman Sutama, Iwan Dewantama, Luh Kartini, Viebeke Lengkong, Bangun Nusantara, Wayan Bagia, as well as Pak Rebo, for their support and hospitality.

I have also been supported by my big family in Tabanan, Batubulan, and Gianyar, colleagues in Denpasar (Agung Alit & Hani Duarsa; Pak Arca; Taman 65—Termana, Ika, Putra, Degung, Candra; Arisan 2 Are; Yayasan Wisnu—Pak Suar, Denik, Lisa and Atiek; Komunitas Pojok—Dewa Ketha and Wiss; and Tjok Agung Tresna networks—Ngurah Karyadi, Sri Widhiyanti, Agus Samijaya, Bob Tirja, Made Nurbawa, and Giriyasa) as well as the Balinese community in Perth (Bli Wika and family, Bli Satrya and family, Bli Eka Sucahya and family, Bli Made Kurniawan and family, Bli Komang and family). I have been very fortunate to be accompanied, motivated, and supported by my beloved Yogi Mitha and the boys, Chanakya and Bhanu, during difficult times in completing this book.

Moreover, the Faculty of Law, Universitas Gadjah Mada, has been very supportive in the publication of this book. Here, I would like to express my gratitude to the Dean, Prof. Sigit Riyanto, and the Deputy Deans (Dr. Dahliana, Dr. Herliana, and Dr. Mailinda), academic staffs, colleagues in the Department of Environmental Law (Pak Harry, Mas Yun, Mas Totok, Bu Fajar, Mba Dinar), and the MIH Jakarta management (Prof Sulistiowati, Siti, Beta, Debby, Donald, Elsa, and Pak Yono).

Last but not least, I would like to express my special thanks to Murdoch University for awarding me a Murdoch International Postgraduate Scholarship (MIPS) from which this study was generously funded. Without the scholarship, this book would not have been possible in the first place. I believe that there is no such thing as an individual achievement, and my achievement in completing this piece of work to a larger extent has been shaped by generous people around me. Without their contributions, I would not have undergone this intellectual journey. All errors in this book, however, remain solely mine.

Yogyakarta, Indonesia
June 2018

Agung Wardana

Contents

Abbreviations

AAA	Akademisi, Agama, Adat
AMDAL	Analisis Mengenai Dampak Lingkungan
ANDAL	Analisis Dampak Lingkungan
ASITA	Association of the Indonesian Tours and Travel Agencies
BAL	Basic Agrarian Law
Bappeda	Badan Perencanaan Pembangunan Daerah
Bapedalda	Badan Pengendali Dampak Lingkungan Hidup Daerah
BBI	Bali Benoa International
BBM	Bali Benoa Marina
BNPB	Badan Nasional Penganggulangan Bencana
BNR	Bakrie Nirwana Resort
BPD	Badan Perwakilan Desa
BPG	Bali Pecatu Graha
BPN	Badan Pertanahan Nasional
BPS	Badan Pusat Statistik
BTDC	Bali Tourism Development Corporation
BTI	Barisan Tani Indonesia
BTID	Bali Turtle Island Development
CDM	Clean Development Mechanism
CMEA	Coordinating Ministry for Economic Affairs
CSR	Corporate Social Responsibility
DPD	Dewan Perwakilan Daerah
DPRD	Dewan Perwakilan Rakyat Daerah

FPM	Forum Peduli Mangrove
HGB	Hak Guna Bangunan
ICOMOS	International Council on Monuments and Sites
ILIC	Indonesia Land Investment Company
IMB	Izin Mendirikan Bangunan
IUCN	International Union for Conservation of Nature
Kadin	Kamar Dagang dan Industri
KIPEM	Kartu Identitas Penduduk Musiman
LEKRA	Lembaga Kebudayaan Rakyat
LPM	Lembaga Pemberdayaan Masyarakat
LPPM	Lembaga Penelitian dan Pemberdayaan Masyarakat
MCT	Ministry of Culture and Tourism
MP3EI	Masterplan Percepatan dan Perluasan Pembangunan Ekonomi Indonesia
MUDP	Majelis Utama Desa Pakraman
NGO	Non-Governmental Organisation
Pansus	Panitia Khusus
PDAM	Perusahaan Daerah Air Minum
PDI-P	Partai Demokrasi Indonesia Perjuangan
PEMSEA	Partnership in Environmental Management for the Seas of East Asia
Perda	Peraturan Daerah
PHDI	Parisada Hindu Dharma Indonesia
PHR	Pajak Hotel dan Restaurant
PMO	Project Management Office
PNI	Partai Nasional Indonesia
PT	Perusahaan Terbatas
Repelita	Rencana Pembangunan Lima Tahun
RKL/RPL	Rencana Pengelolaan Lingkungan/Rencana Pemantauan Lingkungan
RPJM	Rencana Pembangunan Jangka Menengah/ Mid-Term Development Plan
RTRW	Rencana Tata Ruang Wilayah
SAP	Structural Adjustment Program
SARBAGITA	Denpasar, Badung, Gianyar and Tabanan
SCETO	*Societe Centrale pour l'Equipement Touristique Outre-Mer*
TBTR	Tanjung Benoa Tolak Reklamasi
TWBI	Tirta Wahana Bali Internasional

TWNC	Tambling Wildlife Nature Conservation
UNDP	United Nations Development Program
UNECE	United Nations Economic Commission for Europe
UNESCO	United Nations Educational, Scientific and Cultural Organization
UNOCD	United Nations Office on Drugs and Crime
UPT	Unit Pelaksana Teknis
WALHI	Wahana Lingkungan Hidup Indonesia
WHC	World Heritage Committee

List of Figures

List of Tables

1

Introduction

In late 2017, Mount Agung erupted. Villages surrounding the mountain were evacuated in panic and confusion. The last time the biggest mountain in Bali situated in Karangasem District erupted was in 1963, causing a thousand deaths. One important source of confusion was in fact triggered by inconsistent information provided by the state institutions, especially on the level of eruption and those responsible for management of the emergency response. The Badan Nasional Penanggulangan Bencana (BNPB/National Body for Disaster Management) declared the scale of eruption as a provincial-level disaster, and in the end of November, it announced the highest level of warning of '*awas*' (alert). The announcement was covered widely by national as well as international media, resulting in a negative reaction from the tourism industry and high-ranking officials, who accused the coverage of being economically motivated by Bali's competitors in terms of tourism, especially Thailand (*Radar Bali*, 12/12/2018). The representatives of the tourism industry protested BNPB's declaration as it might affect tourist visits and result in visitor cancellations. According to the Minister of Tourism, this might cause a US$ 1.2 billion potential economic loss because the end of the year is the high season of Bali's tourism (Topsfield 2017).

A. Wardana, *Contemporary Bali*, https://doi.org/10.1007/978-981-13-2478-9_1

In December, the Indonesia Hotel and Restaurant Association (PHRI) of Bali sent a letter to President Jokowi demanding the national government to take a necessary action to restore the situation (*Kompas*, 13/12/2018). The letter also stated that the industry would undertake mass labour redundancies if tourist visits continued to decline. Eventually, the national government responded to these demands by downgrading the level 4 '*awas*' (danger) into the level 3 '*siaga*' (alert) and downscaled it to a district-level disaster. In late December 2017, President Jokowi even visited Kuta Beach to send a message to the world that it was safe to travel to Bali. The direct promotion from the president seemed to manage a gradual increase in tourist visits to the island. Meanwhile information and matters related to managing the response to the eruption have been localised reaching only villages surrounding the mountain. When the initial level 4 warning was declared by the BNPB through mass media coverage as well as social media, people across Bali and beyond spontaneously mobilised donations and transportations for evacuees and offered the refugees places to stay and build refugee camps (*Antara News*, 24/09/2018). As the result of localisation and downgrading, refugees staying in refugee camps beyond Karangasem District became less exposed to public eyes, leaving them under-resourced.

This crisis experience demonstrates the influence of the tourism industry in Bali. The declaration of a natural disaster that is supposed to ensure human safety and security as the first priority was compromised for the industry's benefits. Cok Ace, the Chairman of Hotel and Restaurants Entrepreneurs Association and the future Vice Governor of Bali (2018–2023), suggested the tourism industry to capitalise the disaster as a new tourist attraction (*Bali Post*, 03/10/2017). Interestingly, the spokesperson of the National Body for Disaster Management, Sutopo Purwo Nugroho, also proposed a similar response that watching Mount Agung's eruption should be developed as a potential disaster tourism, as it would be a unique, once in a lifetime experience (*The Strait Times*, 29/10/2017). Tourism, as MacCannell (1992, 1) puts it, "is not just an aggregate of merely commercial activities, it is also an ideological framing of history, nature, and traditions; a framing that has the power to reshape culture and nature to its own needs". In other words, tourism is an economic structure that has the power to inform the ways in which a society should conceive of and perceive itself. In Bali, introduced by the

Dutch Colonial in the early twentieth century, the tourism industry has been growing rapidly, in the process compromising environmental sustainability and commodifying local culture (Picard 1996; Vickers 2012). The marginalisation of local communities, social and cultural displacement, as well as violence, contributed to the expansion of tourism on the island under the authoritarian regime of Suharto and has continued since (Aditjondro 1995; Warren 1998).

Following the fall of Suharto's authoritarian regime in the late 1990s, the state structure was reconfigured through a process of decentralisation. Here, decentralisation should be seen as a form of downward rescaling in which governance is transferred from the national to the regional government. This reconfiguration of space and governance was a response to internal pressures from disaffected regions and to external pressures from the World Bank and the International Monetary Fund seeking to liberalise the Indonesian economy (Schulte Nordholt and van Klinken 2007; Hadiz 2010; von Benda-Beckmann and von Benda-Beckmann 2013). In this process, authorities were notably transferred from the national government to district rather than to provincial level government, in part, because decentralisation to the provincial level was considered to threaten national integrity (McCarthy and Warren 2009, 5), but also because decentralisation to the district level had long been regarded as a mechanism for promoting neoliberal development and deregulation agendas (Hadiz 2010). Hence, under this new regime, the district government has become a new locus of power to pursue development across the archipelago.

Under decentralised governance, Bali's eight districts and one municipality[1] have acquired a strong sense of authority to govern their territories (Wardana 2015). Economically, Badung is the richest district in the province because of its administrative and geographical position, where mature tourism infrastructures, including Kuta and Nusa Dua as well as Ngurah Rai International Airport, are situated. In 2014, Badung's local revenues (PAD—*pendapatan asli daerah*) reached US$ 195 million—

[1] These are the districts of Badung, Gianyar, Tabanan, Jembrana, Buleleng, Karangasem, Bangli, Klungkung, and Denpasar Municipality.

much larger than the other eight districts' revenues combined (BPS Bali 2015, 422).[2] More than 70% of Badung's revenue is derived from the tourism sector, primarily from hotel and restaurant taxes (*Tribun Bali*, 01/04/2015). The economic success of Badung from the tourism industry has had a 'demonstration effect', encouraging the other districts in Bali to follow Badung's path of development.

All districts have been competing to attract tourism investments and to extract revenues from such investments within their territory. In doing so, they often disregard the impacts of development beyond their territorial borders, not to mention side effects within. Promoting tourist investment provides opportunities for regional elites to engage in rent-seeking practices and chase easy money from granting permits or acting as local brokers. Hence, tourism and its related industries, especially the real estate and property businesses, have spread across the island while the provincial government made little effort to control district competition and the alarming path of development although it has the authority to supervise these.[3] In fact, despite its proclaimed concern for balancing development and protecting the island's culture and environment, the provincial government has also pursued policies that exacerbate these problems.

These accumulative impacts in the development of the tourism industry in Bali have affected social and environmental conditions in contemporary Bali. Many scholars have observed Bali reaching its tipping point that has led towards a socio-ecological crisis (Reuter 2003; Lewis and Lewis 2009; Suryani et al. 2009; *Bali Post*, 11/01/2009; Fox 2012). Productive agricultural land is converted to support tourism infrastructure (resorts, hotels, villas, and golf courses) in the framework of a mass tourism-oriented model of development, at a rate of around 1000 hectares

[2] In 2014, these districts' local revenues were A$ 8.9 million (Jembrana); A$ 27 million (Tabanan); $A 42 million (Gianyar); A$ 9.8 million (Klungkung); A$ 7.6 million (Bangli); A$ 24 million (Karangasem); A$ 22 million (Buleleng); and A$ 69.8 million (Denpasar) (BPS Bali 2015, 422–424).

[3] One example of the ineffective policy by the Provincial Government was 'the moratorium' of new hotel development in 2011. The appeal was not fully respected by investors and the district government (see *Detik News*, 09/02/2011).

per year (Warren 2009), threatening the *subak*—the traditional irrigation society—which is regarded by many observers as the foundation of Balinese culture (MacRae and Alit Arthawiguna 2011). Conflicts over public space, including coastal areas and sacred sites, have become more common (see Suartika 2005; *Bali Post*, 20/9/2011; Wardana 2014b; Strauss 2015). Tourism is also a water-intensive industry that diverts water from basic needs and is predicted to lead to a water crisis by 2025 (Cole 2012; Cole and Browne 2015) causing conflicts between the *subak*, the government, and the tourism industry (*Bali Post* 26/3/2007; 10/1/2011; Strauss 2011; Kurnianingsih n.d.). Pollution and rubbish have also increased alarmingly (Dharma Putra 2009; Marshall 2011).

Analysis of the contemporary crises in Bali above is conceived politically and intellectually based on three perspectives. The first one is the rational-choice approach, which considers that these are natural transformations that are the product of a rational calculation of costs and benefits to maximise individual wealth. In the context of the crisis of Bali's agrarian heritage, for instance, the approach has been dominantly used to examine the trend of land conversion from agricultural land into tourism facilities, which is seen to be caused by the unprofitability of agriculture compared to tourism (Sutawan 2001; Indonesia. MCT 2011; Pitana and Adi Putra 2013). Accordingly, policies to provide incentives through agro-business, agro-tourism, as well as village tourism by integrating agricultural activities as a cultural practice into the tourism industry have been introduced. Regarding the process as driven by the individual choices of local farmers, however, this approach fails to bring accumulation and dispossession into the picture of the agrarian crisis in the island.

The second analytic framework is the conservative approach, which treats the crisis as a product of external forces, such as globalisation. These forces in turn have altered Balinese culture and values that are essentially rooted in the doctrine of *Tri Hita Karana* (three causes of happiness)—a balanced relation to the spiritual, social, and natural worlds. Accordingly, Balinese society that was supposed to be collective, religious, and harmonious has turned into a society based on individualism, materialism, hedonism, and conflicts (Atmadja 2010a). Such changes in the cultural values have brought Bali into social, cultural, and environmental crises which should be addressed, according to this approach, by reinforcing the Balinese identity as articulated in the *Ajeg Bali* movement, in order to prevent the negative aspects of globalisations. Schulte Nordholt (2007) points out the paradoxical nature of the conservative project and calls BaliBaliisland as "open fortress". On the one hand, Balinese culture is protected by establishing a fortress guarding it from external influences; on the other hand, Bali is economically dependent on the tourist economy supported by the flows of foreign tourists to the islands. Hence, the conservative approach consciously or unconsciously props up the tourism industry, the main driver of globalisation on the island, by searching for a marketable alternative or 'authentic' Bali.

A third perspective is based on the institutionalist approach. It treats the crisis as one primarily caused by changing the institutional structures from centralism to decentralism, which transferred authorities to district governments in a relatively small province of Bali. Since the mid-2000s, the establishment of district autonomy has been challenged by many forces. Provincial government officials, members of the Provincial House of Representatives (DPRD Bali), academics, and even civil society organisations appear to agree that decentralisation at the district government level has accelerated the socio-ecological crisis (Pansus Otsus 2007; Atmadja 2010a; Suharyo 2011; *Antara News*, 25/09/2014). Proposed solutions based on this approach include restructuring the regional governmental institutions further by pushing the regional autonomy regime 'upward' under the banner of 'one island one management' through special autonomy at the provincial government level, and 'downward' to recognise the autonomy of the *adat* village (*desa pakraman*) (Pansus Otsus 2007; Ramstedt 2013). Moreover, regional autonomy is also pushed 'outward' by transferring state authority governing space to private enterprise, as we shall see in the case of Benoa Bay. Such rescaling strategies are undertaken in order to avoid compromising the unitary structure of the Indonesian state, the ultimate basis for political consensus in the country.

For those three perspectives, the enactment of the new Spatial Planning Law No. 26/2007 provided an opportunity to address the crisis by pursuing the 'one island one management' project. This project was assumed to enable the creation of a comparable tourist economy across the island, the reunification of the fragmented Balinese cultural identity, and the control of development and rent-seeking practices at the district levels as the impact of decentralisation. For the Provincial Government of Bali, this was undertaken by designating areas within district territories that are considered provincially significant in terms of economy, security, ecology, and culture to become 'provincial strategic areas'. Accordingly, Memorandum of Understanding (MoU) No. 075/06/KB/B.PEM/2008 was signed in 2008 by the governor of Bali and all district/municipal heads in Bali to establish 'provincial strategic areas', including the three case study sites investigated in this book—the Uluwatu Temple Complex (Chap. 4), the Jatiluwih Rice-growing Areas (Chap. 5), and Benoa Bay (Chap. 6). The governance of these areas would be rescaled up to the provincial government for efficient and effective spatial governance. The MoU is indeed a legal strategy to bind the district governments in the decentralised era to submit their planning to the provincial government's direction, and also to anticipate future conflicts in governing those areas. In 2009, the MoU was incorporated within the new Provincial Regulation on Spatial Planning for Bali Province (Perda RTRW Bali No. 16/2009), which is used as a legal instrument by the provincial government to re-establish its regional predominance and reconfigure spatial organisation across the island.

The process of reorganising space, however, does not take place in a social vacuum. The institutional approach overlooks the fact that reorganising space through spatial planning remains embedded in existing power relations. Due to the significant material and symbolic values, contestations in accessing and controlling designated strategic areas have occurred not only within the state structures, but also between the state institutions and local communities. Not to mention, 'space' in Bali is not merely an economic resource, but is also the 'place' as the immediate site where meanings are invested and societal, cultural, environmental, as well as economic common goods may be pursued (McCarthy and Warren 2009). Consequently, a single unit of physical space is likely to be imagined and regulated divergently by different actors and institutions pursuing a range of interests and visions of the social world. The notion of spatial governance comes into this picture. Here, spatial governance refers to rules, processes, mechanisms, and institutions set and practised by state and non-state actors for articulating their interests and exercising their power over space, people, and resources. Unlike Razzaque (2013) who defines governance optimistically as a form of power sharing between state and non-state actors to pursue the sustainable management of natural resources, in this book, I am concerned with the contests of power that are shaped by antagonistic interests and competing visions of the social world.

In this book, I examine the dynamics of spatial governance in defining and regulating space, people, and resources, through contests over and accommodation to the state's spatial planning regime under the reform era of Indonesia. The particular focus of this book is on the ways in which such contestation and accommodation engage with the contemporary crisis confronting Bali. In so doing, I address three research questions: how spatial planning is used as a development strategy to address the rapidly changing environmental, socio-economic, political, and cultural contexts in contemporary Bali; how the complex legal and institutional configurations of decentralised governance interface with the spatial planning regime in advancing particular interests while constraining others; and how social forces respond to the reorganisation of space and its institutional arrangements. In answering these questions, an adequate analytical framework is needed to comprehend the fragmented and pluralistic nature of political and legal life and its socio-spatial implications in post-authoritarian Indonesia (Warren 2007; Aspinall 2013a; von Benda-Beckmann and von Benda-Beckmann 2013).

Spatial Governance and the Law

Spatial Planning: The Technocratic and Political Streams

In general, there are two main streams in spatial planning literature. The first one is the technocratic stream. In this stream, spatial planning is primarily studied as a scientific exercise in organising space. It also concerns how spatial planning should be conducted and improved by establishing adequate institutions (Healey 1997; Kidd and Shaw 2007; Faludi 2010) and introducing new approaches (Beard 2002; Schroll et al. 2012;

Kawakami et al. 2013) including information technology (Hermann and Osinski 1999; Wegener 2000). In this stream, the questions of ideology, power relations, and legal-political dynamics in planning practices are beyond its horizons. The second stream in spatial planning literature is the political stream that draws heavily on critical geographic literature, among others, Lefebvre (1991), Brenner (2004), Massey (2005), and Harvey (2005b). This stream seeks to understand the underlying rationales behind spatial planning policies and practices, for example, pursuing economic growth (Galland 2012; Ionescu-Heroiu et al. 2013), opening markets and expanding investment (Priemus 1997; Moroni 2007; Shibata 2008; Allmendinger and Haughton 2013), and establishing socio-economic and spatial segregation (Butler 2003; Peters 2009; Blank and Rosen-Zvi 2010).

The political stream is particularly relevant for analysing the use of spatial planning in the contexts of developing countries. This is because in these countries spatial planning has been an important component of development strategies to modernise and rationalise land use and accelerate economic growth. As Ionescu-Heroiu et al. (2013, 152) observed, spatial planning becomes essential for coordinating and directing investments into particular geographical spaces so that their positive impacts on economic development could be maximised. Structural reform to open up the market economy may also be served by spatial planning, as has been done in the post-Soviet countries. In those countries, spatial planning has been used to create value and property rights in land so that it could be "traded freely by agents who are thought to be the best judges of the locations most favourable for increasing their well-being and profitability" (Ionescu-Heroiu et al. 2013, 32; see also UNECE 2008).

Predominantly, spatial planning in the political stream is framed by liberal political theories. In this regard such planning is seen as a state instrument to protect land as a property right to direct productive use, and to control unreasonable or harmful uses against other property owners (Priemus 1997; Platt 2004; UNECE 2008; Ionescu-Heroiu et al. 2013). In other words, a spatial planning policy "theoretically both encourages and restrains the profit seeking behavior of private property ownership" (Platt 2004, 31). There is a fundamental tension in this liberal spatial planning approach between property ownership, which is intended to maximise its owners' personal profit in the private sphere, and objectives that aim to exercise governmental power in regulating the use of land according to public interest and environmental sustainability (Platt 2004; see also Priemus 1997). Accordingly, the state, assuming its neutrality within plural societal interests, has become the central institution to balance this tension within the frame of a constitutionally inscribed common goal. However, this liberal planning seems to be problematic within East Asian developing countries, where the distinction between public and private spheres is more or less blurred and the state is far from neutral due to its close collusion with vested interests (see Robison 1986; Jayasuriya 1999).

Spatial Planning in Neoliberal Times

More recently, scholars have pointed out that neoliberalism has been the prevailing idea of the century. Neoliberalism here refers to a "theory of political economic practices that proposes that human well-being can best be advanced by liberating individual entrepreneurial freedoms and skills within an institutional framework characterized by strong private property rights, free markets, and free trade" (Harvey 2005a, 2). The practices have brought important changes to spatial planning policies and practices. In the neoliberal time, space is 'reterritorialised' to accelerate circulation of "people, commodities, capital, money, identities and images through global space" (Brenner 1999, 431), in what many critical geographers call a 'neoliberalisation' of space (Peck and Tickell 2002; Brenner et al. 2010; Allmendinger and Haughton 2013). In this context, 'neoliberalism' is seen as a regulatory transformation process to pursue a free-market economy that is "variegated, geographically uneven, and path dependent" (Brenner et al. 2010, 327). Within this process, spatial planning plays an important part to reconfigure the existing spatial configuration and to re-scale its spatial governance 'upward', 'downward', or 'outward' to suit the expansion of market forces (Brenner 1999; Reed and Bruyneel 2010). 'Upward' governance refers to the transfer of the existing governance of a spatial unit to a higher tier of state institutions, for example, from regional to national governments, and 'downward' is undertaken by transferring spatial governance to a lower tier of government, for example, through decentralisation, while 'outward' refers to the transfer of spatial governance to non-state entities or to a state/non-state collaborative governing institution (Reed and Bruyneel 2010).

Accordingly, spatial planning becomes an essential instrument to establish neoliberal spatial governance (Allmendinger and Haughton 2013). In governance, the state itself is not absent but plays its role as both a governing partner and a meta-regulator, providing a legitimate framework for its arrangement (Santos 2005). In other words, the role of the state in the era of neoliberal governance becomes "less hierarchical, less centralised, and less *dirigiste* in character" (Jessop 1998, 43) in order to establish its claim to offer a more efficient, effective, and democratic governing technology (Sorensen and Triantafillou 2009).

In these neoliberal times, terms like efficiency, participation, and the rule of law have become mantras in spatial planning. Efficient spatial planning enhanced by public participation and the rule of law, Ionescu-Heroiu et al. (2013) argue, would lead to better economic outcomes, because it has a strategic role in driving development and curbing market inefficiencies. As a state policy to govern its territory, spatial planning, which used to be hierarchical and centralised through national government, has been transformed into a more inclusive model as a coordinative framework in enhancing governmental effectiveness and efficiency, the central aspect of good governance (UNECE 2008; Ionescu-Heroiu et al. 2013). In this regard, the state is not the only actor in planning the use of space, but the private sector and civil society also now have increasing opportunities to become formally involved in spatial planning, from design to implementation (Hudallah 2010; Galland 2012). Decentralisation in spatial planning is also encouraged to foster diversity in land use and spatial organisation, as well as competition between regions or localities for capital investment (Galland 2012; Allmendinger and Haughton 2013; Rukmana 2015).

Indonesia is not an exception in responding to these global forces. In the post-Suharto era, environmental and spatial governance has more or less been informed by these global neoliberal forces (see Arnscheidt 2009). Due to the reorganising of the state's institutional structures from centralism to decentralism, the 1992 centralistic spatial planning law

(Law No. 24/1992) was considered no longer relevant for pursuing development under the regional autonomy regime and contemporary market-oriented policies (Rukmana 2015). In 2007, a new spatial planning law (Law No. 26/2007) was enacted hand-in-hand with the adoption of new laws dealing with investments (Law No. 25/2007),[4] as well as coastal area and small island management (Law No. 27/2007)[5] and following the adjustment of natural resources-related legislation. These legislative changes were part of a post-crisis reform package outlined in the Government of Indonesia—International Monetary Fund (IMF) Letters of Intent (LoI) which sets out how the structural adjustment and legal reform agenda in post-crisis Indonesia should be undertaken by the government. It stipulated reform not only in the financial, investment and banking systems but also reform in environmental, natural resources, as well as energy sectors to bring them into line with global markets.[6] Hence, the environmental and spatial governance during this era has become a product of the 'amalgamation of law' in which "various elements from different legal systems" have been adopted to fit changing Indonesian structural conditions (Bedner 2008, 172).

The new spatial planning law uses a comprehensive spatial planning approach that not only deals with plan making (*perencanaan ruang*), but also space utilisation (*pemanfaatan ruang*) and space utilisation control (*pengendalian pemanfataan ruang*) by giving bigger roles than before for regional government to implement those tasks (Hudallah 2010; Rukmana 2015). Hudallah (2010) argues that this new spatial planning law is the

[4] For the first time, Investment Law No. 25/2007 does not conceptually differentiate between 'foreign investment' (*penanaman modal asing*) and 'domestic investment' (*penanaman modal dalam negeri*); consequently, they have similar treatment under the Indonesian economic law regime (Article 6 of Law No. 25/2007). This legal framework follows the World Trade Organisation's (WTO) basic principle of 'non-discrimination', especially the norm of 'national-treatment' in which a state party should treat economic actors equally regardless their country of origin.

[5] The Coastal Area and Small Island Management Law No. 27/2007 gave the authority to the government to grant a *hak pengusahaan perairan pesisir* (HP3/the right of business in coastal waters) to non-state enterprises in utilising and managing a designated water area. However, in June 2011, the provisions on HP3 were finally revoked by the Constitutional Court because they violated the 1945 Constitution by opening coastal water areas to privatisation and commercialisation, which might disrupt local livelihoods within such areas (see Putusan MK No. 3/PUU-VIII/2010).

[6] See LoI on 16 March 1999; 20 January 2000; 7 September 2000; 31 December 2001.

product of domestic institutional and neoliberal globalising forces aimed at opening up new circuits for capital, labour, and commodities in Indonesia (see also Hudallah and Woltjer 2007). Under this current model, spatial planning is directed to provide sufficient information, protection of property rights, zoning regulations, and incentives that would assist markets to calculate cost and benefit in making proper decisions for investment. In some sectors, such as housing, water supply, and infrastructure development, the role of the private sector is strongly encouraged under public-private partnership or purely private investment schemes (Hudallah 2010). Unlike the previous law that only gave the authority to designate a special purpose area (*kawasan tertentu*) to the national government, the current law gives similar authority to all tiers of government to designate their own strategic areas (*kawasan strategis*) in terms of economy, environment, socio-cultural matters, security, and defence (Rukmana 2015). As will be seen in the case study chapters, these designations have become highly contentious in Bali.

In brief, the political stream planning literature provides an important insight for unpacking the underlying political-economic logics behind spatial planning. Paradoxically, although the planning system is usually defined as a "system of law and procedure that sets the ground for planning practice" (Healey 1997, 72; see also Hudallah 2010; Moeliono 2011), the question of the role of law tends to be ignored in the literature. Indeed, spatial planning is not merely a state policy, but relies upon law through which the policy is implemented and imposed upon a populace. By ignoring the role of law in planning, this approach consequently also overlooks the implications of such laws on social, economic, political, and cultural domains. Therefore, in the next subsection, I will look at the literature on legal geography in which the relationship between space, law, and development, including in the context of spatial governance, has been the specific object of inquiries.

Space, Law, and Development

The spatial turn in socio-legal studies has become one of the most significant developments in legal theory over the past two decades, by forcing law to be grounded (Philippopoulos-Mihalopoulos 2012). A number of scholars have devoted their work to theorising and examining the interrelations between law and space by borrowing approaches from other disciplines, including political geography (Blomley et al. 2001; Butler 2003; Delaney 2005; Blank and Rosen-Zvi 2010), political economy as well as hermeneutic (Santos 1987; Blomley and Clark 1990; Blomley 1994; Mahmud 2011), and post-structural frameworks of analysis (Taylor 2006; Philippopoulos-Mihalopoulos 2010a, b).

In his seminal book entitled *Law, Space, and the Geographies of Power* (1994, xii), Nicholas Blomley attempts to elaborate the interrelationship between law and space in society, and argues that neither space nor law is "an empty or objective category"; both directly relate to the way "power [is] deployed and social life [is] structured". Santos (1987, 282), for instance, treats law as a map, observing that "the relations law entertains with social reality are much similar to those between maps and spatial reality. Indeed, laws are maps; written laws are cartographic maps; customary, informal laws are mental maps". Mahmud (2011, 105) coins the term 'geo-legal space' to describe the relationship between law and space in facilitating the global system of domination and exploitation under capitalism, which at the same time provides "the field of possibilities for both operations of power and subaltern resistance".

Heavily informed by the 'interpretive turn' in the social sciences, these scholars tend to confine themselves to the "symbolic use of space as metaphor for indeterminacy, contingency and difference" (Butler 2009, 316). Avoiding the merely metaphorical or symbolic use of space in legal geography, Butler (2003) and Blank and Rosen-Zvi (2010) employ Lefebvre's theory of space to examine the production of suburbia in post-war Australia and the production of social space in Israeli contexts respectively. They similarly note the illuminating framework of Lefebvre's (1991) *The Production of Space*, which analyses space along three dimensions—physical (referring to its physical features), mental (referring the subjective aspects of space, particularly how space is conceived and designated by planners or state institutions), and social (referring to intersubjective dimensions, especially how space is socially experienced by its inhabitants). In this regard, these scholars examine the relational production of space by emphasising how spatial planning (mental space) shapes and is shaped by the other two dimensions.

Despite such important developments, the emerging field of legal geography suffers from two related problems. First of all, it is mostly developed within urban and industrialised country contexts. Secondly, although several of these writers complicate the notion of law by criticising its liberal legal character in the case of Kedar (2003), or by expanding its concept of legal production in the case of Philippopoulos-Mihalopoulos (2010b), to a large degree they retain the state legal system as the centre of gravity. Accordingly, for them, almost nothing is 'law' but state law. In fact, given the different historical, socio-economic, political, legal, and cultural conditions of developing countries, these approaches are not well-equipped to grasp the interfaces between the complex legal and institutional constellations—ranging from state to international, as well as customary and religious legal orders—and to cover multiple scales of spatial construction in developing countries (von Benda-Beckmann et al. 2009).

In developing countries, the mutually constitutive interrelationship between law and space can closely be analysed in the field of spatial governance. However, in Indonesia, legal geography, as a relatively new theme in legal studies until recently, remains under-explored. Only few legal scholars have attempted to analyse the relationship between law and space in the Indonesian spatial planning regime, including Moeliono (2011), Lisdiyono (2008), Rijadi (2004), and Silanawa (2008). All of them, however, still confine their approaches within the paradigm of 'legal centralism' (Griffiths 1986) in which spatial planning is examined solely as the product of state legal frameworks (Rijadi 2004; Lisdiyono 2008; and Silanawa 2008) and analysis of the socio-legal gap between 'law-on-the-books' and 'law-in-action' (Moeliono 2011). Moeliono (2011), for example, frames his thesis around the Indonesian concept of *Negara Hukum* (a state based on the Rule of Law) where the law is seen as the primary instrument of the state for pursuing its objectives. In this regard, Moeliono tends towards a form of 'legal centralism', where legal pluralism is seen as a barrier to the unification of the state legal system that should govern the society and that is more appropriate to 'nation building and modernisation'. None of these writers attempt to examine the pluralistic legal and multiple spatial configurations of Indonesia by broadening their analysis of the legal construction of space as relational, plural, and an ongoing process, and less inclined to explore why socio-legal gaps exist and are exacerbated in Indonesia's decentralised era.

The question then becomes: how are the discussions of space, law, and development relevant in the contexts of contemporary Bali? To answer this question, it is important firstly to consider the meanings of space in Bali. Lorenzen and Roth (2015) have pointed out that space has very diverse meanings involving different interests and visions of the social world, which sometimes involve ambivalence between its instrumental values and its intrinsic values. Warren (2005b, 62), for instance, observes how community mapping precipitated fundamental debates within Balinese communities regarding the meanings of space and resources attached to it, especially land, between social and cultural values tied to place and market-oriented economic values commodifying space. Clearly, space remains an important locus where people's conceptions of a 'commonweal'—a domain organised to pursue collective goods, including economic, social and cultural values—is grounded (Warren and McCarthy 2009). These identities of place, as Massey (1994, 5) put it, "are always unfixed, contested and multiple". Thus, reducing the multiple meanings attached to space and identities of place into a merely instrumentalist value would create new ambiguities, complexities, tensions, and even conflicts over space and place (Lorenzen and Roth 2015).

The ways in which social actors become involved in conflicts over space has been made more complicated by the rapidly changing conditions of legal and institutional pluralism in contemporary Bali (Warren 1993, 2007). This pluralistic legal and institutional constellation arises not only within the state structures resulting from contemporary decentralisation, but also within Balinese society as a historical condition since the pre-colonial period, including the dual *adat* and *dinas* village governance institutions, as well as other local institutions dealing with specific aspects of community organisation, for example, *subak* (Balinese traditional irrigation society), *seka* (common interest groups), *dadia* (clan groups), and others (Geertz 1959; Warren 1993). These local institutions, as 'semi-autonomous social fields' (Moore 1973), are capable of employing their own rules and frameworks in the governance of space, resources, and people within their designated territories or social spheres. Hence, their role in the study on spatial governance in Bali should not be underestimated.

Problematising the Notions of Space and Law

In an edited book entitled *Spatializing Law*, F. von Benda-Beckmann et al. (2009) push legal geography further to examine the connection between law and space in a pluralistic legal setting. Many of these attempts to fill the gaps, however, continue to be oriented towards a metaphorical use of space that characterised the earlier geography of law (see Whitecross 2009; Griffiths and Kandel 2009; Anders 2009; Wilmsen 2009). With the exception of contributions by Wiber (2009), F. von Benda-Beckmann and K. von Benda-Beckmann (2009), and Bakker (2009), chapters in the book mostly examine the interactions between what Lefebvre (1991) calls mental space and social space, especially how the pluralistic legal constructions of space shape or perpetuate the ways people perceive space and identities. Those interactions leave aside the third dimension of physical space. Consequently, they are unable to examine systematically how both mental and social spaces are grounded in physical space and, of course, with what material consequences for inhabitants and their environment (von Benda-Beckmann 2009).

The book, especially its introduction, provides important insights for a legal geography research agenda within the context of developing countries where the law is far from a single, unified, or coherent system, as it is commonly conceived in industrialised countries. Indeed, F. von Benda-Beckmann et al. (2009) as the editors critically interrogate the notion of law in space by employing the analytical concept of law inherited in the legal pluralism tradition as their point of departure. In this tradition, the law is seen as "a dimension of social organisation, which defines the extent of the autonomy of a society's members" through providing "frames of meaning that offer points of orientation for human conduct" (von Benda-Beckmann and von Benda-Beckmann 2013, 18). Law conceptually "cannot be more than an umbrella concept, an abstract cover term for a large variety of social phenomena of legal character" (von Benda-Beckmann and von Benda-Beckmann 2013, 19). This legal character involves shared principles, rules and sanctions, political and institutional legitimacy, as well as social validity (see von Benda-Beckmann 2002; von Benda-Beckmann and von Benda-Beckmann 2011).

Consequently, this reconceptualisation responds to the theoretical necessity of recognising law not simply as the jural embodiment of the state, but also as a normative system beyond the nation state, including religious law, *adat* law, and of increasing importance, international law. Furthermore, beyond broadening the conception of law, its reconceptualisation in the light of legal pluralism also provides an illuminating framework for understanding how those legal orders and their institutional underpinnings interact and shape each other as 'semi-autonomous social fields' (Moore 1973). Therefore, in analysing the law and space nexus in developing countries, F. von Benda-Beckmann et al. (2009, 4) convincingly argue that

> legal pluralism deserves a central position in the analysis of law in space. For it highlights the ways in which legal constructions of space in state and international law, religious and traditional law operate with their own spatial claims for validity. Under plural legal conditions … diverse and often contradictory notions of spaces and boundaries and their legal relevances come to coexist.

Accordingly, space in this context is understood as "a grounded, physical setting in which law affects the life of people. At the same time space also presents a more intangible universe" (von Benda-Beckmann et al. 2009, 22). This understanding of space corresponds to Massey's (2005, 9) theory of space conceived as "the product of interrelations" constituted by multi-scaled interactions, and consequently also "always under construction". Reconceptualising space based on Massey's propositions would lead the analysis to focus on interrelations between pluralistic legal settings and multiple spatial configurations. This would reveal not only "the extent to which law is a powerful tool that is constantly in the making and that is used in a variety of ways by different social actors to create frameworks" for governing space (von Benda-Beckmann 2009, 266), but also the extent to which constantly changing spatial configurations reflect back on social and legal structures.

Jayasuriya (2012) provides an insight into how to consider complex legal constellations in developing countries from a critical political economy perspective. He argues that legal pluralism should be "understood as a technology of jurisprudence that provides templates for institutional entrepreneurs such as transnational agencies as they develop novel institutions of legal governance" (Jayasuriya 2012, 145). Accordingly, "[i]nstitutions, not the diversity of legal culture, need to be at centre stage in the study of legal pluralism" (Jayasuriya 2012, 145–146). Institutions should be understood not as simply a consciously collective design to set "the rules of the game" in society (North 1990), but as mechanisms for allocating and distributing power and resources that are deeply embedded in social relations (Robison and Hadiz 2004; McCarthy and Warren 2009).

In this matter, scale is essential to the analysis of spatial organisation (Platt 2004). Smith (1995, 60–61) argues that "geographical scales are the product of economic, political and social activities and relationships; as such they are as changeable as those relationship themselves". Hence, 'scale' should be understood as 'fluid and dynamic', because it is "produced, contested, and transformed through a range of socio-political and discursive processes, strategies and struggles over what that social space contains" (Robertson et al. 2002, 475). The analysis of scale will reveal the extent to which material resources available at a given scale within pluralistic legal frameworks are mobilised, expanded, negotiated, and contested across multiple and superimposed geographical scales and jurisdictions by social actors in their struggles over the governance of space, people, and resources. As F. von Benda-Beckmann et al. (2009, 12) correctly say, "the scales at which social and ecological issues are perceived and addressed with legal means to a large extent define what the issue is". In Bali, this means that societal problems may be perceived differently according to the scalar location of the actors concerned.

As a result of this reconceptualisation, in this book, I use the terms 'spatial planning' and 'spatial governance' in two different contexts. The former refers solely to state policies for managing space, as reflected in spatial planning laws and regulations, while the latter refers to a broader conception of how space is governed by different institutions, either state or non-state institutions, through their respective forms of legal embodiment. This distinction is important to make for at least two reasons. First, it follows the current tendency in spatial planning that shifts from an exclusively government enterprise into collaborative spatial governance within state institutions or between state institutions and non-state entities, known as co-governance (Galland 2012). Secondly, given multiple meanings and interests over space, which are legitimately constructed through different forms of legality in many developing countries, including Indonesia, a spatial unit is not only governed by state institutions through the spatial planning regime but is also engaged with non-state modes of spatial governance.

As an interdisciplinary study, this book could be located within Bali Studies literature where debates have centred around the 'reinvention' of the Balinese cultural identity by the Dutch Colonial regime. In this literature, contemporary Balinese society is conceived within the framework of the continuity/discontinuity of pre-colonial and/or colonial construction under globalising processes. Here, globalisation is understood as a flow of capital, labour, commodities, and cultural items across the globe, through which Balinese culture and identity is implicated (see Darma Putra 2003; Schulte Nordholt 2007; Picard 1996; Lewis and Lewis 2009; Atmadja 2010a). This book adds consideration of another dimension of globalisation that is the fixed and immobile component of globalisation. This involves the reorganisation of space and scale for developing infrastructure and technology, as well as constructing global metropolitan networks, in which all are grounded in physical space and have both symbolic and material consequences (Brenner 1999).

This book is also intended to contribute to the literature on Law and Development in Asia. The dominant themes in the legal literature covering intellectual property law (Heath 2003; Sardjono 2007), judicial and institutional reform (Assegaf 2007; Thanadsillapakul 2012), commercial law (Antons 2003; Juwana 2004, 2005; Van Uytsel 2012), human rights law (Juwana 2007), constitutional law (Harman 2007; Harding 2012), labour law (Cooney et al. 2002; Uwijono 2007), and the rule of law (Jayasuriya 1999; Peerenboom 2004; Lindsey 2004; Sumiya 2012). However, within Asian law and development research, it appears that the studies of spatial planning remain unattractive despite the fact that spatial planning as a state legal instrument to govern its territories for designated purposes plays a vital role in value transformation for economic development. Given this role, spatial planning in Asian law and development contexts deserves much more attention than it has received to date. The book adds to this by putting the power struggles across governance scales under the lens to analyse the interplay between competing interests and identities in the complex structural setting and fragmented socio-spatial configuration of contemporary Balinese society.

The book demonstrates the process of defining, organising, and regulating space pursued by policymakers to respond to Bali's contemporary crisis, which was in turn caused by massive tourism development in the first place. Ironically, such reorganisation of space through spatial planning has in fact resulted in an expansion of the tourism industry even further. At the theoretical level, I argue that the 'production of space' (Lefebvre 1991) in developing countries could not be explained from perspectives that solely focus on the dynamics within the centres of power, namely, the state. Analysis needs also to incorporate a perspective that considers the complex legal and institutional setting, which would define the extent to which power is effectively exercised or even challenged at a given scale by different social actors whose identities and interests are embedded in those spatial configurations. Like law, space also exhibits indeterminacy, as it is continuously crafted by different, sometimes antagonistic, conceptions of space underpinning diverse interests over its use and resources. What is stipulated in the spatial planning is actually the 'representation of space' defined by the planners and policymakers with a set of particular interests—often claimed to be a 'public' interest—at the expense of others, and this stipulation will never be fixed as the strategies for pursuing such interests change. The case of Bali shows that social forces, whose vision of the world and interests are implicated in such 'representations of space', have created spaces of resistance by navigating Bali's pluralistic legal and institutional setting of the contemporary era.

Methodology

This book employs a qualitative method combining fieldwork and case studies with documentary analysis. Qualitative research enables the researcher to uncover the deeper meaning and significance of human behaviour and experiences and to explore the contexts in which spatial meanings are constructed, as well as the reasons behind the positions adopted by a range of actors in making decisions. By applying these methods, it is expected to gain a rich and complex understanding of the interrelationship of law, society, and economic development in contemporary Bali.

A case study method is also used in this book to provide in-depth and cross-scale analysis on how recent development within the complex legal and institutional settings of contemporary Bali is conceived, articulated, and contested by different social actors located across scales of interaction. This method may also help to prevent the tendency of over-generalisation and monolithic characterisation of a very complex, dynamic, and often ambivalent, contemporary Balinese life in the literature. There are three case studies explored in this book: the contested sacred space of Uluwatu Temple, the rescaling of the World Heritage listed Subak Landscape of Catur Angga Batukaru, and the Benoa Bay reclamation project. Their choice is justified because the three cases are the most concrete examples of spatial governance issues and processes in the context of contemporary development policy in Bali, which also represent island-wide tendencies. Secondly, they have triggered debate not only at the local level but also at the provincial, national, and even international governance levels regarding the trajectory of economic development on the island and its implications for social, cultural, and ecological conditions.

Several research techniques are used in this book, including documentary research, semi-structured interviews, and participant observation. With regard to documentary research, the important literature concerning spatial planning and environmental management, world heritage, customary law, development policy, and social and environmental justice issues in Bali and beyond are all reviewed critically. Among these documentary sources are spatial planning laws and regulations, legal cases, government submissions and reports, news articles, press releases and statements, local *awig-awig* (written customary rules), meeting minutes, environmental impact assessment (AMDAL) documents, project proposals, village profiles and reports, official maps, and so forth.

Around 108 semi-structured interviews have been conducted in order to gather information and opinions from key informants representing local communities (52%), government officials (14.50%), non-governmental organisations (11.80%), the private sector (10%), academic researchers (6.20%), and religious organisations (5.50%). These interviews were conducted in the Balinese and Indonesian languages, taking place in several different locations in Bali, including Denpasar, Tabanan (Jatiluwih, Mengesta, Babahan, Piling, Senganan Villages), Badung (Tanjung Benoa and Pecatu Villages), Gianyar (Ubud and Batubulan Villages), and Buleleng (Gobleg Village) during a preliminary field trip in May 2013 and a nine-month fieldwork period from November 2013 to September 2014. In addition, I also used two interviews conducted by my former PhD supervisor, Dr. Carol Warren on August 2012 in Pecatu. Interview participants were asked to describe their personal background, local issues concerning their environment, economic conditions, social relations, and their opinions on how the local and state institutions deal with these issues. Finally, they were asked to give their perspectives on how these problems should be handled by local people, village institutions, as well as the government. Because the majority of participants were male (80%), there may be some gender-based biases in their opinions, an issue that I have not been able to systematically explore in this book.

Book Structure

This book is divided into eight chapters providing an introductory overview of the background and relevant literature, three case studies, a comparative analysis of the case studies in Chap. 1, and a concluding chapter in Chap. 8. In Chap. 2, I outline the politics of development in Bali since the colonial period and especially under the forces of globalisation brought by the tourism industry. The chapter describes the complex relationships between local institutions in Bali, including the *adat* village, administrative village, traditional irrigation association (*subak*), and wider governmental structures. These complex relations are important to provide a basic understanding of local governance frameworks before analysing the case studies in the following three chapters. Chapter 3, 'Crisis and Reorganisation of Space', seeks to show how crisis in contemporary Bali is conceived and addressed accordingly. One of the strategies for addressing the contemporary problems of cultural and environmental integrity in Bali has been the enactment of the spatial planning regulation in which areas within district territories are designated as 'provincial strategic areas'. Three among those designated provincial strategic areas—Uluwatu Temple, Jatiluwih, and Benoa Bay—are sites of the three case studies explored in this book. Each of these cases iconically represents important spatial governance issues affecting the environment, culture, and socio-economic viability of local communities in Bali.

The first case, covered in Chap. 4, concerns conflict over the sacred space of Uluwatu Temple located in Pecatu Village of Badung District. I examine how the changes in physical landscape, economy, and socio-cultural conditions of the village due to massive tourism development has affected the ways in which local people perceive sacred space. Here I show that the entanglement between the 'production' of Uluwatu Temple's sacred space and the 'profane' forces of the mass tourism industry provoke complex cross-scale alliances and resistances to claim responsibility for and ownership of the space's material and symbolic significance. The second case study concerns the rescaling of the Subak Landscape of Catur Angga Batukaru elaborated in Chap. 5. This chapter examines the inscription of the Subak Landscape of Catur Angga Batukaru to UNESCO's World Heritage Regime in attempts to integrate the conservation of Bali's cultural heritage with the global tourism market as value added development. Without carefully assessing the complex institutional and legal constellation and its implications for the social dynamics within which the landscape is produced, the inscription has led to contestations not only among state institutions, but also among local communities, in their efforts to access the benefits and control the negative externalities arising from UNESCO's World Heritage Listing. Chapter 6 concerns the current heated controversy over a large-scale development project proposed for Benoa Bay by a powerful national tycoon, who plans to build a massive enclave resort within the bay. This chapter explores the alliance between the state and private interests that continues a model of crony capitalism forged under the New Order, but also the deployment of legal plural strategies by local social forces to articulate their dissent.

Chapter 7 is a comparative analysis of those three case studies. I examine a common feature shared across the cases, which is the development of new modes of spatial governance aimed at expanding tourism development. The second feature is the use of law and institution as a resource in social conflicts in contemporary Bali. The third feature is the character of power struggles that pose diverse meanings of space and place against narrow commercialisation and private interest. In some cases, resistance takes the form of an open struggle challenging vested political and economic interests, but in other instances opposition is revealed in 'everyday forms of resistance', when open struggle is considered culturally inappropriate and may disrupt local social cohesion.

Finally, I close my book by drawing several conclusions. Firstly, the designation of 'provincial strategic areas', which at first was regarded as an attempt to address contemporary Bali's institutional, economic, environmental, and cultural problems caused by the rapid expansion of mass tourism and property speculation on the island, has been deflected to accelerate this expansion yet further. Legal and institutional pluralism in decentralised Bali has provided more arenas for social actors to advance their interests, as well as to constrain the trajectory of tourism expansion with mixed and uncertain outcomes. Moreover, the book challenges the common characterisation of customary institutions as antiquated, elite-dominated impediments to progressive development. On the contrary, the case studies demonstrate the various ways in which customary institutions and law become arenas where local actors negotiate, accommodate, or challenge the state and private models of development. Finally, I propose the importance of adopting a wider analytic approach in examining complex legal and institutional configurations in post-authoritarian Bali and beyond.

2

The Politics of Development in Bali

In 2007, *National Geographic Traveler* released a report based on an assessment conducted by 522 experts of 111 tourist islands across the globe. Bali was identified as one of the "islands in the balance" referring to "a mixed bag of successes and worries, with the future at risk" due to "[g]orgeous scenery and endearing local traditions as well as awful coastal tourism ghettos—unplanned and reflecting the worst excesses of package tourism" (Tourtellot 2007, 124). Nonetheless, from a business point of view, Bali has become increasingly attractive for tourists and property investors. For instance, in 2011, the Australian tourism and business magazine, *the Informer*, put Bali's resort and property investment opportunities as its main theme targeting potential Australian investors and providing legal advice on how to invest in Bali. It stated that,

> Bali has become well known around the world as a glamorous retirement and lifestyle destination [;] many feel they are living the dream. The very friendly, always smiling Balinese people, are very tolerant of expats living in Bali … It is not only the lifestyle but many great business opportunities that are bringing increasing numbers of foreign nationals to live in Bali. The very low cost of living, abundance of local labour and low rates of pay for local workers offer a viable business strategy. (McEwon 2011, 24)

A. Wardana, *Contemporary Bali*, https://doi.org/10.1007/978-981-13-2478-9_2

In the same year, however, Andrew Marshall's (2011) piece in *Time* Magazine, entitled 'Holidays in Hell: Bali's Ongoing Woes', sparked a polemic on the future of Bali's tourism industry. Although somewhat exaggerated, Marshall (2011) explains how the realities of uncontrolled development, crime, traffic congestion, as well as environmental degradation, are in contrast with the image of Bali as 'paradise'. Then followed a debate between Ngurah Wijaya, the chair of the Bali Tourism Board, and Vyt Karazija, an expat and foreign journalist in Bali. Wijaya, in an interview (*Jakarta Globe*, 25/04/2012), blames 'stingy' tourists for causing Bali's contemporary problems, such as traffic congestion, waste, pollution, and water shortages, for which they have made little contribution to the local economy.[1] From a tourist perspective, Karazija (2012) argues that, from the day of their arrival in Bali, their experience is a disappointment—paying "the same prices as at home for mediocre Western-style meals", faced with unsatisfactory hotel services, dishonest money changers, impolite street vendors, garbage, rabies, and the list goes on. In other words, Bali is far from what the travel brochures offer to visitors. Hence, for Karazija, it is not that stingy tourists have caused the problems but rather the converse: the problems experienced by tourists have caused tourists to become 'stingy'.

Much of this debate is confined within a framework of Bali as a tourism 'brand' (Hobart 2011). Accordingly, the two opposing arguments that are raised in the debate reflect two different positions within Bali's tourism industry, that is, between the producer and the consumer (Wardana 2012). Placing the debate within a wider context, in fact, they both are concerned with the sustainability of the island's tourism industry, and their arguments are shaped by a similarly imaginary and instrumental construction of Bali, either as a 'paradise' or a 'hell'. The questions of the historical trajectories of capitalistic tourism development in Bali—and how social forces respond to them—are beyond their horizons.

[1] There was also the earlier controversy along the same lines in the *Bali Post*'s '*Giliran Anda*' column entitled *'Bali: Keranjang Sampah'*, *Bali Post*, 1–18 December 2004. Unlike the Wijaya's narrow scapegoating, among these comments, there is also considerable introspection evident, attributing blame to investors, politicians, and ordinary Balinese as well.

Appearing not only within the practices of the tourism industry, the image of 'paradise' is not uncommon in the literature on Bali Studies. Its uses vary as romantic or ironic tropes (Noronha 1979; Kam 1993; Vickers 2003; Harnish 2005; Lewis 2006; Hitchcock and Darma Putra 2007). It appears in academic literature beyond tourism studies, for example, in psychological studies (Suryani et al. 2009), architecture and urban studies (Suartika 2005), cultural studies (Agung 2005; Vickers 2012), or even the analysis of political violence (Robinson 1995). The image of 'paradise' seems to be strongly attached to the way Bali is imagined and the way in which the 'real' Bali is interpreted. Thus, it is necessary to provide a more critical account of contemporary Bali as a site of struggles. This chapter highlights the interaction between external forces and internal dynamics that has shaped Bali's development trajectories.

A Changing World of Bali

The Colonial Construction of Bali

The interaction between external forces, especially the Dutch Colonial administration, and Balinese society has been the crucial 'conjuncture' in Bali Studies literature. This is not only due to the abundance of publications, notes, reports, and archives on Balinese society that were made accessible to Western scholars. More importantly, this period in its history has to a large extent shaped Bali's development trajectories up until the contemporary period. Historically, at first, the colonial administration had little interest in the island of Bali as it had limited commercial resources to be traded for the European markets (Pringle 2004). Early Dutch interaction with Bali, especially North Bali, primarily revolved around slave trades of which Bali, together with Makassar, was regarded as 'the dual axis' of the slave trade network in Netherlands Indies (Vink 2003, 143). The Balinese rulers were actively involved in this trade, both to export Balinese slaves and to re-export slaves from eastern Netherlands Indies (Vink 2003; Pringle 2004; Fagertun 2017b). As Pringle (2004, 78–79) notes, rulers' attempts to secure incomes through the slave trade in order to buy opium, luxury items as well as arms to compete with other Balinese rulers had intensified warfare on the island because war prisoners could be brought into slavery. As a result, during 1653–1682, out of 10,000 slaves brought by vessel to Batavia during this period, almost 24% of them came from Bali, and more than 41% came from South Sulawesi (Vink 2003, 143). As the abolition of slavery took place in the early nineteenth century, Balinese rulers changed their revenue base by turning into cash crops, namely, coffee (Pringle 2004).

In terms of colonial revenues on Bali, opium and land tax were two significant sources for the administration. The Dutch Colonial rulers imposed a Netherland Indies-wide opium monopoly by selling an affordable dose for common persons and this encouraged wider consumption among Balinese (Pringle 2004, 115). In the context of land administration, the Dutch governed by establishing land registration in order to extract land tax. Eventually, Balinese farmers found the heaviest land tax in the Netherlands Indies imposed upon them, causing an increase in extreme poverty among farmers, and especially sharecroppers who were responsible to pay the tax while they were only allowed to keep one-third of their harvests (Pringle 2004).

The colonialists also attempted to reorganise village governance. Influenced by F.A. Liefrinck's concept of *dorpsrepubliek* ('village republic'), which regarded the village as the fundamental and authentic social unit of Balinese society, they attempted to distance the village from the Balinese kingdoms that were considered to be a Javanese despotic interference (Creese 2016). To control village populations, the Dutch introduced dual *adat* (customary) and *dinas* (administrative) governing village structures (Warren 1993). The *adat* structure was supposed to preserve the 'authentic' element of Balinese villages dealing with religious and customary affairs, while the *dinas* village structure was established to reorganise local social units for the effective mobilisation of villagers through corvée labour (Pringle 2004; Parimartha 2013). Hence, local villagers who were also peasants had a double burden as a result of the colonial administration of land and the restructuring of village governance under which they had to pay a heavy land tax and at the same time to provide corvée labour. As the global market for crops slowed down due to the Great Depression of the 1930s, Balinese farmers were under considerable pressure, "resulting in a surge of landlessness and increasing concentration of land in the hands of the rulers, their families and other aristocrats" (Pringle 2004, 116).

After conquering the whole island in the early twentieth century through a shameful war marked by ritual suicide (*puputan*—the ending), the Dutch applied different governing strategies among the eight kingdoms—which, in the post-colonial era, became Bali's districts. These strategies depended on their degree of cooperation with colonial authorities. A direct rule strategy where the traditional rulers were not officially recognised applied to the Buleleng, Badung, Jembrana, Tabanan, and Klungkung kingdoms that were less cooperative with the colonial government (Pringle 2004). Meanwhile, for more cooperative kingdoms—Bangli, Karangasem, and Gianyar—indirect rule was applied, where the traditional rulers served as regents to the Dutch, having a responsibility to the residents of Singaraja, and to the governor general in Batavia (Pringle 2004). The Dutch Colonial regime also attempted to introduce a modern bureaucracy in Bali (Schulte Nordholt 2000). Schools were established to produce a new generation of Western trained officials who filled the lower ranks of the colonial administration.

In the 1920s, the political climate in the Netherlands Indies changed when the 1926–1927 abortive revolt of the Indonesian Communist Party and the spread of nationalism had pushed the colonial administration to respond. In Bali, a new 'ethical' policy was introduced aimed at 'traditionalising' Balinese society (Schulte Nordholt 2000, 103). Consequently, the policy for modernising the colonial bureaucratic administration shifted, reinstalling the descendants of traditional rulers in the colonial system in order to provide 'a familiar face of traditional authority' (Schulte Nordholt 2000, 103). This was accompanied by the reinvention of the caste system as a rigid social stratification based on birth (Pringle 2004; Schulte Nordholt 2000). The reification of caste divisions and the gradual return of the old royal kingdoms triggered criticisms from north Bali's growing intelligentsia, who objected to the prioritisation of high-caste descendants recruited as colonial officials (Schulte Nordholt 2000; Darma Putra 2011). As a result, dynamic intellectual debates between the opponents and the proponents of the Dutch-imposed caste system took place in the journals *Soerja Kanta* and *Bali Adnjana* (Darma Putra 2011). Both *Soerja Kanta* and *Bali Adnjana* were periodicals published by the Balinese educated classes working as teachers or officials in the colonial administration. While *Soerja Kanta* outspokenly rejected the notion of caste in their advocacy to modernise Bali, *Bali Adnjana* was dominated by conservative authors from three high castes (*tri wangsa*) to counter *Soerja Kanta* propaganda by emphasising the need to preserve the caste system as the foundation of Balinese society (see Darma Putra 2011).

In the legal context, there had been an effort to compile *adat* laws, which contributed to an understanding of the complexities of Balinese legal culture prior to colonial arrival (Creese 2009). There was no other area in which the 'reinvention of tradition' (Hobsbawn 1983) took place obviously than in the establishment of a special Hindu court for Bali, *Raad van Kertha* (Schulte Nordholt 2000). The colonial administration set the court consisting of Brahmana priests as the judges and it introduced two old Javanese legal codes—*Adigama* and *Agama*—to be used as the basis for court decisions. However, the priests acting as the judge had limited knowledge over contents of the codes and they did not even speak the Old Javanese language used in the codes. Eventually, the colonial administration translated the codes into the Malay and High Balinese languages, enabling 'enlightened European' re-interpretation, rewriting, and improvement of the codes so that assessment and control over their application would be possible (Creese 2016). Given the imposed caste system that related to the obligation to provide corvée labour and to the access of colonial administrative positions, many of the cases heard in the court were regarding caste declaration cases claiming to belong to one of the three higher castes (Schulte Nordholt 2000; Pringle 2004; Vickers 2012).

All of these attempts traditionalising Bali are usually referred to as the *Baliniseering* (Balinisation) project with a mixture of political and economic colonial motive. Politically, such a project was to counteract the negative image at an international level after the shameful conquest (Vickers 2012) and also served as an attempt to prevent the spread of nationalism and Islamisation from Java, as well as Christian missionaries, to Bali by making the Balinese proud of their unique Hindu identity 'in a sea of Islam' (Hitchcock and Darma Putra 2007; Picard 2011). There was an aligned interest between the Dutch Colonial and the traditional rulers in preserving the Balinese cultural identity. Ardika et al. (2013, 358) argue that the interaction between the Dutch and Bali was an 'episode of historical change' when the Westerners encountered traditional Bali and gave birth to the reconstruction of the Balinese identity. In fact, as shown above, such interaction did not only result in a 'historical' change, but also resulted in 'structural' changes that have shaped the trajectories of the island up to the present. Economically, the publication of the first Bali guidebook in 1914, only six years after the conquest, by the tourist bureau of the colonial administration in Batavia, marked the birth of Indonesia's international tourism (Adams 2018; Picard 1996). The image of Bali as 'paradise', according to Vickers (2012), was then produced to boost the tourism industry on the island, a colonial image that has persisted as a dominant narrative throughout the modern history of Bali.

Post-colonial Bali and the Mass Killings

In the post-colonial Bali, in spite of being viewed sceptically by leftist intellectuals who regarded tourism as a form of neo-colonialism (Darma Putra 2003), the colonial image of Bali "was given new life, as [Indonesia's first] President [Sukarno] established a palace there and held court regularly, entertained by Balinese dancers, his walls hung with Balinese paintings" (Vickers 2012, 19). The tourism industry was rebuilt on the material and ideational foundations left over by the Dutch Colonial administration and, interestingly, many of the actors involved were former independence fighters who established their own tourism enterprises, such as hotels, art-shops, and travel agencies (Vickers 2011). They were able to succeed in the economic sphere due to their access to state resources by becoming politicians themselves or maintaining a close friendship with local political elites who happened to be their brothers-in-arms during the war for independence (Robinson 1995).

However, for ordinary Balinese, this post-colonial period, especially 1950s and early 1960s, was a period of economic difficulty. A combination of factors, including hyperinflation, the dramatic increase of food prices, poor harvests, and the volcanic eruption of Mount Agung, hit peasant and working class families badly. As observed by Robinson (1995), this economically challenging condition had opened up the possibility for political mobilisation by leftist political parties, especially the Indonesian Communist Party and its affiliated mass organisations—of which the most prominent one in Bali was the *Barisan Tani Indonesia*

(BTI/Indonesian Peasant Front). As a result, for the first time in modern history, the Balinese were highly politicised. Contestations over power, class, and land emerged on an unprecedented scale. The national land reform and equitable harvest share policies of the early 1960s had shaken the foundations of feudalism in the hands of noble families. Landless and smallholding peasants mobilised through the BTI to enforce the policy for land redistribution through government administration or, if necessary, through unilateral actions (MacRae 2003; Sawita 2012).

The events of 30 September 1965, when several military generals were kidnapped and killed in Jakarta, allegedly by an army wing of the Indonesian Communist Party, changed the political landscape not only at the national level, by bringing Suharto to power, but also at the local level. Although the interpretation of these events remains debatable, the evident result was the eradication of the communist influence from Indonesian politics, the disorganisation of civil society, and the consolidation of power in the hands of General Suharto, through the Western-supported mass killings and arrests of those accused of being communists and members of other leftist organisations in 1965–1966 (Heryanto and Hadiz 2005; Roosa 2006). In Bali alone, it is estimated that around 80,000–100,000 people, or up to 8% of the total population, were killed, among whom were leftist intellectuals, farmers, and labour organisers, women activists, and ordinary people associated with the Indonesian Communist Party and affiliated organisations, especially the BTI (Cribb 1990; Robinson 1995; Vickers 2012). Here, Geertz's (1973) interpretation that regards 'culture' shown in the cruelty and violence impulses in the Balinese cockfight to explain the massacre is clearly ignorant of the historical and political-economy contexts, where contestations and class inequalities during the post-colonial as well as the Cold War periods were essential conditions to understanding the event.

Suharto's New Order and the Jakarta's Colony

A relatively smooth process to advance the tourism industry on the island during the New Order era was partly insured by the traumatic experience of the 1965–1966 mass killings. Previously, leftist intellectuals, especially *Lembaga Kebudayaan Rakyat* (LEKRA/Institute for the People's Culture), were suspicious of tourism, which was regarded as a form of neo-colonialism (Darma Putra 2003). In general, the 1965–1966 mass killings should be seen as paving the way to power for Suharto, enabling the new regime to take away land from farmers and stripping away potential opposition groups and co-opting civic organisations in order to expand the capitalist mode of production. Farid (2005) argues that the 1965 massacre was a form of what Marx (1990 [1867]) calls 'primitive accumulation'. In the case of Bali and Indonesia in general, the ongoing processes of dispossession it facilitated became the basis of the capital accumulation dynamic that continues unabated.

As a result of such dispossession, Suharto's New Order national policies on mass tourism development in Bali were imposed without significant opposition, at least for the first two decades of authoritarian rule. In the New Order government's first five-year national plan (Repelita 1: 1969–1974), Bali was designated as the centre for foreign exchange earnings through tourism. Although the President Sukarno also attempted to develop tourism by building the Bali Beach Hotel, it was under Suharto's New Order Regime that mass tourism expanded at an unprecedented scale on the island. Akin to the promotion of tourism by the Dutch Colonialists after the *puputan* wars, the tourism policy under the regime also served at least two objectives: the advancement of the tourism industry taking Indonesia to the global market, and the utilisation of Bali's colonial romantic imagery as a peace-loving and harmonious society to replace the violent and traumatic memories of Suharto seizing power (Picard 1996; Adams 2018).

In pursuing mass tourism development on the island, Suharto's New Order Regime had been assisted by international institutions. Planned by the *Societe Centrale pour l'Equipement Touristique Outre-Mer* (SCETO), a Paris-based consulting group, and funded by UNDP and the World Bank, the national government focused development on building a mass tourist enclave on the southern peninsula of Nusa Dua (UNDP/USAID/World Bank 2006; Hitchcock and Putra 2007). This enclave, managed by the Bali Tourism Development Corporation (BTDC)—now the Indonesia Tourism Development Cooperation/ITDC—Nusa Dua, was planned to concentrate mass tourism accommodation on what was considered as dry and relatively unproductive land in order to contain the negative impacts of tourism on local culture (World Bank 1974; Picard 1996; see also Noronha 1979). McCarthy (1994, 107) observes that there were several reasons why the government of Indonesia encouraged enclave tourism: first, in terms of market, enclave tourism was targeting upper-class tourists for high value foreign exchange; second, there was an assumption that enclave tourism would have less impact on local culture; third, the use of global marketing networks through international travel agents for a high-end travel experience would attract tourists in substantial numbers; finally, the symbolic value of having luxury tourist accommodation was a boost to national pride.

However, the development of a tourist enclave on the island was never without conflicts. In Nusa Dua, at the beginning, it created conflicts with local people, albeit on a small scale. Local farmers were forced to sell their land below the market value for agricultural land, which triggered resistance from the famers against the BTDC (Pratiwi 2004). In one case, Pratiwi (2004, 238) reported that, after being 'intimidated' by the state officials, her respondent gave up and "finally decided to sell [his 1-hectare plot of land to the BTDC] after the *Kecamatan* (sub-district) officials called him [to the office] twice". In the period of the New Order's authoritarian regime, being called in by government officials was relatively frightening for local farmers—who feared that it might be a death call. The use of the 'clean environment' (*bersih lingkungan*) discourse played a decisive role to push local community to 'clean up' their neighbourhood from communist influences and to scrutinise any suspicious activity that might disrupt law and order. No one would dare to look politically 'different' for fear of being labelled a 'communist' or 'anti-development' (*anti pembangunan*), with serious implications not only for himself or herself but also for his/her family and property. More importantly for Balinese whose social lives were heavily dependent on local social and cultural relations with their neighbours for conducting rituals or borrowing money, the label might have the consequence of being expelled from the community (*kasepekang*) in order to keep the community 'clean' from communism.

Following the establishment of BTDC, Balinese intellectuals introduced the concept of 'cultural tourism'. This concept aimed at keeping the tourism industry in the hands of the local populace as the owners of Bali's cultural heritage. Picard (1996, 2003, 108) argues that it later became conflated with 'touristic culture' where tourism 'proceeds from within' as reflected in the doctrine of the 'Seven Charms' (*Sapta Pesona*)—security, friendliness, orderliness, beauty, comfort, cleanliness, and memories—that became an 'ethic' to meet the need of the tourism industry for a friendly climate. More significantly, disciplining Balinese society was pursued through the vital conjuncture with the continued use of coercive force to impose tourism development, as in the BTDC case above. In order words, the mass killings and their aftermath contributed to a form of 'accumulation by dispossession' (Harvey 2003), where local farmers' lands were forcefully appropriated to build tourism infrastructures through the presence of the state apparatus and local strongmen, supported by the internalisation of the 'clean environment' and seven charms doctrines, as well as the New Order rhetoric of 'developmentalism'.

With the dominance of the Washington Consensus in the 1980s, the role of the private sector was prioritised, including in tourism development (Hawkins and Mann 2007; Wardana 2016). In the context of Bali, New Order government policies directed the tourism industry to move away from the enclave scenarios of the SCETO planners by expanding mass tourism beyond Nusa Dua through the designation of 15 'tourist areas' (*kawasan pariwisata*) in 1988, expanded to 21 areas across Bali in 1993, covering 24.7% of the province (Picard 1996, 66; UNDP/USAID/World Bank 2006, 4). As a result, in the following years, tourist visits to Bali increased significantly. The average annual growth is estimated to have been 12–15% between 1971 and 1997, taking off in the late 1980s after a slow start. Total amount spent by the tourist more than doubled in only five years—from US$ 198 million to US$ 406 million between 1985 and 1990 (Hassall and Associate 1992, 13). This dramatic growth in tourism and tourism dollars led to a dramatic increase in investments in resorts, hotels, restaurants, golf courses, and other facilities. According to Warren (1998, 230) the deregulation of the banking system in 1987 led to "an unprecedented investment boom resulting in a 10-fold increase in foreign and domestic investments between 1987 and 1988, and almost doubling again the following year".

Under the centralistic authoritarian government of the New Order, the key players during that period were closely linked to Suharto. This was a time when Bali was referred to as 'Jakarta's Colony' by Aditjondro

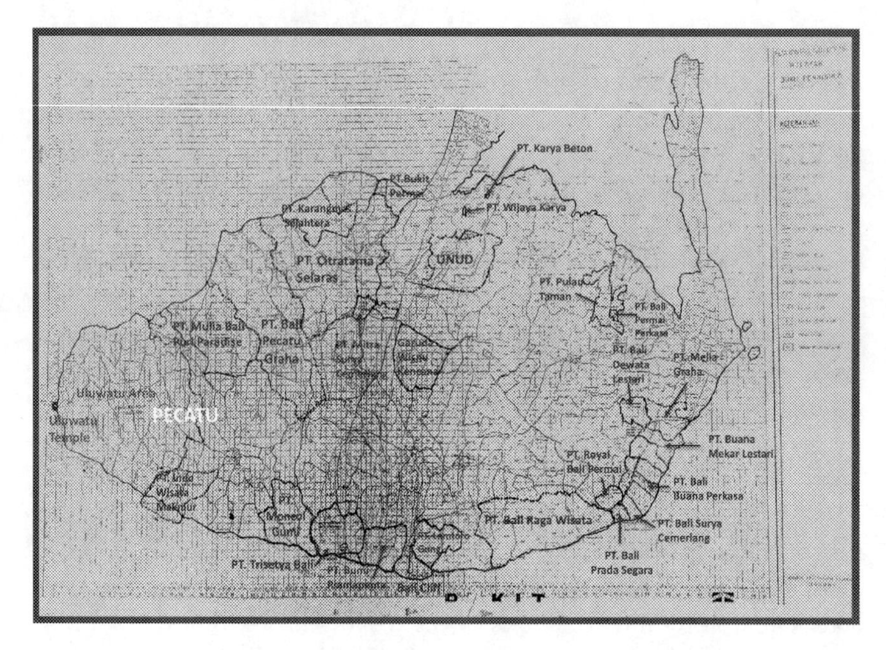

Fig. 2.1 Concessions in Bukit Peninsula, southern Bali. Adapted from Peta Kontrol Lokasi Wilayah Bukit Peninsula 1994 [the 1994 Location Map of Controlling Interests on the Bukit Peninsula]

(1995). As shown in the Fig. 2.1 below, Bukit Peninsula in Southern Badung, where tourist development is concentrated, was blocked out, and concessions in the form of *Hak Guna Bangunan* (HGB/Building Rights Title) on state land (*tanah negara*) were granted by the national government to several companies owned by Suharto family members and allies in the early 1990s. These conglomerates had dominant interests in several controversial projects at Serangan, Pecatu, and Tanah Lot (see Warren 1998; Suasta and Connor 1999). McCarthy (1994, 37) observes that, during the centralistic period, the national government was the institution in charge of tourism policies, while the provincial government was not in a position to curb the investors. But by focusing on the Jakarta elite (Aditjondro 1995) and the national institution (McCarthy 1994), Aditjondro and McCarthy overlook the role of local brokers from among Golkar functionaries, regional government officials, and local noble families, who were able to navigate Jakarta's conglomerates for their own rent-seeking and networking interests. Those local brokers then become future tourism entrepreneurs and political-economic elites during decentralisation. Ketut Sudikerta from Pecatu, a Golkar politician, former vice-district head of Badung (2005–2013) and vice-governor of Bali (2013–2018), as one of the prominent local brokers for Tommy Suharto's projects, is a perfect example of these local conduits. As a result, significant tracts of land across Bali's Bukit Peninsula came to be occupied by the Suharto family and its cronies through corrupt, manipulative, and coercive practices (Lewis and Lewis 2009).

Decentralisation and District Competitions

The fall of the Suharto Regime in 1998 brought an era of political reform, not only at the national level, but locally as well. Governmental structures were decentralised after heavy pressures were exerted by local elites and international development agencies (the World Bank and IMF) (Schulte Nordholt and van Klinken 2007; Warren and McCarthy 2009; Hadiz 2010). In 1999, the first law on decentralisation was issued (Law No. 22/1999), which transferred several authorities (*kewenangan*) to the district level. The national government only retained its authority in matters of security, religion, fiscal responsibilities, and international relations. Decentralisation to the district government rather than provincial government scale was chosen as a rescaling downward strategy, because there was a perception that decentralisation to provincial authority might threaten national integrity (McCarthy and Warren 2009, 5). However, the transfer of power to the districts also considerably decreased central control. For this reason, under the Megawati presidency, the law was revised and replaced by Law No. 32/2004 on Regional Government, in which provincial governments were given a role as supervisors of district governments to oversee their exercise of autonomy. This role has been strengthened by Law No. 23/2014 on Regional Government.

In Bali, decentralisation has substantially changed the political structures of the island province. Since its inception, Bali's eight districts and one municipality have been able to exercise strong authority to manage their own resources to maximise local revenue. This new control structure in turn has led to widely criticised district 'arrogance', and elite capture on a new scale (Hadiz 2010; Schulte Nordholt and van Klinken 2007). Badung has become the richest district in Bali benefiting from the well-established tourism infrastructure—such as the Ngurah Rai international airport, Nusa Dua, and Kuta that are located within its boundaries. Local politicians from other districts regard Badung as a role model of development for their own districts. They are driven by the prospect of more revenue from investment in tourism in their districts. Thus, they have been actively and sometimes competitively involved in expanding tourism and inviting investors. Fees and commissions may be gained easily from investors, not to mention outright bribes, as local politicians become rent-seeking middlemen finding land and facilitating the granting of permits to investors. By 2014, it was reported that there were 28,811 international standard rooms across the island, 18 times the original limit of 1600 rooms set by SCETO planners (World Bank 1974, ii; BPS Bali 2014a).

Bali Bombings that occurred twice, in early and mid-2000s, did not slow down the pace of tourism expansion. The Bali Bombing I in 2002 severely affected the tourism industry as the number of tourists visiting Bali decreased dramatically. In that nadir, policymakers and Balinese intelligentsia encouraged Bali to reduce its economic dependency on the fragile tourism sectors by turning back to agriculture, which has proven to be more resilient. MacRae (2005) notes two strategies pursued to maximise the profitability of the agricultural sector in a moment of crisis; they are the agro-industry and agro business, which focuses on a shifting from subsistence towards market-oriented cash crops; and organic farming to enhance human health and environmental sustainability. However, the idea of turning away from tourism was then set aside once tourism gradually recovered, following massive injections of funds to undertake recovery programs, from international agencies, including the World Bank and UNDP, foreign governments, as well as travel agencies. In the moment of crisis, procedures for investment were also relaxed to attract investors who might stimulate the local economy. Consequently, tourism infrastructures as well as a villa style of tourism accommodation—considered more private and secured—have continually developed across the island, including in Pecatu (Chap. 4).

A recent national policy to expand the tourism industry even further was promulgated through the Master Plan for the Expansion and Acceleration of Economic Development (*Master Plan untuk Perluasan dan Percepatan Pembangunan Ekonomi*/MP3EI) by Presidential Regulation (*Peraturan Presiden*/Perpres) No. 32/2011, under President Yudhyono. The master plan divides the country into several economic regions based on their competitive advantage in the global market. This spatial division of labour has continued to designate Bali as the centre of the nation's tourism economy, with East Nusa Tenggara (NTT) and West Nusa Tenggara (NTB) as its supporting sub-regions. Under this development scheme, it was projected that Indonesia would be visited by 20 million tourists annually, with Bali alone projected to receive 7 million tourists (Indonesia. CMEA 2011, 142). In order to meet this target, the rise of the middle class in China is seen as a potential market (*Jakarta Post*, 04/07/2013). In fact, Chinese tourists increased by 51.29% in 2015 over the 2014 numbers, to become the second largest group of foreign visitors in Bali (13.51%) after Australians (27.88%) (*Kompas*, 02/02/2015). Since 2017, Chinese tourists have outnumbered Australians to be the largest group of foreign visitors to the island (*Kompas*, 03/01/2018).

The MP3EI policy framework not only reconfigured the space for economic expansion and growth, but it also enabled several preferred corporations to bypass procedural requirements at the local level in order to advance their capital accumulation agendas, including, for example, Benoa Bay's 'revitalisation' project by the Tirta Wahana Bali International (TWBI), owned by Tomy Winata, a powerful national tycoon, the case study to be covered in Chap. 6. The master plan illustrates the contradictory nature of spatial governance in Indonesia. On the one hand, the MP3EI is a product of a neoliberal policy framework aimed at opening up space for a market economy based on competition. On the other hand, the master plan commits itself to several preferred actors who have formal or informal connections to state officials and political elites. Although enacted during the Susilo Bambang Yudhoyono presidency, there is no indication so far that it will be revoked by President Jokowi. In fact, Jokowi has instructed his ministers to continue the projects designated by the master plan without using the MP3EI label, but incorporating it into his *Rencana Pembangunan Jangka Menengah* (RPJM/Mid-Term Development Plan) (*CNN Indonesia*, 18/12/2014).

Complex Socio-legal Configurations

The Nexus Between Land and Caste/Class

As in Bali, like in other agricultural societies, access to and ownership of land define social relations in Balinese society for centuries. Several types of land regimes include *tanah ayahan desa* (village-owned land), *tanah milik* (privately owned land), *pelaba pura* (temple-owned land), and *tanah pecatu* (king-owned land). *Tanah ayahan desa* (AYDS) is a customary land regime in which the ownership of the land is at the hands of the *adat* village. This land is usually used as a residential area for the *adat* village members, with a reciprocal obligation to contribute labour and finance for the *adat* affairs, including ceremonies. The guardianship of this land can only be transferred through inheritance but if the guardian has no descendant, it will return to the *adat* village and may be transferred to other members who need a place to live. Privately owned land is the land whose ownership is held by individuals that may derive from inheritance, land distribution, trading, and so forth. *Pelaba pura* is a piece of land owned by a temple, which is usually cultivated with certain crops needed for the temple's ceremonies. *Tanah pecatu* is a plot of land granted by the king or noble families to be worked by ordinary peasants with an obligation to provide harvest shares as well as labour for the king when needed.

In the present era, the expansion of the tourism economy has implicated the nature of landownership. As observed by McCarthy (1994, 48), the needs of land to build tourist infrastructure in prime locations increased land value and triggered land speculation and conflicts within families. Land that was owned and managed by extended families was sub-divided based on the number of heirs in the family. Once it was individually owned, the land might be sold to tourism investors as the owner wished, a decision that was more difficult when the land remained collectively owned by the extended family. It has often been the case that local people sold their land to investors without any capacity to manage the money arising from the sale and ended up becoming gardeners for tourist accommodation built on their previously owned land. The sub-divided land was no longer sufficient to support their family;

hence, they were added to the proletariat and forced to sell their unskilled labour in the tourism industry. This is what Fagertun (2017b) considers the third wave of dispossession in Balinese society as a result of economic modernisation and industrialisation, especially the transformation of an agriculture-based economy to a tourism economy. According to her, in Bali's modern history, there have been three waves of dispossession that are closely related to the emergence of class in Balinese society (Fagertun 2017b).

The first wave of dispossession took place under the Dutch Colonial period. This was when the colonial administration 'reinvented' a strict caste system from the notion of *wangsa*, a relatively loose social stratification through which the lower castes would be subjected to provide corvée labour and imposed by heavy land tax obligation (Fagertun 2017b; see also Robinson 1995; Ramstedt 2013). Consequently, farmers belong to lower castes were forced to sell their land to noble or higher caste families as they found serving corvée labour and paying taxes too difficult. This perpetuated the massive ownership of land by noble families, and landlessness became common among lower caste families (Robinson 1995; Pringle 2004; Fagertun 2017b). In order to survive, they had to work as sharecroppers to the noble families, of which the class relation between the sharecroppers as the 'direct producer' and the noble families as the 'tribute-takers' was consolidated, which in turn shaped and reproduced patron-client relationships not only within the economic sphere, but also political and cultural spheres (Fagertun 2017a, 333).

The second wave of dispossession, according to Fagertun (2017b), was taking place in the post-colonial period. Through a nationalist economic policy, the newly independent state nationalised foreign companies and facilitated the rise of an indigenous capitalist class. In Bali, Fagertun (2017a, 332) suggests that the "first capitalists were aristocrats with close relations and political links to the protectionist local state … who were involved in many different political parties, which provided them with influential positions over questions of subsidies, licenses and contracts". In the early 1960s, through the enactment of Basic Agrarian Law (Law No. 5/1960) and the land reform policy, individual landownership was restricted to two hectares for wet agricultural land (*sawah*) and seven hectares for dry agricultural land (*tegalan*). Those who owned land beyond the limits were subject to the redistribution of their land to the sharecroppers and landless peasants. Reluctant landowners circumvented the policy by secretly transferring their surplus land to their relatives or producing false reports on their land assets. Facing reluctance from the landowners, the *Barisan Tani Indonesia* (Indonesian Peasant Front), a peasant-wing of the Indonesian Communist Party, took unilateral actions to occupy landowners' land and distributed it to their members. Following the 1965–1966 mass killings, lands owned by victims of massacres were taken back by the old landowners, perpetrators, or even the state.

Based on those three waves of dispossession, Fagertun (2017b; see also 2017a), following Parker (2003) and Robinson (1995), observes the continuity of the Dutch-imposed caste system and the rise of the capitalist class in contemporary Balinese society. In other words, for those authors, the class formation has seen convergence with the caste system in which the wealthy class tends to be associated with the three higher castes (*triwangsa*) whose privileges given by the colonial administration, and whose resistance to land reform in mid 1960s, made it possible to concentrate landownership. During the booming of the tourism industry on the island since the 1970s, they have been able to capitalise their means of production—the land—to establish their own tourism enterprises, or to sell or rent for tourism facilities. However, it might be also the case that noble families have substantial land because they have been successful in the tourism business, and not necessarily due to family inheritance.

Hence, the above observation is only partly true. The convergence between caste and class positions was clearly evident as the result of the first wave of dispossession. But, for the second and the third waves, the picture is far more complex. When considering the ten richest capitalist figures in Bali, the data shows a more nuanced and complex picture of the caste background of the capitalist class, rather than caste and class being tidily overlapped. Despite the data being rather outdated, it gives a sense the relationship between caste and class in contemporary Bali. It shows a comparable caste background in the ten figures in which five come from a commoner background and five from the *triwangsa* caste, including Cok Ace of Ubud Royal Family (the 6th), the former District Head of Gianyar (2008–2013), and the current vice-governor of Bali (2018–2023) (*Berita Bali*, 05/07/2011).

There are at least three problems with the assumption behind this line of argument. First of all, those authors, especially Fagertun (2017b) and Parker (2003), assumed that there was a monolithic association between caste and political affiliation. Put simply, those from a high-caste family are assumed to affiliate politically with conservative political parties; meanwhile, those from the lowest caste families would be close to progressive and working class-based political parties. In fact, as Birkelbach (1973, 158) puts it: "[t]he *Brahman* and *Ksatria*-educated elites tend to embrace radical Western ideologies. A large number of Balinese Communists who were massacred in the 1965–1966 Indonesian coup-counter-coup were of higher castes." Robinson (1995, 268) notes that two out of three district heads from Indonesian Communist Party (PKI) in Bali during 1964–1965 came from high-caste families. In Denpasar, many of the victims of the mass killing belonged to *ksatriya* families, who were active in leftist political parties (Alit 2012). At least one *brahmana* high priest (*pedanda*) was also reportedly killed during the event (Vickers 2012).[2] Even the Governor of Bali Gusti Bagus Sutedja, from a noble family of Jembrana, disappeared and was believed to have been assassinated due to his political affiliation to Sukarno and left-wing politics. Hence, the social-political context at the time of the massacre was far more complex than an assumption of the convergence of caste and class interests would suggest.[3]

Secondly, those authors ignore the geography of capitalist value by assuming that land, as a means of production, has a comparable value across the island. Accordingly, the feudal class across Bali linearly transformed themselves into a capitalist class engaged with the tourism industry. In fact, as tourism is developed unevenly across the island, the value of land from one place to another differs considerably. Thus, a commoner family owning a plot of land in one of the prime locations of tourism

[2] Vickers (2012, 236) writes: "Stories of killings tell of magical battles going on as the Left exterminated. One youth who took part in the execution of a PKI *pedanda* (brahmana high priest) described to an Australian tourist how his sword failed to cut into the priest's flesh, until another *pedanda* could be brought in to sprinkle holy water and break his power, enabling the PNI killers to decapitate the first priest and hack him to pieces."

[3] As Roosa (2006) and Robinson (1995) have shown, the role of military forces, and even foreign governments, especially the US and the UK, has been decisive in this humanitarian tragedy.

development—Sanur, Bukit Peninsula, Ubud, or Kuta—may be in a better position to join the capitalist class by capitalising on their land, than would be a *triwangsa* family owning a much larger plot of land somewhere outside the tourism zones. Finally, the capitalist class in Indonesia did not emerge in isolation from the political sphere, but it in fact was given birth and nurtured by the political powerholders (Robison 1986). In Bali, especially during its period as Jakarta's colony, the interests of Suharto's family and cronies in developing tourism facilities necessarily involved local brokers whose social background crossed the caste system. Accumulating capital derived from serving these rent-seeking activities, local brokers, regardless of caste, were able to turn themselves into a capitalist class within the tourism industry, with support from the centres of power.

Adat and Dinas: Dualistic Village Governance

Decentralisation has not only brought about fragmented state structures, but has also expanded possibilities for fostering and adapting a new range of local governance variations. Geertz (1959, 991) noticed the complexities of Bali's local governance in his article 'Form and Variation in Balinese Village Structure' by saying that, "[a]s all things Balinese, Balinese villages are peculiar, complicated and extraordinarily diverse." He conceptualises those complexities through seven overlapping planes: "(1) shared obligation to worship at a given temple (*desa adat*); (2) common residence (*banjar*); (3) ownership of rice land lying within a single watershed (*subak*); (4) communality of ascribed social status or caste (*wangsa*); (5) consanguineal and affinal kinship ties (*dadia*); (6) common membership in one or another 'voluntary' organisation (*seka*); (7) common legal subordination to a single government administrative official" (*desa dinas*) (Geertz 1959, 992–1001). These institutional complexities do not only act as a Balinese framework for political and social action, but also construct local subjectivities grounded on them. In the context of this book, four of these planes have been of particular importance, which are: *desa adat*, *desa dinas*, *subak*, and *banjar*—the sub-village structure usually defined by common residence, where *adat*/*dinas* dichotomies are less clearly demarcated (Warren 1993).

Across Bali, according to the *Majelis Utama Desa Pakraman* (MUDP/ Supreme Assembly of Customary Villages), there are eight main typologies on how *desa adat* and *desa dinas* structures (including *kelurahan* in this category) relate to one another. They are: (1) one *desa adat* consisting of one *desa dinas/kelurahan*; (2) one *desa adat* consisting of several *desa dinas/kelurahan*; (3) one *desa adat* consisting of a single hamlet (*banjar*); (4) one *desa dinas/kelurahan* consisting of several *desa adat*; (5) one *desa adat* with several *desa dinas/kelurahan* located in different sub-districts (*kecamatan*) within one district administration; (6) one *desa adat* consisting of several *desa dinas/kelurahan* located in different *kecamatan* and different district administrations; (7) one *desa dinas/kelurahan* in which one of its *banjar* belongs to another *desa adat* outside the *desa dinas* administration, but is located within a single *kecamatan*; (8) one *desa dinas/kelurahan* in which one of its *banjar* belongs to another *desa adat* beyond the district administration (MUDP Bali 2014; see also Mulyanto 2015).

Historically, the division of labour between the sphere of religious/*adat* affairs within the domain of *desa adat*, and the sphere of law and administration within the domain of *desa dinas* has been the legacy of Dutch Colonialism (Warren 1993). Parimartha (2013), a Balinese historian, however, argues that if '*dinas*' is understood as the representative of state administration at village scale, then the division of labour has its roots going back far before the colonial period when the Gegel Kingdom in Bali with its Majapahit ancestral relations appointed *perbekel* as controllers of village life in the fourteenth through the seventeenth centuries. The Dutch Colonialists took over the *perbekel* role and institutionalised it under the colonial administration for political-economic purposes, such as providing *corvée* labour and revenues, as well as cultural preservation (Parimartha 2013). The establishment of *desa dinas* alongside *desa adat* was informed by Westerners' notions of the separation of religion and politics. Empirically, this was justified by the studies on Bali's mode of governance by two Dutch scholars: Friedrich's hierarchical model of noble governance for *desa dinas* and Korn's model of autonomous and egalitarian village governance, or the so-called village republic, for *desa adat* (Schulte Nordholt 2010).[4]

[4] See, for examples of Dutch scholarship on religious and cultural dimensions of local governance, essays by Liefrinck (1969[1886–1887]), Korn (1984 [1926]), and Friedrich (1959 [1849–1850]).

The relationship between *desa dinas* and *desa adat* is not always harmonious. During the New Order, especially after the enactment of Law No. 5/1979 on Village Government, village structures across the country were standardised and made uniform using the Javanese village model "in the name of efficient development" (Warren 1990, 1). Despite marginalising *desa adat* during this period (Parimartha 2013), Warren (1993) argues that, nonetheless, community life for ordinary villagers continued to revolve primarily around *adat* institutions. This was particularly the case at *banjar* level, where *dinas* functions of the sub-village administrative '*dusun*' under the Village Government Law were effectively encompassed by the *banjar adat*.

The decentralisation policy through the Law No. 22/1999 concerning Regional Autonomy opened up possibilities to develop more responsive village government. However, the state's logic of 'legibility and control' (Scott 1998) was more or less retained with regards to the *kelurahan* structure in urban areas and politically sensitive rural villages. Otherwise, the position of elected village chief (*kepala desa*) was now subjected to a check-and-balance mechanism based on liberal democracy through the village assembly, *Badan Perwakilan Desa* (BPD/village representative body). At the same time, decentralisation has empowered the *desa adat* to widen its domain beyond that previously understood by strictly 'religious' and '*adat*' issues and to take leadership in village governance (Warren 2007). In this matter, although far from an idealised 'village republic', in many cases, *adat* institutions in Bali have shown themselves capable of change and of operating as intermediaries, able to negotiate, adapt, or challenge external vested interests (Warren 2005a, 2007).

More recently, through the enactment of Village Law No. 6/2014, the state structure has been pushed down further to encourage initiatives and entrepreneurship at the village scale. Thus, persistent debates in Bali over whether the division of labour between *adat* and *dinas* village institutions should be maintained (Haruya 2005; Warren 2007) have gained new momentum as the law opens up the possibility to choose *adat, dinas*, or *kelurahan* village structures as the recognised village governance system through district government registration (Vel and Bedner 2015). Based on his historical account, Parimartha (2013) argues that the Balinese should retain the dual structures, because both structures have been complementary for centuries, analogous to a husband-wife relationship. In Sidemen, Karangasem, for instance, Pedersen (2007, 206) shows how the local customary leaders suggested that they "cannot be completely independent of the administrative villages". Accordingly, the supporters of *desa dinas* registration suggest that district and provincial governments in Bali should register *desa dinas* in order to balance the power between *adat* and *dinas* at the village level instead of getting rid of one of them.

In the other camp, however, the supporters of registering *desa adat* embrace the idea that *desa adat* should be legally recognised. Once the *desa adat* becomes a 'legal subject' (*subjek hukum*), it may have legal ownership of land and other collective assets recognisable by state law, and its autonomy will be respected so that the state cannot easily interfere in its internal affairs (*Bisnis Bali*, 06/08/2014; *Bali Post*, 07/01/2015). Nyoman Partha, a Bali DPRD member and Chair of the Special Committee (Pansus) on Village Law, for example, supports the registration of *desa adat*, given its formal marginalisation under previous legislation. He argues that the enactment of Village Law No. 6/2014 should be used as a legal opportunity for giving the *adat* institution acknowledgement, respect, and support with sufficient resources for its maintenance.[5] For him, this was also the background logic for the enactment of Bali's Provincial Regional Regulation No. 3/2001 on Desa Pakraman. In the legislation, the term '*desa adat*' is changed to '*desa pakraman*' to stress its common membership and collective governance authority, rather than the narrow connotations of '*adat*' as tradition-bound custom (Warren 2007). The term '*desa adat*' was previously used in Perda No. 06/1986 concerning Desa Adat. The change to '*desa pakraman*' was pursued because the term '*adat*' is considered alien to the Balinese, as it was derived from the Arabic language and introduced by colonial scholars. Instead, '*pakaraman*' or '*karaman*' itself can be found in many old Balinese scripts, for example, Prasasti Dausa Pura Bukit Indrakila (942 AD) and Prasasti Buahan A (994 AD) (Parimartha 2013; see also Goris 1954).

A closer look at the debates on village government in Bali, including, more recently, concerning Village Law 6/2014, shows that they tend to

[5] Interview with Nyoman Partha, a DPRD member, on 13 October 2013.

be focused on the notion of autonomy. Both the proponents who wish to register *desa dinas* and those who wish to register *desa adat* share a common position in identifying the 'autonomy of *desa adat*' as the point of departure. However, they disagree on how that autonomy should be positioned in relation to the state. Generally, both conflicting stances seem to be confined within the institutional framework. They also tend to be based on a linear assumption of a relation between autonomy and collective welfare, in which greater autonomy would automatically lead to greater welfare of the villagers. In fact, neither *desa adat* nor *desa dinas* are immune from elite capture, albeit with different degrees of susceptibility. This is a particularly salient concern, given that the annual budget for village institutions has been increased significantly by the national government to more than US$ 72,000 per village annually.

Although the debate remained inconclusive regarding the implications of the two alternatives, and significant differences among district government inclinations emerged, Bali's district governments took a decision to register *desa dinas*.[6] From the outset, the Provincial Government of Bali had declared that its stance was to retain the dual system of village government in Bali, and this option came closer to retaining the status quo in practice. As Vel and Bedner (2015) suggest, it is unsurprising that government officials tend to choose *desa dinas* at the expense of *desa adat*, since registering *desa adat* would mean extra work involved in restructuring local institutions. This would include providing policy support in terms of a regional regulation on its recognition, technical support in terms of determining delineation of its territory that is very often unclear and does not tidily overlap with *desa dinas*, as well as political support by not intervening in its internal affairs. More importantly in the context of Bali, choosing *desa adat* would compromise the government's ability to control decision making on lucrative development projects upon which the rent-seeking practices of government officials are based (Wardana and Warren forthcoming). As will be shown in Chap. 6, *adat* institutions very

[6] The divided stance within the district level was especially between *Majelis Madya Desa Pakraman* (*Adat* Village Assembly at the district level), district government officials, and *Forum Kepala Desa/Perbekel* (the forum for administrative village chiefs).

often become a site of struggles against external vested interests when other local institutions, *desa dinas*, or *kelurahan*, are 'well-disciplined' by the state (see also Warren 2007).

In summary, complex village governance has been shaped by power dynamics within Balinese society or between Bali and outside forces. During the Dutch Colonial reign, dualistic village governance was introduced to organise Balinese society to make the extraction of corvée labour and land tax possible with minimal disruptions to local culture. Through the hand of local rulers and the politics of non-intervention towards *adat* village institutions, the colonial administration aimed to conduct indirect rule in Bali, which served the economic interests of the administration to extract revenues and the political interests to prevent a wave of nationalism imported from Java by treating Balinese culture as 'unique', and regarding nationalism as an alien force that might disrupt this uniqueness (Vickers 2012).

This colonial imagery has informed the ways in which Balinese intellectuals responded to any attempt by the national government to change the pre-existing village structures. Even when an opportunity to return to the *adat* village governance as a single village institutional structure was given by the new Village Law, Balinese elites have retained the dualistic village structure inherited by the Dutch Colonialists. Many scholars would agree that if only Bali chose the *adat* village structure, Balinese identity politics would more easily be fostered. So far, the decision to retain the dualistic structure in practice represents a qualified version of Ramstedt's (2013) suggestion of Bali pushing decentralisation downward to the *desa adat* level. In fact, downward decentralisation does not mean to return to the pre-colonial village structure in the hands of *adat* villages, but rather, enhancing its power to be able to work in balance with its *dinas* counterpart.

Subak: Between Autonomy and Dependence

Akin to the debate on the nature of the *adat* village, scholarly debates have occurred in the context of how *subak* relations to 'outside' structures—the state and *desa adat*—are to be understood. Theoretically, the debate pits revisionist interpretations by Schulte Nordholt (2011) and Hauser-Schaublin (2003) against those of Geertz (1980) and Lansing (2006, 2007 [1991]). Geertz (1980) stresses the autonomous nature of *subaks*, a position affirmed by Lansing (2007 [1991]), who adds another feature to the argument on the paramount role of the water temple in *subak* relations, a thesis that is used as the theoretical foundation in the nomination of the Cultural Landscape of Bali Province to the UNESCO World Heritage Regime (Chap. 5). On the other hand, Hauser-Schaublin (2003) shows the important role of kings in managing *subak* relations in pre-colonial and early colonial Bali. Against the romanticisation of *subaks*, Schulte Nordholt (2011) criticises both Geertz and Lansing, by arguing that the notion of *subak* autonomy is a product of a colonial myth in order to side-line institutional structures beyond the village. Birkelbach (1973) notes that *kelihan subak*, or the *pekaseh* in pre-colonial Bali, were chosen by *sedehan yeh*, the king's appointed irrigation controller, as the intermediary between the *subak* and the pre-colonial state. This debate is far from conclusive, as both stances represent each extreme side of the pendulum.

Many observers have shown that the development of *subak* institutions at the local level is not uncontested and is far from harmonious. Like any other irrigation system, the work of the *subak* irrigation association is part of a political process in which rivalry to maintain domains of control and access to resources, most importantly water, is implicated (Mosse 1997; see also Roth and Sedana 2015). Parker (1989, 2003) describes the case of *subaks* in Brassika, Klungkung, which divided their memberships into 'active members' and 'passive members' as a result of incidents associated with the land-reform movement and mass killings during 1965–1966. A *subak* member who was a PKI sympathiser was killed in the *subak* water temple area. Concerned about spiritual 'pollution' caused by the murder, the *subak* leaders decided to build a new *subak* temple and asked its members to contribute labour and funds. Given the heavy burden of building a new temple, several of the members did not show up during the construction. They were then accused of being 'communist' and labelled as 'passive members' of the *subak* (Parker 2003). Although a passive member might still have access to irrigation water and retained the obligation to participate in *subak* affairs, he could not be appointed as a *subak* leader, or *pekaseh*.

Subak institutions may also develop strategic alliances internally or externally in order to pursue their collective interests. Their relative autonomy may become politically advantageous in a broader structural context, as shown by Spiertz (2000) in Subak Gegulung, which is administratively located across two districts: Gianyar and Klungkung. Subak Gegulung uses its administrative good fortune to access government projects, for example, the improvement of tunnels and canals, from both neighbouring district governments. As will be shown in Chap. 5, after being listed as a UNESCO World Heritage Site, Subak Jatiluwih, and other *subak*s within the landscape, are in constant negotiation with *desa dinas, desa adat*, as well as external structures of the state, and even international regulatory bodies.

As Hauser-Schaublin (2003, 162) noted, the debates on the relationship between Balinese *adat* institutions, including *desa adat* and *subak*, and the state should not trap us into "black-and-white thinking", but require an alternative approach. In this matter, the legal pluralist approach provides a different understanding of these two counter positions in the debates concerning the relationship of *desa adat* and *subaks* to the state. The work of Sally Falk Moore (1973) is particularly useful. Moore (1973, 720) develops the concept of a 'semi-autonomous social field', which embraces the idea that an entity has the authority to "generate rules and customs and symbols internally, but that it is also vulnerable to rules and decisions and other forces emanating from the larger world by which it is surrounded". In other words, a social field regulates its domestic affairs, including creating rules of conduct for itself, but at the same time it cannot escape from the external structures that set the framework for its existence. This conceptual framework requires a cross-scale analysis to provide a better understanding of how the boundaries between autonomy from and dependence of a social field upon its wider structural context are drawn, confirmed, negotiated, or contested in particular circumstances.

Thus, both *desa adat* and *subak* in Bali should be seen as 'semi-autonomous social fields', which are internally relatively autonomous and, at the same time, externally relatively dependent upon the wider structural setting (Lorenzen and Lorenzen 2005; Pedersen 2006). This understanding is used throughout the book to escape from the unhelpful dichotomy between the autonomy and dependence of *subak* and *desa adat* in Bali and their relationship to their memberships and wider structural contexts. This conceptual framework enables us also to explain the diversity of structural accommodations between institutional scales that are found across time and space.

Adat Law and the Bhisama Religious Ruling

Several scholars have argued that the conditions of legal pluralism have been the product of colonial indirect rule (Mamdani 1996; Merry 2012). In Bali, however, the conditions of legal pluralism have been a hallmark of Balinese legal culture since the pre-colonial era. Creese (2009) elaborates upon these conditions and notes that, in the pre-colonial period of Bali, there were two models of normative order defined by their jurisdiction, the state (kingdom) scale ('the Indic-influenced law codes' applied by the *Kerta*, a council of priests and judges), and the village scale (local norms or customs applied through assembly, *sangkep*, and *paruman*).

The conceptual framework of the 'semi-autonomous social field' helps to clarify the relationship between institutions with their legal embodiments and the wider structures in which they are embedded. It looks at the interaction between normative orderings not only between a social field and its larger society, but also within the social field itself. In this context, it is no longer possible to consider coexisting legal orders to be exclusively isolated from one another, as they are related and superimposed towards 'inter-legality' (Santos 1987). The normative orders, from *adat*, religious, state, and international laws, rather than being treated as building blocks that must be placed in a rigid hierarchy, should be seen as a constellation that may be adjusted, negotiated, as well as contested, based on the internal logic of the field, and depending upon the power dynamics that are developed within and beyond it. Similarly, in Bali, *adat* law should be understood in relation to other legal orders—state law, religious law, as well as international law—by which it informs and is informed.

With the emergence of an international human rights discourse well before the fall of Suharto, the development of *adat* law in post-authoritarian Bali has been strongly informed by this narrative. Wayan

Windia (2010), an *adat* law professor, advocates a shift in the Balinese *adat* law principle of *Desa Mawacara*—the principle reflected in the adage *desa-kala-patra* (place-time-circumstances) that makes *adat* law in Bali internally flexible and plural—towards a new principle of *Bali Mawacara*, a single, centralised, and unified *adat* law that would apply across Bali, akin to state law. Against this external intervention, Rideng et al. (2015) argue that *desa adat* should be governed based on *Desa-Kala-Patra*, rather than *Bali Mawacara*, to respect its local grounding and autonomy, as well as to prevent its bureaucratisation.

The rationale behind this *Bali Mawacara* narrative is derived from the reality of *desa adat* dynamics, revolving around issues of human rights violations, gender-bias, feudalistic practices, inter-village conflicts, and pointing to the need for an *adat* or religious court system. Windia and others assume that by unifying *adat* law in Bali, it would be easier to mainstream and supervise *adat* law at the village scale to ensure that it complies with human rights and gender equality standards. This standardisation would enable the establishment of an *adat*/religious court based on a hierarchical dispute settlement process mirroring the state court system from the village, to district and provincial levels (Windia 2010). Furthermore, Haruya (2005, 69) argues in the context of *desa adat* in Gianyar District, that in order to 'democratise' *adat* law, will need to grapple "with the inveterate habit of hierarchical social relationships that are maintained under the name of local customs". For him, revitalisation of customary norms at the village level would also lead to "a revitalisation of old feudal power and prestige" (Haruya 2005, 69).

However, feudal practices in *adat* spheres should be seen as arising at least as much from its relationships to the state, as from any distinctive or essential component of *adat*. In *adat* cases across the island, families from higher castes have been expelled from the *adat* village and participation in ritual affairs if they refused to carry out local obligatory *adat* duties given their traditional status. Furthermore, Pedersen (2007) shows in her study in Sidemen, Karangasem District that although the old noble families may regain their power, they do that by "incorporating contemporary values", be that through community empowerment, gender equality, human rights, and so forth (Pedersen 2007, 209). She adds that the tension between hierarchy and egalitarianism is not a new experience in Balinese society, where local people do not follow local leaders blindly (Warren 1993; Pedersen 2007; see also Warren 2016). Even within so-called liberal democratic society, hierarchical structures based on class, gender, race, or sexual-orientation still persists (see Grahn-Farley 2008). There too, formal political institutions are to a large extent dominated by economically and politically powerful elites, as many scholars of Indonesian oligarchy have shown (Winters 2013; Hadiz and Robison 2013).

Bali Mawacara would require a hierarchical institutional arrangement to supervise and superimpose its standards upon *desa adat* at the village scale. In this regard, the reform era *Majelis Desa Pakraman* (*adat* councils) from sub-district up to provincial levels, whose current roles are limited to advisory and promotional functions, would be transformed into a hierarchic structure of authority in which *desa adat* would be the lowest level. In order to make its task effective, the *Bali Mawacara* centralised institutional arrangement necessarily requires the standardisation of customary law, including in the form of written *awig-awig*. Warren (1993, 4) notes that *adat* in Bali is far more complex than the conventional concept of customary law implies. It involves *tata krama* (local practice), *sima* (rules and norms), and *dresta* (*adat*/custom) as "a field of meanings covering ritual obligation, social institution, legal regulation and ancestral evocation". Indeed, *adat* in Bali has "always been embodied in what is essentially community praxis, a practice and procedure whose authority rests on relations between the living and the dead, in which codified forms could only be partial expressions" (Warren 1993, 296). Accordingly, *adat* in Bali is highly diverse, involving rich meanings and practices, since local praxis itself is different from one locality to the others. Hence, codification of *adat* law would mean reducing this rich meaning to a written legal regulation which compromises its flexibility and plurality (Pedersen 2007) and more importantly risks shifting the power balance between *adat* and *dinas* institutional authority (Warren 1993). The *Bali Mawacara* narrative appears to be deeply informed by the 'seeing-like-a-state' logic (Scott 1998). This does not only aim at simplifying the dynamics of *desa adat* and making them legible to higher authority, but by design to transform the *desa adat* itself into being like a state.

A similar tendency to unification and formalisation has also been occurring within the context of the *subak* system. Modernisation of *subaks* has been undertaken through *lomba subak* (*subak* competitions) since the 1980s. As with *lomba desa* (village competitions) in the same period, one of the components to be judged is whether the *awig-awig* has been converted into written form with a standardised format (Pedersen and Dharmiasih 2015; Lorenzen 2015). Subak Jatiluwih has never been nominated for the *subak* competition because it has no written *awig-awig*, or *subak* meeting hall. With the UNESCO World Heritage designation, however, it eventually decided to enact a written *awig-awig* as required by the management plan for governing the site (see Chap. 5). Besides a written *awig-awig*, the other requisite is the recognition of *subaks* by the state law regime in the form of a government regulation. Thus, the provincial government enacted a Provincial Regulation on S*ubak* (Perda Subak No. 9/2012), which defines *awig-awig* as "*norma-norma adat yang disuratkan yang mengatur tentang subak* [customary norms that are written to govern *subak*]". Clearly, this undermines the nature and role of informal and unwritten rules that are very often more important as the basis of daily decision making (Warren 1993; Lorenzen and Lorenzen 2005).

Another aspect of the normative legal order in Balinese society has been the religious rulings based on Hindu manuscripts, known as *Bhisama*. In the context of spatial and environmental governance, the *Bhisama Kesucian Pura* was declared by the PHDI in 1994 at the height of public protests against mega-project developments facilitated by the New Order. Those projects have dramatically altered the character of the Balinese economy and initiated an increasingly politicised Balinese society (Warren 2009, 198). The landmark case was the Bakrie Nirwana Resort (BNR) mega-project owned by Aburizal Bakrie, a national tycoon close to Suharto (see Warren 1998; Suasta and Connor 1999).[7] The plan was to develop the agricultural areas surrounding the Tanah Lot Temple into an integrated tourism resort complex, including hotels, golf courses, condominiums, and other facilities. The most sensitive argument presented in the media by those of the Balinese populace who were opposed to the project was a symbolic and religious one, namely, the fact that it

[7] More recently, the BNR has been taken over by Hari Tanoesoedibjo, a national tycoon, who collaborates with Trump Hotel owned by Donald Trump, the US President (*Tempo*, 23/01/2017).

was too close to Tanah Lot Temple, which is one of the holiest shrines for Balinese Hindus. The Tanah Lot mega-project was one among many development proposals believed to disturb the sacredness of numerous sites and came to symbolise popular disaffection with a range of cultural, environmental, socioeconomic, and political impacts arising from the new direction and scale of tourism development.

Accordingly, the government-recognised Hindu organisation, *Parisada Hindu Dharma Indonesia* (PHDI), conducted a *Mahasabha* (general assembly) in 1994 to discuss the issue, and then finally released the *Bhisama* concerning the sphere of temple sanctity. The *Bhisama* translates the radius of the temple's sacred space, depending on a hierarchical classification of temples, into standard measures: (1) *Kahyangan Tiga* at the village scale with a radius of *apenimpug* (a stone's-throw), or quantified as 25 metres; (2) *Dang Kahyangan* at the district scale with the radius of *apeneleng alit* (normal human line of sight), quantified as two kilometres; and (3) *Sad Kahyangan* at the provincial scale with the radius of *apeneleng agung* (exceptional line of sight), quantified as five kilometres. In spite of failing to prevent the project, the *Bhisama* remains a pivotal ruling. In 2005, the Provincial Regulation on Spatial Planning for Bali (Perda RTRW Bali No. 3/2005) incorporated the *Bhisama* into the state's legal regime (Article 19). Hence, it is no longer merely a spiritual ruling with spiritual sanctions, but has also become a legal claim, which many civil society actors have used to reject development projects that are perceived to jeopardise Balinese culture and the environment (see Wardana 2015).

Conclusion

Contemporary Bali has been shaped by a series of historical conjunctures. In this chapter, I have shown several of them dated from the colonial period. The image of paradise created by the Dutch Colonial administration is an essential myth that has been the foundation for the tourism industry on the island to date. The polarisation of former freedom fighters in the post-colonial period led to contestations over power and resources that provided a local context to the 1965–1966 mass killings. This humanitarian tragedy was a form of 'accumulation by dispossession' that paved the way for Suharto into power and opened up capitalist modes of production in the country. In Bali, this was pursued through development of the mass tourism industry employing systematic persuasions, displacements, indoctrination, and even coercions. Following the fall of the Suharto Regime, the politics of development in Bali have never changed, but have even expanded sporadically where local political and economic elites incubated under the authoritarian regime played a decisive role. The changing in government institutional structures from centralism to decentralism has perpetuated more complex legal and institutional conditions in the islands. As we shall see in the following chapters, these local institutions play a more significant role than ever in the development process.

3

Crisis and Reorganisation of Space

In the previous chapter, we have seen how the historical conjunctures shape contemporary Bali not only in terms of its economy, but also in terms of its legal and institutional constellations as well as social and political dynamics. In fact, the unintended consequences of these conjunctures have brought Bali towards socio-ecological crisis. In this chapter, I will demonstrate how such a crisis is conceived and the solutions are put forward in public policy. Here, it is observed that there are three dominant perspectives used to understand the current crisis, which are rational-choice, conservative, and institutionalist perspectives. The chapter will show how those perspectives have failed to provide an adequate understanding of the crisis due to their inherent flaws. Finally, this is then followed by a particular focus on the use of spatial planning to respond to the crisis through the designation of 'provincial strategic areas'.

Conceiving Crisis in Contemporary Bali

Tourism sectors have had a significant impact on Bali. As Picard (1996) argues, Balinese culture is deeply influenced by tourism. Economically, the tourism sector provides 481,000 jobs directly, providing employment

A. Wardana, *Contemporary Bali*, https://doi.org/10.1007/978-981-13-2478-9_3

for 25% of the work force and contributing 30% of the Gross Domestic Product of Bali Province in 2009 (Cole 2012, 1224). From the national point of view, Bali is 'the gateway' for the tourism economy in Indonesia: around 40% of the total tourist visits to Indonesia in 2010 arrived through Bali, which has 15% of the total hotel capacity in Indonesia (Indonesia. CMEA 2011, 142). Despite its significance, tourism as a capitalist industry must face up to its inherent contradictions in terms of displacement of local communities, resource exploitation, intensified commodification of culture, and labour exploitation (Bianchi 2009; Fletcher 2011). In Bali, its negative environmental, social, cultural, as well as local economic, impacts have become public concerns among the Balinese public.

Many observers have argued that Bali has reached its 'tipping point' and is on the verge of 'self-destruction' (Reuter 2003; *Bali Post*, 11/01/2009; Lewis and Lewis 2009; Fox 2012, 13). Bali's agricultural heritage is declining, as shown by the acceleration of land conversion (Warren 2012) as well as the impoverishment of farmer households (MacRae 2003; Lorenzen and Lorenzen 2005). Waste and pollution have been chronic issues (Dharma Putra 2009; Marshall 2011; Oliphant 2017). Forest cover has been reduced to well below the 30% total land area threshold, which is only 22.42% (PPPE Bali & Nusra 2015, 9). This will have adverse effects on the water table. In fact, it is predicted that Bali will face a water crisis by 2025. The extraction of water, particularly ground water, is also alarming, as it now far exceeds its natural hydrological cycle (Cole and Browne 2015; Sunarta et al. 2015; Sunarta and As-syakur 2015). Around 260 out of 400 rivers have reportedly run dry (Cole 2012, 1234).

Conflicts over space and natural resources have also become more common. In Tabanan alone, almost 65% of its water resources are transported to tourism areas in Southern Bali, especially Badung (Cole 2012, 1234); this has resulted in an escalation in water conflicts in the region (Kurnianingsih n.d.; Trisnawati n.d.; *Tempo*, 14/01/2013). Moreover, there have been contestations over common space, such as beaches, forests, and lakes (McCarthy 1994; Suartika 2005; Strauss 2015; see *Bali Post* 20/9/11). The coastlines, especially along non-touristic beaches, are severely eroded by up to 30%, which in turn may lead to the shrinking of terrestrial areas of mainland Bali (Arida 2008, 120). Sacred areas that are important not only for religion and culture, but also for conservation have been encroached (Wardana 2014b; Strauss 2015). Moreover, social inequalities and crime rates targeting and involving tourists have increased rapidly (*Jakarta Globe*, 08/01/2012; Cassrels 2014; *Pos Bali*, 21/10/2014; *Antara*, 26/07/2015).

In this section, I trace the ways in which socio-ecological change and crisis in contemporary Bali is understood within the sphere of public policy. There are three perspectives that dominated public policy: the rational-choice, the conservative, and the institutionalist frameworks. I argue that such understandings of change and crisis in contemporary Bali are flawed and cover up the underlying foundations of the crisis. Alternatively, I examine the notion of socio-ecological change and crisis through the wider configurations of power, representing "'the focal points of conflict' where competition and struggles to access power and resources involving different social forces take place within a particular geographical scale or across scales" (Rodan et al. 2006, 8; Gerard 2014). Furthermore, particular constructions of the 'crisis' are necessarily political. To say this does not mean that the crisis facing contemporary Bali is not real, but rather speaks to the need to uncover the political opportunism taking advantage of these concerns. This is exactly because "[c]rises … provide an opportunity for contending groups to assert their interests. Note that the power to declare a crisis is itself contingent upon power—having a voice and a constituency to hear and support it. Resolutions of crises reflect the coming into power—or failure to achieve it—of contending groups" (Lees 2001, 55). In other words, how a crisis is declared and solutions to the crisis put forward necessarily involve a power exercise through which particular interests are advanced while others are hindered.

The Rational-Choice Assumption

Agriculture, according to many observers, has been the backbone of Balinese culture, in which the *subak* has played an important role. It is estimated that there are 1559 *subaks* covering around 81,625 hectares of wet-rice *sawah*, 14.48% of Bali's landmass (BPS Bali 2013). Although the *subak* system is argued to have been highly resilient due to its flexibility, the combination of internal and external pressures in the contemporary period, including climate change, has created more challenging issues than ever (MacRae 2003; Lorenzen and Lorenzen 2005; MacRae and Alit Arthawiguna 2011). One notable challenge faced by *subaks* is the rapid conversion of agricultural land into non-agricultural land nowadays, especially for constructing tourism and real estate facilities, such as golf courses, resorts, hotels, and other commercial sites. The rate of land conversion since the 1990s has been 1000 hectares annually (MacRae 2005, 211–212; Warren 2009, 198).

It is frequently argued that farmers choose to sell their land leading to massive land conversion when farming is no longer economically profitable due to the high price of fertiliser, seeds, and other production costs, while the market product remains limited (Indonesia. MCT 2011; Pitana and Adi Putra 2013). The dossier of the Nomination for the Inscription of the Cultural Landscape of Bali Province on the UNESCO World Heritage Regime clearly states this by saying that "[a]s long as farmers can only grow cheap hybrid rice, rising land prices and increasing living costs tempt them to sell their land and seek alternative professions" (Indonesia. MCT 2011, III-5). On a similar note, Sutawan, Udayana University Professor of Agriculture, argues that:

> The shrinking of farmland has been rapid, especially in the locations that are close to urban areas because the price [of land] tends to be high. It appears that farmers tend to sell their land instead of utilizing it as the harvest is not really promising. The farmers are more likely to deposit the money from selling the land in a bank and wait for the monthly interest paid which maybe bigger than the income from utilising the land. (Sutawan 2001, 3)

The rational-choice assumption above embraces the notion that every individual is a wealth-maximising entity in which his or her decision is merely determined by a cost-benefit calculation. In this regard, the rational-choice assumption sees the rapid land conversion leading to the crisis as the product of inefficiency of the agricultural sector. It concludes that the conversion of productive rice fields is because agriculture is no longer economically attractive and beneficial. Based on this assumption, the solutions proposed are very often related to maximising the profitability of agricultural activities, as well as providing added value by integrating it with the tourism market. Hence, farmers who are typically involved in subsistence agricultural practices are directed to develop their entrepreneurial skills by orienting to the market demand either to grow cash crop for the global markets through agri-business or to grow organic food for New Age-minded tourists and expatriates in Bali.

The other dominant solution to address Bali's agricultural crisis is by making an added value for farming. It embraces that in order to conserve Bali's agricultural landscape from rapid conversion, alternative income sources should be provided to farmers. The integration of agriculture into tourism market is seen as the most feasible solution. Hence, the agriculture heritage of Bali involving cultural practices and scenic landscapes are then packed and promoted as a tourist's gaze based on the assumption that the revenues from tourist visits to the agricultural landscape can be used to support farmers dealing with their economically challenging conditions. This assumption has also been the underlying motivation behind the inscription of several *subak* landscapes to the UNESCO World Heritage Regime. Following the flocks of tourist visits to the agricultural landscapes with a brand of being a World Heritage Site, namely, the Jatiluwih Rice Terrace, which in turn increased local revenues, initiatives to develop village tourism projects in rural areas across Bali have been pursued sporadically either through the financial support from local governments and universities or by means of self-funding from the village fund.

Historically, the village tourism project was started in 2005 to develop in three rural villages in which Jatiluwih Village where the core zone for the World Heritage Site for Bali Province is situated was one of them (Yamashita 2003). Since 2013 onward, the project then has expanded further, with an ambitious plan of the Government of Bali Province to develop 100 more village tourism objectives. In 2017, through this program, it had managed to establish 67 village tourism objects across the island (*Bisniswisata*, 21/02/2017) in addition to the existing 160 of them funded under the PNPM Mandiri schemes and many other objects developed independently by the local community (*Kompas*, 10/04/2014). This is claimed to offer different types of tourism experiences so that the target of 7 million tourists—almost twice Bali's total population—in 2018 can be reached (*Kompas*, 10/04/2014; *Tempo*, 19/12/2017). Consequently, competition between villages to attract tourist visits will be more common in the future, and the pressures on the environment should not be overlooked.

The Conservative Viewpoint

Many scholars of Bali Studies attribute what has been happening in Bali is related to the impacts of globalisation and modernisation brought by tourism through which Balinese cultural values are compromised with the introduction of modern values (Lewis and Lewis 2009; Atmadja 2010a; Vickers 2012 [1990]). Lewis and Lewis (2009, 8) posited that "the crisis of Bali is fundamentally associated with its meaning and the different way in which these meanings are created by different social groups". Using a conservative tone, Atmadja (2010a, 84), an Undiksha anthropologist, observes that "modernisation and westernisation striking Balinese nowadays has not only caused changing in the physical culture (*kebudayaan fisik*) and the social system, but also in the cultural system, such as in the spiritual aspect". According to him, Balinese Hindu spirituality has been replaced by what he calls 'modern spiritualism' involving individualism, hedonism, consumerism, and so forth (Atmadja 2010a, 86–87). Hence, based on a conservative approach, the crisis in contemporary Bali is regarded as the product of cultural change within Balinese society, in which such change itself is caused by external forces.

As discussed in the previous chapter, conceiving external forces as a jeopardy to the Balinese cultural identity is not a new mode of identity politics in Bali's history. During the colonial period, the Dutch administration introduced an ethical policy of '*Baliseering*' or 'Balinisation' of Balinese society based on a colonial ideal conception of 'Balinese-ness', from dress, arts, architecture, social system, *adat* law, and even religion (Schulte Nordholt 2000). During this period, the fear of external forces such as nationalism, Islam, and Christian missionaries were seen as threats to the colonial administration and the traditional structure of the society that brought the Dutch Colonial and Balinese traditional rulers together with mutual objectives, retaining their power and resources. In both colonial and contemporary understandings of threats to Bali, the conservative framework necessarily involves essentialising Bali's cultural identity as distinctively given, and the construction of the 'other-ness', be it nationalism, Islam, modernisation, globalisation, and more recently immigrants, which allegedly may destroy such an identity.

When it comes to the economy, instead of defining the economic actors in terms of class, or their position in the ownership of the means of production, the conservative framework defines them in terms of cultural identity, Balinese and Non-Balinese. In this respect, it is estimated that around 80–85% of the US$8 billion total assets of Bali's tourism industry is in the hands of non-Balinese (Lewis and Lewis 2009, 76; MacRae 2010, 20). In fact, Balinese hold only 1.7% of top management positions in the industry, while the rest are occupied by non-Balinese, either foreigners or other Indonesians (*Bali Post*, 16/02/2006). Nowadays, Fagertun (2017a, 336) claims that migrant workers from parts of Indonesia are counted to be 10% of Bali's total population. Responding to this, Anak Agung Ngurah Alit, the Chair of Badung's Chamber of Commerce, argues that "this condition is very dangerous for Bali's economy. Thus, the role of local [Balinese] investors should be *diperkuat* (reinforced)" (*Kompas*, 25/11/12). In the context of the reclamation project in Benoa Bay, Windia (2015), an Udayana Professor of Agriculture and the Chairman of Subak Study Center, in an opinion published by the *Bali Post*, argues,

> If the reclamation project of Benoa Bay is allowed, migrants staying in Bali will be multiplied. They need land for residency and this may convert rice fields and subak landscape in Bali yet further. Once the landscapes and fields destroyed, Balinese culture rooted in agrarian culture will also be destroyed. If Balinese culture is destroyed, there nothing can be relied upon (*dipertaruhkan*). Bali will be disappeared, like in the case of Majapahit Kingdom.

The conservative gesture is not exclusively the property of old generations. The young Balinese generation may also share a similar one. This is best represented by two young public figures in Bali. The first one is

Jerink of Superman Is Dead—a rock band from Kuta—who is a leading figure in ForBali, the opponent group against the Benoa Bay reclamation project (Chap. 6). The second is Dr. Arya Wedakarna, son of Wedastera Suyasa, a local figure of the Indonesian Nationalist Party (PNI) in Bali who was responsible for Bali's political polarisation leading to the 1965–1966 mass killings (Robinson 1995). Jerink, in an interview with a magazine, influenced by a Malthusian thinking, regards overpopulation as the biggest threats to future Bali's environment. When asked about his activism, he declares that "[i]n principle, I am not *anti pembangunan* (anti-development). My colleagues in Forbali are also not anti-development. But what we demand is simple, that is *pembangunan yang benar* (right development). Development that is not hurting social structure of Balinese society (*tidak melukai struktur sosial masyarakat Bali*) and not hurting or destroy ecology" (Apriando 2014). The crisis in contemporary Bali is in fact the product of the existing social structure based on hierarchy and unequal relations of power. Preserving the existing social structure would mean retaining the existing relations of power—the root cause of the crisis.

For Balinese conservative groups and intellectuals, the era of Majapahit Kingdom is very often used as a reference for lesson learnt with regards to what has been happening to Bali lately. The fall of the kingdom is attributed to the spread of Islam in Java during the rule of Brawijaya in the sixteenth century, where Muslim traders had gained influence and dominated the economy (Atmadja 2010b). Prof. Windia's reference to Majapahit implies that the history of the fall of the Majapahit Kingdom would repeat itself in Bali if Muslim immigrants were not quickly brought under control. A similar reference to Majapahit, but in an optimistic version, has been employed by Dr. Arya Wedakarna. To build its image and popularity, Dr. Wedakarna spends around IDR 1 billion annually for media outreach, especially in the *Bali Post*'s column of pseudo-news (Muhajir 2013). Through this media, he utilised the myth of *Sabda Palon*, a Javanese Hindu version of the chosen one, and proclaimed himself to be the one—or the next—King of Majapahit to bring back the glory of Hinduism in the archipelago. In the 2014 general election, by exploiting a conservative idea of Hindu nationalism, he managed to win a significant vote running a set in the senate-like Regional Representative

Council (DPD). Indeed, as a young and ambitious politician supported by adequate financial resources, he certainly will not stop here. He seeks to capture executive positions, especially the post of governor, where he can bring his right-wing Hindu Nationalism to be a formal government agenda.

Rather than seeing those environmental, economic, and cultural concerns as being rooted in the political-economic structures of the tourism industry, dominant responses to those concerns have been a narrow identity politics of 'Balineseness'. One most popular response employing the conservative assumption has been the *Ajeg Bali* movement. First initiated in the early 2000s by Satria Narada, the media mogul who owns Bali's main media outlet—the *Bali Post* Group—the movement attempted to establish public discourse in considering Bali's contemporary social, economic, cultural, and environmental issue in their relations to development (Lewis and Lewis 2009, 152). The discourse gained momentum to attract more widespread public attention among the Balinese populace following the 2002 Bali Bombing, and it became the campaign tagline to Mangku Pastika, the former Chair of Bali's Police Department, running for the 2008 gubernatorial election with support from the *Bali Post* Group. The institutionalisation of *Ajeg Bali* in Mangku Pastika's first term in office (2008–2013) has caused previous public discourse to take on institutionalised political weight. Governor Pastika, in his address on the 2011 Nomination for Inscription of the Cultural Landscape of Bali Province on the UNESCO World Heritage List, for instance, states that "the government of Bali Province is still committed to proceed the nomination as it is in accordance with the local government's campaign of *Ajeg Bali* to preserve Balinese culture, society, and politics from the effect of globalization" (Indonesia. MCT 2011, I-2). Schulte Nordholt (2007) notes that this movement is a modern version of the *Baliniseering* policy, for strengthening and preserving Balinese culture from external forces.

Besides the institutionalised form of *Ajeg Bali*, it is also a different interpretation from several conservative Balinese intellectuals. Prof. Bawa Atmadja (2010a, 3), for instance, argues, "*Ajeg Bali* movement related to the preservation of Balinese cultural identity is not only important but also a state of urgency; a must for the sustainability of Balinese society and Balinese culture". However, Atmadja's version of *Ajeg Bali* differs from that of the *Bali Post* in the construction of 'other-ness' (Wardana 2013). While the *Bali Post*'s version of *Ajeg Bali* defines non-Balinese immigrants as the 'other', Atmadja's version widens the horizons of the 'otherness' to consider the flow of globalisation as the main threat to Balinese culture. For him, the issues of Non-Balinese immigrants, especially from the neighbouring islands, should be seen as a symptom or derivative of globalisation. He says that although the immigrants are also a threat to Bali because they can "take Balinese jobs and space", the destructive degree of this threat is far less than that of globalisation (Atmadja 2010a, 496–501). However, they both represent what may be called as 'the paradox of Balinese culture'—on the one hand, the conservative groups praise Balinese culture to be uniquely resilient; on the other hand, they demand that the culture should be preserved, protected, and guarded from outside forces, be they migrants, modernisation, or globalisation. The need for protection is itself showing its weaknesses and fragility. Moreover, the defence of Balinese cultural identity, consciously or unconsciously, also serves the tourism industry, the main driver of neoliberal globalisation in the island, in searching for the 'authentic' Bali to be consumed by global tourists.

The role of media is important in the spread of *Ajeg Bali* and other conservative ideas. Ramstedt (2009, 360) once observes that "the 'dark side' of a free press in a burgeoning civil society with competitive election in the fluid institutional contexts of a weak state (like decentralising Indonesia) consists of the fact that it tends to promote ethnicization, and is thereby likely to trigger communalist violence". In Bali, and other regions, the 'dark side' of free press has created severe competitions among media companies and in turn led to a 'pragmatic press' through which elites with strong financial resources may use the media to boost their image and popularity, like in the case of Dr. Wedakarna. Consequently, the mass media in the contemporary period of Bali has been an outlet for promoting *Ajeg Bali* and other conservative political ideas. Such promotion may lose its appeal when the media stops its coverage due to a split among the elites. In the case of *Ajeg Bali*, for instance, the discourse of *Ajeg Bali* has lost its appeal following the conflict between Satria Narada, the owner of the *Bali Post* Group, and Governor Mangku Pastika, once an *Ajeg Bali* political loyalist.[1] Hence, this proves that the ideas of Balinese identity politics, like many forms of identity politics in general, and the sense of insecurity towards external forces, like it was in the colonial period, are in fact fabricated from above by elites in pursuing or maintaining their political, economic, and social interests.

The Institutionalist Explanation

Decentralisation, as claimed by the World Bank, is supposed to bring development and public service closer to the public. However, many scholars have shown the unintended consequences of decentralisation in Indonesia, from the emergence of 'little kings', the spread of corruption, identity politics, as well as environmental degradations (Schulte Nordholt and van Klinken 2007). Similarly, decentralisation has been attributed to the contemporary environmental crisis in Bali. It is frequently argued that regional autonomy in the hands of district and municipal governments is not suitable for Bali's geographical, ecological, economic, and cultural situation (Pansus Otsus 2007; Atmadja 2010a; Suharyo 2011; *Antara News*, 25/09/2014). Thus, a 'one island one management' development concept has been popularised by the Balinese intelligentsia, who were concerned with the competition among district governments in attracting investments by disregarding its impact within and beyond their administrative boundaries.

The concept of 'one island one management' is inspired by the idea of 'eco-region' in environmental management and planning literature. In this literature, eco-region is defined as a large area with similar characteristics in terms of climate, land, water, and biodiversity conditions in which such an area should be managed based on these ecological characteristics, rather than being based on its political-administrative boundaries. Following such definition, it assumes that Bali Province is having similar ecological characteristics and connections where a management

[1] Preceding the 2013 gubernatorial election, the *Bali Post* group switched its support from Governor Mangku Pastika who wanted to run the office for his second term to support Puspayoga, the vice-governor, running of the governor position.

based on districts' political-administrative boundaries may cause severe impacts on this characteristics and connections. Accordingly, the management of the eco-region of Bali should be under the Provincial Government of Bali so that it may oversee developments taking place within the district boundaries and direct them in accordance with ecological sustainability for the whole region. This concept had an appeal not only for government officials and political elites at the provincial level, but also for intellectual, and civil society organisations concerned with the impact of district regional autonomy.

Politically, the realisation of such a concept has been pursued by different strategies. The most notorious one is the proposal of special autonomy for Bali Province. The discourse to change the institutional structure of the province through special autonomy, akin to Aceh, Papua or Yogyakarta, had been circulated in the early 2000s, following the implementation of the regional autonomy regime. In the mid-2000s, a special committee on special autonomy (*pansus otonomi khusus*) was established by the Regional People's Representative Council (DPRD) of Bali supported by the academics of Udayana University, with a mandate to formulate an academic study and a draft of Special Autonomy Law for Bali Province. After working for at least two years, the committee managed to finish both the study and the draft. Indeed, since 2007, the draft has been submitted to the National House of Representatives to be discussed and expectedly to be adopted as a law. From those, the special autonomy proposal attempted to give greater authority into the hands of the provincial, instead of district-level, government, in order to provide an integral approach to island-wide environmental and cultural issues (Suharyo 2011; Ramstedt 2013; see also Wardana 2015). The proposed changes to institutional structure follows after the Jakarta institutional model, in which mayors are appointed by the governor and the Provincial House of Representatives is only located at the provincial level for an effective and efficient government (Pansus Otsus 2007).

Observing this issue, several scholars note that the call for special autonomy in Bali is merely about Balinese identity politics. Ramstedt (2009, 361), for instance, claims that "[t]he rising xenophobia and the growing anxiety over the increasing fragmentation of Balinese society in the wake of the regional autonomy legislation intensified, and therefore calls for special autonomy status for Bali". It is true that the uniqueness to justify the proposal is an essentialist understanding of Balinese culture, customary institution, and religion. However, the underlying motive is less about preserving the fragmented Balinese identity affected by decentralisation at the district level, but more about provincial elites' political economic interests. Bali contributes significantly to the national government from foreign exchange. It is calculated that approximately IDR 47 trillion (US$ 3.4 billion) from non-oil sectors particularly tourism is transferred to the national government (Tempo, 09/09/15). However, revenues from the tourism sectors are not a subject of *Dana Bagi Hasil* (DBH/ revenue sharing fund), a scheme for sharing revenue between national and regional governments deriving only from tax, excise, and natural-resource extraction and exploitation.[2] Accordingly, Bali, a province with limited natural resources, receives a very small amount of the shared revenue fund deriving only from land taxes and tobacco excise. For Balinese elites and the intelligentsia, this shared scheme is considered unfair to the Balinese. Hence, the Balinese identity as an immediate cultural pool has been used by the elites for legitimising access to tourist revenues.

Unsurprisingly, however, it has been more than a decade, and there is no sign the draft of special autonomy for Bali Province will be discussed in the near future. This is not only due to the competition with several similar proposals that have also been put on the table by other provinces (Ramstedt 2013) but, more importantly, because the proposal is viewed suspiciously by political elites both at the district and national levels. For district government politicians, the abolition of the District House of Representatives and the removal of elected district and municipal heads in the draft Law on Special Autonomy for Bali is among other very controversial proposals that implicate the informal incomes of local elites from rent-seeking practices that pervade permit-granting processes. For political parties, it would also mean losing a source of income from their individual parliamentary members in the form of contributory fees (*iuran partai*). Every member has to pay a fee

[2] East Kalimantan, one of the richest provinces in terms of oil and gas resources, in 2014, for instance, received revenue sharing fund (DBH) around US$553 million (*Katadata*, 22/01/2015).

of around US$ 725–1800 per month, almost a half of his/her salary (*Tempo*, 23/04/2013). The proposal would also remove potential checks for such practices that would then be monopolised at the provincial level.

More recently, the discourse of 'one island one management' has re-emerged. This has followed the decision of the District Government of Badung to allocate 15% of Badung's total Hotel and Restaurant Tax (PHR) revenue directly to six relatively lower-middle income districts in Bali. This decision was taken by Giri Prasta, Badung's newly elected district head, from PDI-Perjuangan Party, representing an end of a decade rule of the Golkar Party in the district, to support the other districts mostly ruled by PDI Perjuangan, such as Jembrana, Buleleng, Tabanan, and Bangli. Previously, based on a Memorandum of Understanding (MoU) between the Provincial Government of Bali and the district and municipal governments in Bali made in 2013, the financial allocation for those districts was channelled through the provincial government, which was ruled by PDI Perjuangan. The decision taken by the District of Badung was considered politically motivated by the provincial government because of it Governor Mangku Pastika who was from a Golkar-Democratic Party coalition. It risks significantly decreasing the provincial budget and may erode the influence of provincial government at the district levels while patronising Badung as the 'savoir' of the other districts.

As a response, the provincial government has re-mobilised the discourse on 'one island one management'. The Tourism Bureau of Bali Province, for instance, argues that Bali's tourism should be managed based on the 'one island one management' approach because Bali is not very wide and its resources should be allocated fairly among districts (*Antara News*, 18/02/2017). Following the inscription of the Cultural Landscape of Bali Province to the UNESCO World Heritage Site in 2012, the provincial government established a governing model influenced by such an approach located at the provincial level to manage the conservation and tourism of the World Heritage Site that is located across districts. However, as we shall see in Chap. 5, the model has been a subject of contestations between the provincial and district governments to access the benefits from the listing, especially tourist revenues. In the case of Benoa Bay's reclamation (Chap. 6), the investor was clearly backed by the provincial government. Hence, it is safe to say that neither the regional autonomy in the hands of district governments nor the special autonomy in the hands of the provincial government would lead to the sustainability and fair distribution of resources. As the relations of economic and political power remain intact, both provincial and district government structures are not immune from elite capture in pursuing their vested interests.

The Structure of Disfranchisement

Agrarian Heritage and Capitalist Development

In the nomination dossier of the Cultural Landscape of Bali Province to the World Heritage List, agriculture is used as the main 'selling point' for justifying the inscription. It claims that Bali's agrarian heritage has recently been threatened by four main issues: (1) the loss of soil fertility due to the overuse of chemical fertilisers and hybrid-rice seeds that were introduced with the Green Revolution's intensification program under the New Order; (2) low income from rice farming due to the high cost of inputs and the small size of landholdings; (3) forest degradation that affects the water supply for *subak*; and (4) land conversion due to uncontrolled development (Indonesia. MCT 2011).[3] A close examination of those threats would reveal that they are largely products of government policies and practices within the political economy of capitalist development.

The Green Revolution was the policy of the New Order imposed upon farmers for the modernisation of the agricultural sectors in the country through intensification. This included the introduction of high-yielding varieties and the constructions of new and modern weirs with support from international financial institutions (the World Bank and Asian Development Bank). Many scholars have noted the negative impact of

[3] Many *farming* households that were unable to cope with those threats decided to transmigrate to the outer islands of Indonesia, such as Sulawesi. However, in the new place, they also faced many challenges and conflicts over property rights, including over water irrigation (see Roth 2009).

this policy as it paid little regard to the existing complex and sophisticated cultural-ecological agricultural systems operating on the ground (Birkelbach 1973; Spiertz 2000; Lansing 2007 [1991]; MacRae 2010). Low incomes from farming are due to population growth, unequal distribution of land, and generally poor terms of trade for agricultural products globally.[4] With regard to forest degradation, the government has granted concessions for several entities to undertake development projects within the island's forest watershed areas. These include, among others, the Bedugul Geothermal Project for power generation and the NBA for luxury resorts in the middle of Dasong Forests between Lakes Buyan and Tamblingan.[5] This demonstrates that, in the context of forest degradation, the government is itself part of the problem.

Due to the massive expansion of the tourism industry, the relationship between agriculture and tourism has been problematic. Given the decline in agricultural land (Fig. 3.1) and the low value of primary products, the agricultural sector that previously contributed 43.30% to the regional economy in 1983 has steadily declined to only 17.69% in 2013 (Erawan 1994; BPS Bali 2014a). In contrast, the contribution of the tourism sector has increased from 10.30% in 1983 to 32.14% in 2013 (Erawan 1994; BPS Bali 2014a). Rhetorically, many scholars and policymakers have proposed a win-win solution by advocating village tourism to balance the desire to pursue economic growth and the need to preserve agriculture (see Pitana and Adi Putra 2013).

In practice, however, the relationship appears to be a predatory one in which the tourism industry exploits agricultural areas, images, and practices for branding and expanding tourism and a real estate industry that has become allied to it. This appropriation is entirely about the com-

[4] Lucas and Warren (2013, 2) observe that agrarian policy and conflicts across Indonesia "embody powerful tensions between elites and popular forces, between regional interests and central government, and between Indonesian national and transnational capital".

[5] At this stage, construction has been done on 25.88 hectares out of an 83-hectare total concession and around 2 hectares of a 20.3-hectare concession granted by the Ministry of Forestry (*Kompas*, 15/12/2011; interview with Ketut Artina, Secretary of *Catur Desa Dalem Tamblingan*, on 16 February 2014). However, until recently, both projects have not operated effectively and could not expand their concessions due to protests from local *adat* communities and NGO activists (see *Mongabay*, 14/05/2012; *Kompas*, 11/05/2012; Strauss 2015).

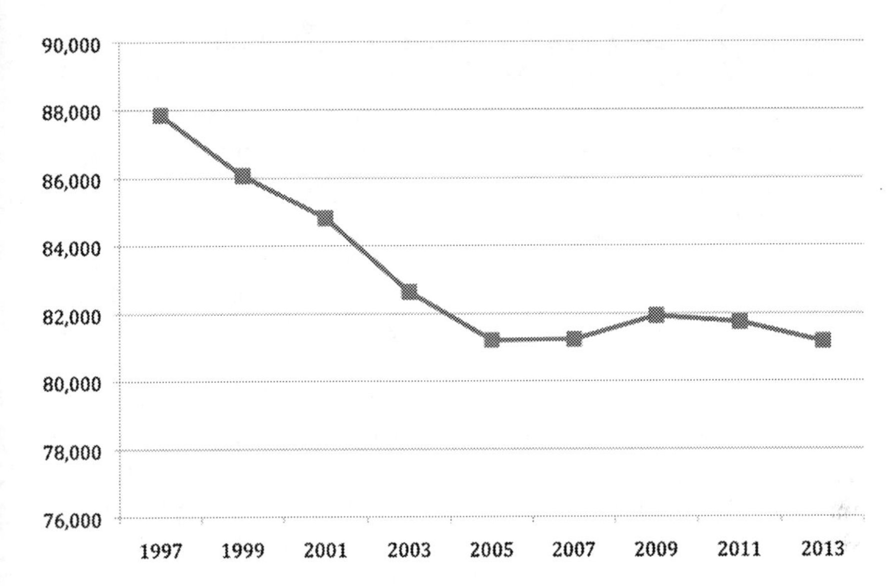

Fig. 3.1 Decline of agricultural land in Bali (Ha). Adapted from: BPS Bali (1997, 2001, 2003, 2005, 2011, 2014b)

modification of increasingly displaced icons while contributing little to farmers in return.[6] Panundiana Khun, one of the prominent capitalist figures in Bali and the chairman of the Bali chapter of Apindo (Indonesian Entrepreneurs Association) stated in an interview that Bali's land was no longer feasible for agricultural activities. He then proposed that government aid Balinese farmers transmigrate to Kalimantan or Sulawesi, where land is abundant. For him, Bali should be developed specifically for tourism and, if agricultural land in the island is to be preserved, this should serve as the interests of the tourism industry to bring in tourists.[7] After provoking much criticism, he finally revised his statement, saying that

[6] Panundiana Khun, the Chairman of the Bali Chapter of the Indonesian Entrepreneurs Association (Apindo), for example, sees agriculture as no longer feasible in Bali, and suggests that Balinese farmers join transmigration programs to other islands where sufficient plots of agricultural land are available (*Berita Bali*, 15/02/2011).

[7] For more details, see http://www.balidiscovery.com/messages/message.asp?Id=6762; http://www.balidiscovery.com/messages/message.asp?Id=6772. One response to his statement was published by the author of this paper in *Berita Bali* (02/2011).

the journalist wrongly quoted his points without clarifying the points that he really tried to convey. Moreover, in many instances, farmers find themselves forced to negotiate for a 'fair' share from the tourism industry, for example, in Bongkasa (Gianyar), where they demand 'royalties' from a luxury hotel utilising their rice terraces as a 'view' offered its guests (see Warren 2007, 182).

Land conversion in Bali presents a very complex picture. The argument utilising a rational-choice framework as above fails to acknowledge the symbolic meanings of land or to adequately confront political-economic drivers behind this 'choice'. In Jatiluwih, the local community is concerned with preserving their agrarian livelihood as the first priority because it is regarded as a *tetamian leluhur* (heritage from the ancestors to be passed to the next generation).[8] In the case of the Villa Petali development, for instance, Pan Sunasih, a farmer in Subak Jatiluwih (quoted in Prasiasa 2010, 324), states:

> I was forced to sell my land by brokers. They persistently said that my land was not profitable for agriculture .... they pushed me to sell it and told me to find other jobs. Finally, I sold the land and started a small business, but it did not last long. Then, I returned to farming by utilizing my remaining small plot of land. I regret that I have sold the land since the area [where the remaining land is located] is degraded and our temple [Water Temple of Pura Petali] has been *leteh* (spiritually corrupted due to the development of Villa Petali within the temple's sacred sphere).

Pan Sunasih's statement shows how political and economic factors have been important in the process of land alienation. Many cases of land conversion for tourist development projects in Bali, including the Bakrie Nirwana Resort (BNR) in Tanah Lot, the Bali Pecatu Graha (BPG) in Pecatu and Villa Petali in Jatiluwih, have involved physical or psychological intimidation from brokers, the state apparatus, and vigilantes, sometimes with the collusion of local elites. Therefore, land conversion is far more complex than what is assumed in a rational-choice framework that

[8] Interview with Made Buana, the former *Bendesa* of Desa Pakraman Jatiluwih, on 7 November 2013.

blames farmers, assuming the choice is based on his individual economic calculation. The value of land in those communities is not solely a factor of instrumental calculation but entangles with its symbolic significance. In contrast, land taxes in Indonesia are calculated based on market valuation, not land use. Market value is strongly influenced by where the land is located, irrespective of its actual utilisation status or the socio-cultural meanings attached to it.

As the tourism industry matures, other related businesses, in particular real estate and property businesses, develop at their own momentum. Vickers (2012 [1990]) observes that due to the liberalisation of land market in Indonesia since the 1980s, from the 2000s onwards, there has been growth among expatriates living on the island. This has triggered the development of the villa industry, a 'small independent living arrangement', usually in the middle of farmland or other 'exotic' sites, making the fragmentation of agricultural areas even worse (Vickers 2012 [1990], 304). More recently, many transnational corporations have become involved in the real estate and property businesses on the island. One of them is the Indonesian Land Investment Company (ILIC), a "Singapore-based company that buys land in developing areas of Indonesia [especially Bali] on behalf of its shareholders". It claims to be "very well connected with local land owners and government officials" (www.indonesiainvestment.org). As individual foreigners are not allowed to own land under a freehold title (*hak milik*), and other types of land rights, in Indonesia, according to Basic Agrarian Law 5/1960, the company offers an alternative for foreign investors to become a shareholder of the company instead of putting an Indonesian name on the land certificate, which is inefficient and economically and legally risky. To convince its potential investors, the company proudly presents I Wayan Puspa Negara, a Badung DPRD member from the Golkar Party, as the local figure "[w]ith direct connections to the government and handling all legalities and future information regarding new laws, changes and transportation links, his participation [in the company] makes everything easier to access" (www.indonesiainvestment.org).

Indeed, this is just one example of how government officials, politicians, and local elites have become 'local middle-men' for tourism, real estate, and property businesses. These practices have led to a rapid increase of land prices and in turn land taxes, leaving the land in many areas only affordable to big investors, for speculation or tourism and real estate development. In 2010, farmers in Canggu, Southern Badung, refused to pay the land tax due to an increase that made it unaffordable for them (Cole and Browne 2015, 445). Unprecedented increases in land taxes as a result of high land transactions have also led to refusals to pay in many parts of Bali.[9] In Pecatu Village, for instance, the increase in land tax has been used as the reason to challenge the Provincial Regulation on Spatial Planning for Bali Province (Perda RTRW Bali No. 16/2009), which designates a five-kilometre sacred radius around Uluwatu temples. This designation is considered by the villagers to negatively affect the local economy, which is highly dependent on tourism investment since agriculture has become less capable of supporting livelihoods in the village. In fact, the increase in land taxes in Pecatu has been a major consequence of the significant increase in land value as a result of the dramatic increase in land transactions for tourism development.

According to a report by the ILIC, the price of land in five areas in Badung District has skyrocketed, since 2005, by up to 302% (www.indonesiainvestment.org). In those areas, a piece of land was worth around IDR 550–850 million (US$ 40,000–61,000) per *are* (0.01 hectare) in 2012 and continues to rise—a price that is hardly affordable for an ordinary working family with a minimum regional wage in Badung District of IDR 2.5 million per month. Thus, at that price, the land in those areas would very likely be developed for commercial purposes, especially tourism accommodation. Not coincidently, this trend parallels the growth of star hotels in southern Bali, especially in Badung District (Fig. 3.2). The costly land acquisition rates required to build tourist accommodation in South Badung also explains the logic behind the Tirta Wahana Bali International (TWBI) project in Benoa, which plans to 'cre-

[9] In Tabanan District, an increase of 1000% in the land tax triggered a mass demonstration in 2007 (see *Liputan 6 News*, 05/10/2007). In Anturan Village, Buleleng, villagers also protested the increase in land tax by up to 500% (*Berita Bali*, 07/08/2007). Similar complaints also occurred in Legian, Kutuh, and Kuta (Badung District), and some parts of Gianyar and Klungkung Districts (*Merdeka*, 06/06/2014). The increase in land tax was a consequence of changing zonation of rural areas (*kawasan perdesaan*) to the classification of urban areas (*kawasan perkotaan*) in the spatial planning regime.

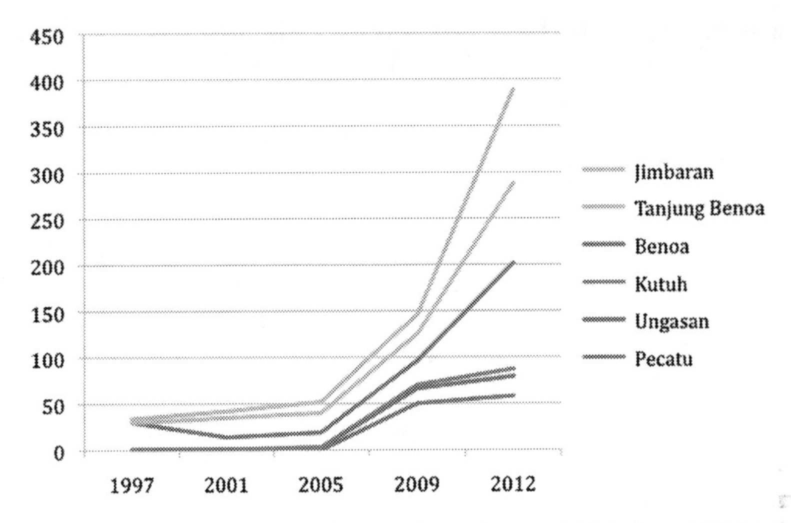

Fig. 3.2 Growth of hotels in Southern Badung. Source: BPS Badung (1996, 2002, 2010, 2013)

ate' land through reclamation to construct a dozen artificial islands for developing a luxury tourist enclave.

Identity Politics in the Absence of Class Politics

Balinese society, in the post-authoritarian Indonesia, has been regarded by many scholars as occupied by xenophobic identity politics. Leo Howe (2005) and Ramstedt (2009), for instance, characterise the Balinese as anti-migrants, especially Javanese migrants, by sweeping up undocumented migrants following the Bali Bombing. This tendency, according to Howe, to a larger extent, has been due to a sense of fear that their distinct culture in which their identity laid upon is being threatened by the Javanese migrants. Observing through the lens of the Balinese-Javanese rivalry, Ramstedt (2009, 361) observes that, in Denpasar Municipality, Muslim migrants had to obtain a temporary resident card and were subject to frequent 'sweeping'; without such a card, they would allegedly be regarded as 'foreign criminals' or even suspected 'terrorists'. A similar tone of characterisation can easily be found in the literature on Bali Studies, and it produces and reproduces through references and citations.

It may be equated by saying that British society is xenophobic due to Brexit and American society is racist due to the ascendancy of Donald Trump as the president.

Such characterisation of Balinese society by Howe and Ramstedt appears to be over-generalisation. My experience in the late 2000s around Panjer, Denpasar, showed a more complex picture. An inspection by the local *pecalang* (an *adat* security force) to check residents' ID card was carried out at every boarding and rented house in the area, targeting those who did not have a Denpasar ID card. Myself, coming from the neighbouring district of Tabanan and happened to rent a room in the area, was also checked during the inspection. Along with me, several students and workers from the other districts in Bali and a few others from outside Bali were also rounded up because we did not have a Denpasar ID card. The local authority forced us to obtain a letter of temporary residence (KIPEM) after paying IDR 25,000 (US$1.8). Through this personal experience, it is safe to say that the ID card inspection is less about identity politics but instead it is more about a strong sense of territorialism justified by decentralisation. In this context, a notion of being migrants or 'outsiders' in Denpasar was not defined by ethnicity or religion but rather by the district's administrative boundary, at a time when competitions between districts in attracting investments and simultaneously protectionism by prioritising labour markets for their own residents had escalated.

By saying this, it does not mean that suspicion and discrimination over non-Balinese migrants is not real. Indeed, there have been small fractions of conservative forces within Balinese society who use racist gestures and discourse in public for their own political and economic interests. In fact, Bali is not unique in this case. Similar gestures and discourse also take place in other societies, including British and American society. As argued above, the category of non-Balinese migrants was a class-based category in which only the working-class non-Balinese, such as those who work in construction or as street vendors, were considered as falling into this category. Meanwhile, the capitalist class regardless of their origins remains privileged. Moreover, the notion of a coherent Balinese cultural identity itself should not be assumed. As a young scholar from Nusa Penida, Dewa Ketha Sudiatmika (2010) has shown that 'Balinese-ness' creates ambiguity among Nusa Penida Islanders due to the geographical condition—the island being separated from the mainland of Bali—and the historical context in which the ancestors of Nusa Penida islanders were expelled from the island by the ruling kingdoms in the mainland due to disobedience towards the rulers. Thus, the 'Balinese identity', assumed to be monolithic and coherent, is in fact fragmented into and contested by different type identities, including the geographical and clan/geneological origins.

An illuminating and comparable observation on the emergence of identity politics in Indonesia has been shown in the works of Robison (2014) and Hadiz (2014). Robison (2014, 27) suggests that Islamic politics, and identity politics in general, should be examined within the wider context of capitalist transformation in a specific time and place, through which new social forces and interests emerge at the expense of other forces and interests. In line with this, Hadiz (2014, 43) observes that the re-emergence of Islamic political dissent in the country represents "the convergence of the aspirations, frustrations and anxieties found among a broad cross-section of society intrinsically related to the social changes brought about by the advance of capitalist development and the pressure of globalization". In the case of Bali, the transformation of the land-based economy which underpins local culture for centuries into the tourism industry serving global markets has not only changed the economy and the geographical landscapes, but also social orders and cultural practices to fit within the current economic structure.

Hadiz and Robison (2012) also note that the resort to cultural pools has been informed partly by the outcome of Cold War. In Indonesia, the social conflicts during this era ended up with the killing of millions of people associated with Leftist political organisations and intellectuals. This then was followed by the elimination and domestification of all forms of organisations representing Leftist political ideologies, and by criminalisation of those who embrace and spread such ideologies (Hadiz and Robison 2012; Farid 2005; Heryanto and Hadiz 2005). Specifically, in Bali, as it was discussed before, the traumatic experience of mass killings and the policies imposed in their aftermath, in particular the imposition of *Sapta Pesona* (seven wonders) and '*bersih lingkungan*' (clean environment) doctrines, had contributed partly to the reluctance of people employing arguments based on class and radical politics, which had been common since the colonial era until the 1965–1966 mass massacres.

As a result, the Balinese people should find ways to express dissent without necessarily being labelled as 'communists', a label that might lead to social and political death. Hadiz (2014) has shown how Muslim communities express their grievances against economic, political, and social dislocation by employing Islamic symbols, terminologies, and imageries. Similarly, Balinese society has turned into an essentialist cultural identity, claimed to be the only resource left in their hands, to express grievances against marginalisation, as well as social, economic, and political dislocations associated with the neoliberal globalisation process. The elites whose privileges are also threatened by such process exploit these dislocations in order to mobilise the Balinese public for defending their privileges and, if possible, for advancing their position in the process. Unlike their Muslim fellows who have been able to form political vehicles, especially political parties aiming at advancing the political, social, and economic position of the *ummah* (Hadiz 2014), Balinese elites remain fragmented and involved in contestations for wider support, cementing traditional patron-client relationship and forming cross-class alliances, by using a collective identity of Balinese-ness (ke-Bali-an) as a political vehicle to preserve the pre-existing social order.

In brief, an essentialist Balinese identity is clearly a myth produced by the Dutch Colonial and, in contemporary Bali, it has been reproduced by the elites by deterring social differences within Balinese society. Such reproduction represents elites' self-defence strategy to deal with the rapid transformation brought about by a globalised flow of capital into the tourism industry. It does not mean that the elites are critical towards the globalised tourism industry on the island, but rather, it shows their ambivalent positions. On the one hand, they tend to embrace the tourism industry through which they aim to elevate their positions in the industry, given their access to capital and their favourable position in the social order. On the other hand, they are also concerned with the fact that the structure of ownership in the industry has been concentrated transnationally (Bianchi 2009), which in turn affects the social order underpinning their social class and status. Meanwhile, the lower-class Balinese has been implicated the most by the tourism industry. They should live in two worlds: the capitalistic labour market which requires them to sell their labour full time; otherwise, they would be expelled from competitions. However, at the same time, they have cultural burdens, being a part of collective identity that requires them to participate and contribute their time and finances in cultural and religious activities within their families, hamlets, or villages. Through these cultural burdens, the competitive nature of Bali's tourism industry has in fact been relied upon. Consequently, as observed by Fagertun (2017a), ordinary people working for the industry have more commonly faced insecurity and unstable labour conditions due to a high risk of losing jobs and are forced to accept longer shifts for lower wages so as to keep their occupations.

Producing Space for Addressing Crisis

In *The Production of Space*, Henry Lefebvre (1991) mentions that the current form of capitalism split regions into two forms, representing the global division of labour. They are regions that are "exploited for the purpose of and by means of *production* (of consumer goods)", known as 'the space of production'; and regions that are "exploited for the purpose of and by means of the *consumption of space*", or 'an unproductive form of consumption' (Lefebvre 1991, 352–353). The latter are the regions that provide a space of leisure and tourism through which the surplus value is invested as a new circuit of capital, a strategy of 'spatio-temporal fixes'—"a metaphor for a particular kind of solutions to capitalist crises through temporal deferral and geographical expansion" (Harvey 2003, 115). These fixes are pursued through: "(a) developing external markets elsewhere in the capitalist world in response to underconsumption; (b) trading with non-capitalist societies to widen markets; (c) exporting surplus capital to establish new production facilities; and (d) expanding the proletariat by separating peasants, artisans, self-employed, and even some capitalists from control over their respective means of production" (Jessop 2004, 149).

In the global and national contexts, Bali, a region with limited natural resources for the global chains of production, from the outset, has been designed as the region for 'the consumption of space' both for national and global tourist markets. This means that Bali has been a circuit of capital that is exploited to provide spaces for domestic and foreign tourists, where their money is spent to satisfy their consumption needs and leisure desires. However, internally, Bali also requires a local scale of spatio-temporal fixes when dealing with the crisis discussed above that resulted from the consumption process. In this regard, the reorganisation of space through spatial planning—"which uses space as multipurpose tool" (Lefebvre 1991, 350)—is employed to pursue such fixes. Here, spatial planning aims at facilitating social control and underpinning the reproduction of social relations and the property relations of production, including landownership, hierarchical orders of locations, designation of new circuits, as well as networks of infrastructures enabling the flow of capital, labour, and the consumption of space.

The turn to spatial planning in Bali to address the existing environmental and governance crisis is considering the unlikelihood of special autonomy being granted in the near future. This was partly made possible by the enactment of Law No. 26/2007 concerning spatial planning in granting opportunities for the provincial government to advance a 'one island one management' agenda. This law follows other laws governing mining, oil, and gas, agro-industries and investment, which had already been issued as a package for the structural adjustment program (SAP) towards economic liberalisation.[10] Without a law concerning spatial planning to meet investment needs under decentralised political structures in the era of regional autonomy, such business-stimulating policies would have been difficult to implement. The law governing spatial planning was considered important to provide legal certainty for investors to promote development across the country. At the national level, spatial planning is considered an essential matter for pursuing Indonesia's strategic interests. Regional governments in the decentralisation era have been given the authority to enact their own regional spatial planning regulations within the framework of regional autonomy, but those regulations are subject to post-enactment 'bureaucratic review', approval by the national government prior to the enactment (Butt and Parsons 2014).

[10] For further discussion on the connection between the spatial planning system and neoliberalism in Indonesia, see Hudallah and Woltjer (2007).

The law mandates regional governments to issue new spatial regulations at the provincial and district levels within two years and three years respectively from the enactment of the 2007 legislation.

The Making of Spatial Planning

Since late 2007, the Balinese public had expressed deep concerns with uncontrolled tourism development that violated the existing spatial plan (Perda RTRW Bali No.3/2005). Almost every day, the public could read in local newspapers about violations of the 2005 Spatial Planning Regulation, in order to build new tourism facilities in Uluwatu,[11] Bukit Mimba,[12] Kelating Beach,[13] Dasong Forest[14] and in other regions. Public protests against these violations were raised by NGO activists, priests, and academics (Warren 2012). Besides that, the public was also demanding the newly elected governor, Made Mangku Pastika, to undertake urgent action to enforce the 2005 Spatial Planning Regulation by demolishing buildings that violated it (*Bali Post* 4/10/2008). The governor responded to the demands by proposing the revision of the 2005 Regulation. He argued that the sanctions stated in the regulation were too weak and unable to provide liability to government officials who issued permits. With a desire to make the government officials accountable for issuing the permits, he started his project to revise the 2005 Regulation by focusing on articles concerning sanctions. Despite the governor's apparently noble intention, there were fears expressed by a con-

[11] The Uluwatu Temple is one of the holiest temples for Balinese Hindus. Tourism development has been growing rapidly surrounding the temple as well as taking place within the temple's sacred boundaries. This case is discussed further in Chap. 4.

[12] Bukit Mimba is located in Karangasem District, in which in the 2005 Provincial Spatial Planning was designated as a protected area due to its geographical condition. However, the District Government of Karangasem issued permits for developing at least two hotel development projects (*Bali Post*, 10/10/08).

[13] The access to Kelating Beach was blocked by luxury villas and hotel complexes in the coastal lines. It was reported that the project was located within a 100-metre coastal setback zone that is supposed to be empty of buildings (Berita Bumi, 27/08/2008).

[14] An eco-tourism site and its luxury facilities were planned to be built in the middle of Dasong Forest that surrounds the lakes Buyan and Tamblingan, Buleleng District. Dasong Forest is the buffer zone of the preserved areas of Batukaru.

cerned public that revising the articles on sanctions would also be an entry point to revise the most crucial articles in the regulation, namely, those on coastal setback rules, protected areas, the *bhisama*, and the protection of common property.[15]

Realising the enactment of the new Spatial Planning Law at the national level, the agenda to revise the 2005 Regulation was changed into having a new provincial regulation complying with the national legislation. In February 2009, for the first time, the provincial government invited the public to a public hearing on a Draft Provincial Regulation on Spatial Planning for Bali prepared by its consultant. During the hearing, the debate was intense in which the participants mostly criticised the draft regulation as primarily geared to support the expansion of the tourism industry, following a 'business as usual' paradigm. Proponents held a firm belief that tourism development required a spatial planning regulation that would support growth through expanding new areas, infrastructure development, and the use of space to serve the tourism industry. Opponents focused on the status of protected areas, in particular, the importance of the *Bhisama* ruling for protecting the relationship between Bali's culture and environment, preservation of permanent agricultural lands (*lahan pertanian abadi*), and the highland watershed areas of Bali. The hearing concluded that the draft should be revised in taking into account the limited carrying capacity of the island, the existing impacts of tourism, as well as global environmental issues that affected Bali, for example, climate change and global warming.

Following such a recommendation, two months later, the provincial government conducted a 'socialisation' forum to announce public regarding the revised draft regulation. During the event, representatives of non-governmental organisations criticised the second draft for retaining the same paradigm as the first draft. Participants also scrutinised the academic research and approach of the consultant for failing to address the existing conditions of Bali on the ground. In light of its inability to convince the concerned groups, especially civil society organisations, to support the draft, the provincial government then decided to establish a new

[15] See the *Bali Post*, 11/2/2009, for the public scepticism on the idea of having a revision of the regulation advocated by the governor.

drafting team involving 22 representatives of NGOs, customary and religious leaders, academics, as well as business sectors, to redo the academic study as well as rework the draft.

Given the establishment of the team, open debates on spatial planning in public articulated in the media had moved into a close room where the team put their interests forward and discussed the matter. As official members of the team, the NGO representatives submitted several concept papers on climate change, agriculture, public transportation, as well as social issues of marginalisation arising from poverty, land alienation, and disability, to be discussed. The customary and religious leaders insisted that the 1994 *Bhisama* concerning sacred space and the sanctity of the temple's sphere to be retained and introduced local concepts of *sad kertih* to be included in the draft. Meanwhile, the representatives of business sectors proposed to omit the provisions for the high-rise building to prohibit buildings that are taller than a coconut tree (15 metres) and to relax the provisions for setback rules for coastal lines, ravines, and rivers.[16] After several months of discussing, formulating, and redrafting the academic study and the draft regulation, the draft produced by the team was submitted by the Provincial Government to DPRD Bali. In late December 2009, the draft was finally adopted by DPRD Bali as the Provincial Regulation on Spatial Planning for Bali No. 16/2009, replacing the 2005 Spatial Planning Regulation for Bali.

Contentious Provisions

There were several contentious provisions drawing wider attention on the regulation of spatial planning. They included the adoption of the 1994 *Bhisama*, concerning sacred space, the setback rules, the high-rise buildings, and the provincial strategic areas. Even before the adoption of the new spatial planning regulation, in October 2009, the alliance of all dis-

[16]Tourism accommodation was not built on a converted agricultural land, but also in the riverbanks and even cliffs for the sake of exotic views. This was the reason when the team proposed to tighten the sanctions for the development in riverbanks and cliff, the representative of tourism industry refused to consider such a proposal. In Bali, there is local wisdom that a building should not be taller than a coconut tree (equated to 15 metres).

trict heads and mayor across Bali raised their voices. They released a joint statement objecting to the adoption of the draft to be a provincial regulation (Arya Utama and Sudiarta 2011). It instead demanded further revisions of those contentious provisions due to their implication in constraining investments at the district level, which in turn might decrease their revenues and limit local rent-seeking practices (Wardana 2015). The sanctions to demolish buildings that violate the regulation[17] and to bring government officials who issue permit for these buildings accountable[18] were also threatening the existing privilege of the district officials. However, the provincial government responded that further revision of the draft regulation could not be carried out because the final draft had been submitted to the Minister of Home Affairs for bureaucratic review prior to their adoption. Sanctions stipulated in the draft were copied verbatim from the 2007 National Spatial Planning Law.

The provisions on coastal, river, and ravine setbacks were controversial, especially for the tourism industry. This is exactly because beaches, ravines, and riverbanks remain prime areas for developing tourist facilities. In the previous legislation, the coastal setback rules, for instance, were classified into different degrees of economic development and wave conditions, where the setback should be applied (Table 3.1). In fact, the 2009 Spatial Planning Regulation for Bali, following the national Spatial Planning Law No. 26/2007, stipulates that the coastal setback rule is at least 100 metres from the highest tideline without further classification. As a result, the district governments and hotel-owners' association were disappointed and argued that the provisions were unrealistic, as many hotels and other tourist facilities had been built within the 100-metre setback rules and it might also be a barrier for future tourism development in coastal areas. They instead demanded to retain the coastal setback rules as they were in the 2005 Spatial Planning Regulation.

[17] Article 150 of Perda 16/2009 stipulates that "after this provincial government regulation putting into force, every use of space that does not correspond to the spatial planning shall be adjusted (*disesuaikan*) through an adjustment process". The word 'adjusted' ('*disesuaikan*') is interpreted as the demolishing of buildings built without a valid building permission prior to the regulation.

[18] Article 148 of Perda 16/2009 stipulates that "(1) Every government official who has an authority to issue permit that is not in correspond to the spatial planning … shall be punished by imprisonment according to the law; (2) Besides imprisonment … the wrongdoer may also be given an additional punishment of impeachment without honour from his/her position."

Table 3.1 Coastal setback rules in the 2005 regulation

	Developmental degree	Wave height	Setback rule
1	Urban and tourism areas	Less than 2 metres high	50–75 metres
2	Urban and tourism intensive areas	More than 2 metres	75–100 metres
3	Rural areas	Less than 2 metres high	100–125 metres
4	Rural areas	More than 2 metres high	125–150 metres

Source: the 2005 Spatial Planning Regulation for Bali Province

The next contentious provision is the maximum height of buildings. Even in the drafting team, this issue had been one of the most debated topics. One member of the team representing the tourism industry argued that the height of buildings should not be regulated in order to slow down land conversion. He argued that the high rate of land conversion in Bali had been driven by the previous prohibitions on building higher than 15 metres (4 floors).[19] The argument seemed convincing; however, the team members from NGOs rejected the proposal on the basis of the experience of Jakarta and other provinces in Indonesia, where the expansion of land for commercial purposes has continued at an alarming rate, regardless of no restriction on building height. Furthermore, considering the fact that Bali has limited sources of water and electricity, the NGO representatives argued that the more high-rise buildings were built, the more pressure exerted on such resources, as well as the more extra land will be required to build supporting facilities, such as parking lots, gardens, and recreational sites.[20]

The adoption of the 1994 *Bhisama* concerning sacred space and sanctity radius of temples in the 2009 Spatial Planning Regulation for Bali

[19] The local concept of prohibiting buildings higher than a coconut tree (quantified by 15 metres) was adopted as an environmental consideration appropriate to a Balinese model of development.

[20] One would argue that more high-rise buildings means less private swimming pools, for instance, with positive effects on water-resource pressures. However, the argument seems to be misleading to some extent. First, private swimming pools are common in villa-type accommodations or real-estate, which is arguably irrelevant in the context of regulating the height of buildings. With or without such regulation, villas and real-estate development will continue to expand, since they have a specific market, namely, expatriates and wealthy elites. Second, deregulation on the height of buildings, particularly for hotels, does not necessarily guarantee preventing the hotels from presenting swimming pools as one of their basic facilities for tourists. Besides swimming pools, the hotels, in generating more profits, would also build as many rooms as they want to, and there would be a bathtub in every single room. Therefore, it would exert more pressure on water as well as electricity.

had been controversial from the beginning. An ahistorical account on this claims, expressed by Ramstedt (2013), that the adoption represents 'sacralisation' of the island in the decentralised era of Bali which goes hand in hand with *Ajeg Bali* movement. In fact, the adoption of Bhisama in the state spatial planning regime had been undertaken far before decentralisation. It was integrated for the first time in the 1995 Spatial Planning for Bali and then followed by the succeeding regional planning regimes, the 1996 and the 2005 regulations, and, more recently, by the 2009 Spatial Planning Regulations. Enacted in 1994 as a response to the mega-project of Bakrie Nirwana Resort (BNR), the Bhisama as religious ruling governing space has two integrated faces, as a spiritual proclamation and an ecological wisdom. As it will be shown in Chap. 7 on resistance in contemporary Bali, the risks of using class-inspired arguments to refuse government-backed projects under the authoritarian structure of Suharto's New Order Regime made resistance articulated by employing cultural-based arguments. Cultural arguments was seen to be the 'safest' weapon to challenge potentially destructive projects as culture also represents the only resource that underpinned central government's objective in developing tourism industry in the island.

Unlike the provisions on setback rules and building height that were adopted without any adjustment, the stipulation of the *Bhisama* was compromised to accommodate rejections and protests from the alliance of district heads as well as from local communities, especially Desa Pakraman Pecatu, which will be discussed at length in Chap. 4. The final regulation in Article 108 (2) subdivides the sphere of sanctity into three sacred zones: *utama karang kekeran* (core zone), *madya karang kekeran* (buffer zone), and *nista karang kekeran* (utilisation zone), and acknowledges the role of the *adat* village in such designation 'according to its circumstances' (see Table 3.2).

Specifically, on the issues of 'provincial strategic areas', the provincial government recalled a 2008 Memorandum of Understanding (MoU) No. 075/06/KB/B.PEM/2008 that was signed by the governor of Bali, and all district heads and the mayor in Bali. The MoU transferred the governing authority of several district areas, which were considered provincially vital in terms of economy, ecology, as well as socio-culture to be designated as 'provincial strategic areas' in the regulation (Fig. 3.3). The

Table 3.2 Classification of *Bhisama*'s sacred space

No	Hierarchy of temple	Traditional concept	Quantification	Zoning system	Note
1	*Sad Kahyangan*	*Apeneleng Agung*	5000 metres	1. Core Zone 2. Buffer Zone 3. Utilisation Zone	1. Core zone used as protected forest, or for agriculture, religious activities, and green space (*ruang terbuka hijau*) 2. Buffer zone used as forest buffer, green space, for agriculture and facilities to support religious activities 3. Utilisation zone used for agriculture, cultivation, local settlement and non-commercial public facilities for the locals. These zones are designated based on physical borders or geographical conditions with an equal metric distance.
2	*Dang Kahyangan*	*Apeneleng Alit*	2000 metres	1. Core Zone 2. Buffer Zone 3. Utilisation Zone	
3	*Kahyangan Tiga*	*Apenimpug*	5–25 metres	Not classified	

Source: Wardana (2015)

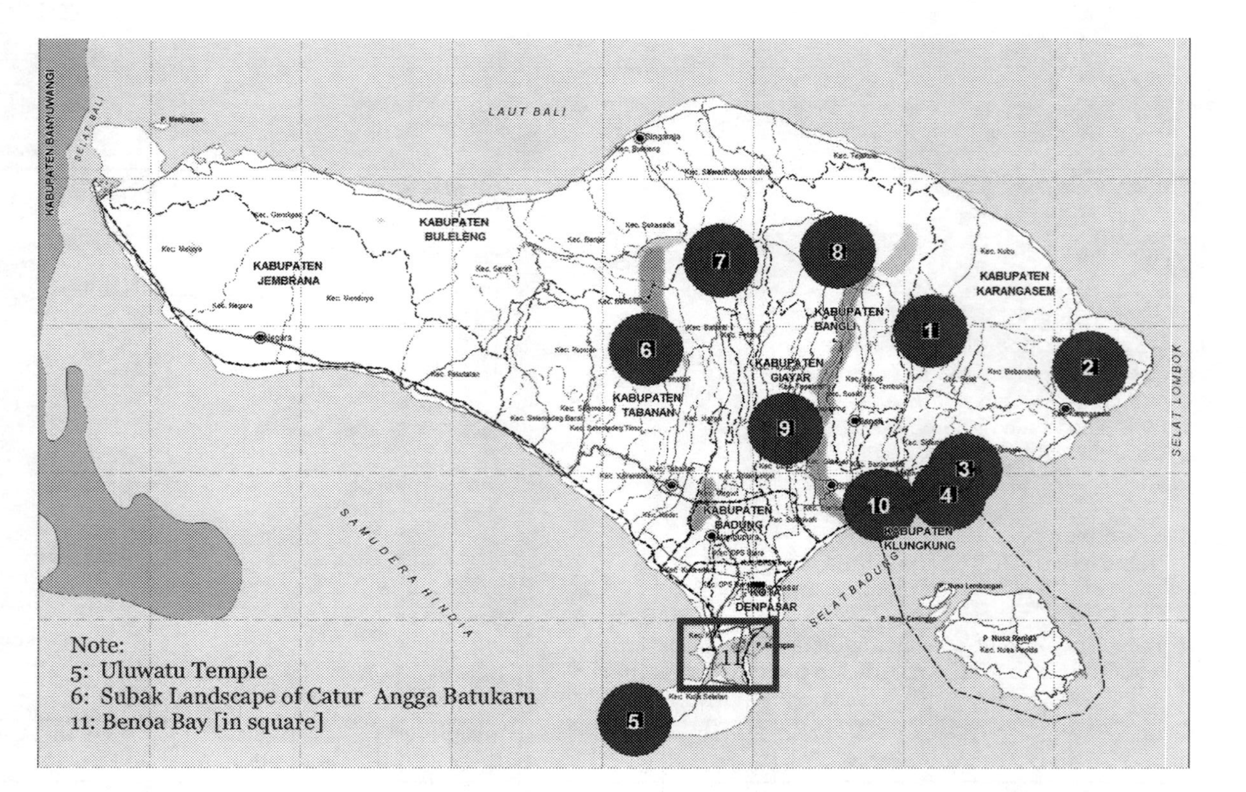

Fig. 3.3 Provincial strategic areas designated in Perda Bali 16/2009. This map is derived from one of the maps of provincial strategic areas in the provincial regulation on spatial planning for Bali No. 16/2009. This is originally the map of provincial strategic areas for social-cultural purposes but, for the purpose of this study, it is then adapted by adding the Benoa Bay area (in the square) that is designated in the map of provincial strategic areas for economic purposes. Source: Perda RTRW Bali No. 16/2009

MoU should be seen as a preventive strategy undertaken by the provincial government to submit the district governments to the provincial government's direction, and also to anticipate future conflicts in governing those areas. These strategic areas—the Uluwatu Temple Complex, the Subak Landscape of Catur Angga Batukaru, and the Benoa Bay areas—were where the case studies were conducted.

Conclusion

The preceding discussions on the Politics of Development in Bali (Chap. 2) and Crisis and Reorganisation of Space (Chap. 3) demonstrate how contemporary Bali has been shaped by the interactions between internal dynamics dominated by vested interests and external neoliberal forces pressing to widen markets and advance the circulation of capital, labour, and goods, including cultural items across the globe through tourism and real estate industry. Turning into spatial planning is pursued to address Bali's contemporary crisis within fragmented state structures in the era of decentralisation. Here, spatial planning is seen as "a strategic capacity and political integration mechanism intended to cement the increasingly fragmented agents of the state, all of whom possess their own agendas, political objectives, strategies, and resources, but who need to cooperate in order to deliver projects and developments" (Allmendinger and Tewdwr-Jones 2006, 17). In other words, spatial planning is used to ensure coordination of the state structures to pursue the state's designated interests. In reality, however, such interests are not necessarily aligned with local interests.

In the making of spatial planning, the provincial government also invited different 'stakeholders' at the provincial level, from NGO activists, academics, *adat*, religious organisations, and business sectors to be involved in the process, and later incorporated them in the institutional arrangement, *Badan Koordinasi Penataan Ruang Daerah* (BKPRD/Coordinating Body for Regional Spatial Planning), dealing with its implementation (see Wardana 2015). In this matter, public participation, a new neoliberal mantra, is used as a strategy to build 'civic constituency' (Sage and Woolcock 2005) in boosting legitimacy for a particular tier of government when it is in contestation with the other government tiers, because their interests are likely to be affected by the expected outcomes.

The ways in which those interests contest and accommodate specific localities will be discussed in the following chapters concerning the contestation over the boundaries of sacred space at Uluwatu Temple, Pecatu (Chap. 4), the designation of the Subak Landscape of Catur Angga Batukaru as a UNESCO World Heritage Site (Chap. 5), and the controversy over the Benoa Bay resort development (Chap. 6). These chapters will explore evolving government policy for reconfiguring space to advance tourism expansion and to analyse local communities' responses within this complex socio-spatial, legal, and institutional setting.

4

Contesting Sacred Boundaries of Uluwatu

In this first case study chapter, I look at conflicts over the governance of a particular sacred space in Bali—that of Uluwatu Temple, a temple of island-wide importance. In doing so, I will focus on the controversy over the adoption of the *Bhisama*, religious ruling, concerning the sphere of temple sanctity in the newest Spatial Planning Regulation for Bali Province (Perda RTRW Bali No. 16/2009). In Pecatu village, where Uluwatu Temple is located, the rapid change of physical, social, and cultural landscape—due to tourism development during and since the New Order Regime—has informed the role and responsibilities of the *adat* community in governing space, particularly the sacred space of Uluwatu Temple. Here, I examine the 'production' of Uluwatu Temple's sacred space within the pluralistic legal and institutional setting of decentralised Bali by interrogating its cross-scale nature, entanglement with 'profane' forces, especially those associated with the contemporary tourism industry, as well as alliances and resistance to claims over ownership of its material and symbolic significance.

A. Wardana, *Contemporary Bali*, https://doi.org/10.1007/978-981-13-2478-9_4

Pecatu Village and Tourism Development

Pecatu, a dryland village of 26.41 square kilometres with an officially recorded resident population of some 7000 (BPS Badung 2012, 8), is situated in the Bukit peninsula of Bali Province. As is the case throughout post-colonial Bali, the term 'village' here represents two overlapping entities, namely, the administrative village (*desa dinas*) and customary village (*desa adat* or *desa pakraman*). The most important difference between the two relates to the division between state-related and customary authorities, despite difficulty in clearly demarcating many of those tasks on the ground. In this regard, the *adat* village structure should be seen as a 'semi-autonomous social field' in which it has authority to produce its own rules and symbols for domestic affairs, but is simultaneously vulnerable from rules and decisions produced by wider external structures (Moore 1973). In Bali, as mentioned in Chap. 2, the relation of *desa adat* to *desa dinas* as a part of the state structure is far from uniform (MUDP Bali 2014; Mulyanto 2015).

Specifically in Pecatu Village, however, the *dinas/adat* relation represents a tidily dual village government model in terms of territory and membership. Pecatu village itself consists of one administrative village (*desa dinas*), Desa Pecatu, which is superimposed over one customary village (*desa adat*), Desa Pakraman Pecatu, comprising three customary/*adat* hamlets (*banjar*), each of which is composed of three administrative hamlets (*dusun*).[1] As a large *desa adat*, direct decision making through members' assembly (*sangkepan*) in Pecatu primarily occurs at the *banjar* level (see Warren 1993) (Fig. 4.1).

Pecatu was a village established through a royal land grant (*tanah catu*), with specific duties and obligations. In this regard, Pecatu Village was designated the caretaker of the Uluwatu Temple Complex,[2] with the

[1] Banjar Kangin comprising Dusun Kangin, Dusun Tambyak, and Dusun Giri Sari; Banjar Tengah comprising Dusun Tengah, Dusun Karang Boma, and Dusun Suluban; Banjar Kauh comprising Dusun Buwana Sari, Dusun Labuan Sait, and Dusun Kauh.

[2] The Uluwatu Temple Complex consists of several temples, which are Luhur Uluwatu Temple, Bajurit Temple, Parerepan Temple, Kulat Temple, Dalem Selonding Temple, and Dalem Pangleburan Temple.

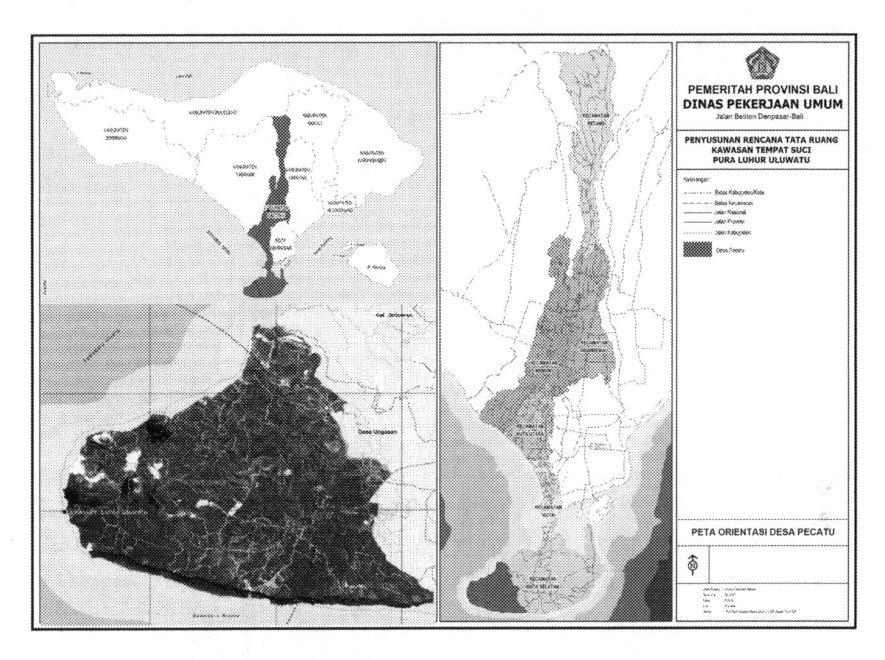

Fig. 4.1 Orientation map of Pecatu village. Source: Wartha Bakti Mandala (2012)

responsibility for maintaining its physical and spiritual condition and conducting routine rituals and major religious ceremonies. The temple itself was built in the twelfth century under King Sri Wira Dalam Kesari, and believed to be the place where Dang Hyang Dwijendra, the highest priest of the Gegel Kingdom in the fifteenth century, achieved moksha—liberation of the soul from the cycle of birth and death. In 1904, two years before the Puputan Badung war that ended in Dutch conquest, Uluwatu Temple, which sits on the cliff facing the Indian Ocean, collapsed. The temple was reconstructed by the Dutch Colonial government and returned to the Badung royal house as a gift for its loyalty to the colonial administration (Adhika 2011a).

After the introduction of the dual village governance model since the late colonial period, Desa Pakraman Pecatu with its autonomous cultural and religious domains has moved gradually from being under the structure of the Badung Royal House to becoming more or less an equal partner of the royal house in managing Uluwatu Temple. The role of

Desa Pakraman Pecatu has been as *pengemong* (supporting congregation), who are responsible for daily maintenance and providing labour during religious festivals in the temple. Badung Royal House, on the other hand, has delegated its role as *pengempon* (trustee) to two small noble families: Puri Agung Jro Kuta (Jro Kuta) and Puri Anom Jambe Celagi Gendong (Puri Celagi Gendong) in Denpasar. These roles and functions have been retained until recently and stipulated in the *Awig-Awig* (*adat* law code) of Desa Pakraman Pecatu.

To support their duties and responsibilities towards the temple, Pecatu villagers were permitted to work the feudal lands within the village owned by the noble families. In the early 1960s, with the national land reform policy, the villagers who had worked the land were entitled to take private ownership in their name while some plots of land, especially *tanah palaba pura* (temple's land) of Uluwatu Temple, remained under the control of the noble families, Jro Kuta dan Puri Celagi Gendong, as trustees. Subsequently, the rights over this land became a contentious object of conflict, not only between trustee families, but also between these families and Desa Pakraman Pecatu (discussed below). Given the arid condition of the land, they were only able to pursue dry farming (*tegalan*) and animal husbandry. I Made Sumerta, the former *perbekel* (*dinas* village chief) of Desa Pecatu, said that "before the tourism boom in the village, the land was unattractive; even if someone was given it for free, he would think twice because it is not productive, made of limestone, with no irrigation water and low rainfall" (quoted in Adhika 2011a, 214). Despite such limitations, during the period 1982–1988, Pecatu became the successful producer of oranges until the spread of the citrus greening disease, leaving the villagers to experience economically challenging conditions (Adhika 2011a).

As enclave tourism development in Nusa Dua matured, the surrounding villages, including Pecatu and Tanjung Benoa, became more involved in the socio-economic transformation taking place. While Tanjung Benoa at first developed its tourism spontaneously from below (Chap. 6), tourism in Pecatu Village to a large extent has been the product of the government policy to expand tourism beyond Nusa Dua through Governor of Bali Decree No. 15/1988. In the decree, Uluwatu Temple, located in Pecatu Village, was at the centre of one among 15 areas on the island to be designated as *kawasan pariwisata* (tourism zones). This decree coincided with the deregulation of the Indonesian banking system (Warren 1998), triggering a boom in investments in tourist accommodation, golf courses, restaurants, cafes, roads, and other public infrastructure, as well as spurring land speculation and real estate developments that have dramatically changed Bali's economy and environment. As shown in Fig. 2.1 (Chap. 2), in the mid-1990s, Pecatu was one of several Bukit areas where the New Order Regime granted building rights concessions (*Hak Guna Bangunan*, HGB) to Suharto's family and allies, including Bali Pecatu Graha, Indo Wisata Makmur, owned by Sinar Mas Group, and the Mulya Group owned by Joko Tjandra.[3]

Under the post-authoritarian regime, the change in governmental structures from a centralised to decentralised state in the hands of district government has brought rapid change in the village landscape. The District Government of Badung has been very actively inviting tourism investment in Pecatu. Ever since, the market trend in tourist accommodation from a semi-public model of hotel or resort developments to a more private house-type villa has also increased the demand for land and construction projects in Pecatu. Adhika (2011a, 3), an Udayana University scholar, estimates that between 1999 and 2008 around 144 *izin mendirikan bangunan* (IMB/building construction permits) for tourist accommodation located in Pecatu Village had been granted by Cipta Karya Bureau, the public works bureau of Badung District. Such accommodation ranges from locally owned homestays to domestic and foreign investment five-star hotels or villas, for example, Bulgari Hotel owned by Mugi Rekso Abadi (MRA)[4] as well as Alila Villas, a Singaporean-based

[3] Bali Pecatu Graha is owned by Hutomo Mandala Putra, known as Tommy Suharto, the youngest son of General Suharto, while the Sinar Mas Group is owned by a Chinese-Indonesian tycoon named Eka Tjipta Wijaya who, together with Joko Tjandra, was a close crony of General Suharto.

[4] MRA is a joint venture between four national conglomerate tycoons: Adiguna Sutowo, Tommy Suharto, Soetikno Soedarjo, and Onky Soemarno (*Jakarta Post*, 15/01/2005). The company controls major businesses grouped in five divisions: (1) food & beverage—bars, cafes, and restaurants, including Hard Rock Café Jakarta and Kuta; (2) mass media—11 radio networks and 16 licences for lifestyle magazines, including *Cosmopolitan*; (3) automotive—exclusive dealerships of Ferrari, Mercedes Benz, Harley Davidson, Ducati, and other luxury brands; (4) hotel and property holdings include Bulgari Hotel and Villas in Pecatu, Four Seasons Hotel and Apartments, and Hard Rock Hotel in Kuta; (5) lifestyle and entertainment—licences for Bulgari Jewellery and other international brands (*Tempo*, 29/10/2013).

Table 4.1 Tourist accommodation within Uluwatu temple's sacred radius

1	Blue Point Hotel & Villa	19	Villa Indah Manis	37	C.151 & Villa
2	Mawar Villa	20	Villa Vijaro	38	The Calyk
3	Wangsa House	21	The Gong	39	Duges Villa
4	Kris House	22	Gobleg Inn	40	Alamanda Villa
5	Bali Villa	23	The Istana Villa	41	Merta Sari Bungalow
6	J. Ni House	24	Bali Villas	42	Kembang Kuning
7	Eduard Sari House	25	Puri Uluwatu	43	Romeo Bungalow
8	Ursula Snati House	26	Moonlight Villa	44	Tepi Laut Bungalow
9	Iskandar House	27	Blue Roose Villa	45	Acapcia Bungalow
10	Charlose House	28	Camplung Villa	46	Leggy Bungalow
11	Tanah at Ulus	29	Rocky Bungalow	47	Bingin Garden Bungalow
12	Tirta Bridal	30	Tete Inn	48	Refture Bungalow
13	Casadulce Villa	31	The Laut Villa	49	Ayu Guna Inn
14	The Cliff Villa	32	Bali Indo Wedding	50	Bulan Putih
15	Hotel Bulgari & Villa	33	Padang-Padang Inn	51	Sacret Garden
16	Villa Kahyangan	34	Mandala Inn	52	Richard Bungalow
17	Villa Alila	35	Villa Pemutih	53	MU Bungalow
18	Villa Canang Sari	36	Villa Bayuh Sabha	54	The Camp

Source: Wartha Bakti Mandala (2012)

transnational corporation. According to Wartha Bakti Mandala (2012), among the hundreds of these in the Pecatu enclave, around 54 are located within the five-kilometre sacred radius of Uluwatu Temple, as shown in Table 4.1 below.

The rapid changes in its landscape due to tourism development have made Pecatu one of the most crowded tourist sites in Badung District and highly dependent on the tourism economy. As a result of the rapid economic growth of tourism, Kuta Selatan Sub-District, including Pecatu village, attracts a large number of migrants from other parts of Indonesia. It was reported that 1578 people migrated to the sub-district in 2009 alone (BPS Badung 2012, 62). Currently, 5 of the 14 tourist beach sites situated in Kuta Selatan Sub-District (BPS Badung 2010) are located in Pecatu Village—Suluban Beach (known as Blue Point), Nyang-Nyang Beach, Padang-Padang Beach, Labuan Sait Beach, Bingin Beach, Dreamland (or New Kuta Beach), and the Uluwatu Temple Complex. Nyang-Nyang and Dreamland beaches are managed privately by a company that owns tourist accommodation at the beachfront, Puri Bali and Bali Pecatu Graha (BPG) respectively. Labuan Sait is managed by the *dinas* village of Pecatu. Suluban, Padang-Padang, and Bingin beaches are

Table 4.2 Numbers of tourist visits and revenues at Uluwatu

Year	Visitors	Revenues (US$)
2006	290,790	45,466
2007	315,652	68,409
2008	390,116	82,380
2009	380,224	82,532
2020	402,351	87,335
2011	378,175	81,959
2012	843,876	1,074,589

According to the District Government of Badung Regulation (Perda Badung) No. 25/2011, since 2012, there has been an increase in the entry fee to the Uluwatu Temple Complex from US$ 0.20 to US$ 1.00 for domestic tourist, and from US$ 0.35 to US$ 1.42 for foreigners, which has made the revenues skyrocket since 2012. This excluded revenues from conducting performances of the Kecak Dance or leasing space for food stalls and parking fees

Source: Yudasuara (2015, 137)

managed by a group of local residents who donated their land for constructing roads and parking lots to the beaches, and initiated tourism development in these areas.

Specifically for the Uluwatu Temple Complex, the district head of Badung through Decree No. 854/1996 has transferred the operative management of Uluwatu's tourism attraction to the local *adat* village, *Desa Pakraman Pecatu*, due to its status as *pengemong* (supporting congregation) in order to support its obligations towards the temple. The *Awig-Awig* of Desa Pakraman Pecatu also stipulates that tourism objects and attractions in the village are assets and under the dominion of the *adat* village (*desa pakraman*). Yudasuara (2015), a local figure and Secretary of the Pecatu village council (BPD), indicates that Desa Pakraman Pecatu is very keen to take over the management of all tourist sites within its territory, but this would need the district government's approval. In terms of tourist visits, provincially, the Uluwatu Temple Complex has been the second most visited site in Bali after Tanah Lot, Tabanan, with over a million dollars in revenues in 2014 (Table 4.2).

Tourist visits contribute significant revenues for the District Government of Badung and Pecatu Village. The revenues are split into 25% for the District Government and 75% for Pecatu Village. For the village, this income is then split further to cover operational management costs (27%) and contributions to the temple (23%). The rest is shared between Desa (*dinas*) Pecatu (30%) and Desa Pakraman Pecatu (70%). The *adat* village chief (*Bendesa*) of Desa Pakraman Pecatu, Ketut Murdana, explains that the share for Desa Pakraman Pecatu is spent on conducting religious festivals for village temples and other *adat*/religious activities so that the *krama* (members of) Desa Pakraman Pecatu are not burdened (*dibebani*) with financial contributions (*pepeson*) for the festivals and are only responsible for contributing their time.[5] Ibu Oka, a boarding house owner, commented that she no longer has to contribute financially for religious festivals in the village temples but still has heavy financial commitments to family temples and other religious festivals. She explains:

> *piodalan* (religious festivals) here [in the village] now are *besar-besar* (very large). They require a large amount of money ... I know this because my mother is a *pedagang banten* (Balinese offering seller) ... For religious festivals in the family temples, *paibon*, we still have to give *pepeson* [financial contribution] .... If we calculate, one household has minimally six temples, and each of them conducts its festival every six months; it means that every month there is a *piodalan* in which we should spend around IDR 2.5–3 million [US$ 180–216] each. This is not to mention Bali-wide festivals like *Galungan*, *Kuningan* and *Nyepi*.[6]

Despite such economic challenges, Ibu Oka says that she should accept this recent trend in conducting increasingly grand religious festivals as the way to show gratitude to God for what the villagers could afford, due to the tourism boom in the village. She mentions, "'how could someone who wears Rip Curl T-Shirts be stingy with the Gods?' That is what people with decent jobs say to us. Usually, they financially back-up the *piodalan* first, then we who do not have money will be paying back their advances in instalments".[7] Indeed, Ibu Oka represents Pecatu villagers

[5] Interview with Ketut Murdana, the *Bendesa* of Desa Pakraman Pecatu, 18 July 2014.

[6] Interview with Ibu Oka, a boarding house owner, on 25 July 2014.

[7] "'*Masak manusianya saja memakai baju RipCurl terus untuk Bhatara dihemat?' Begitu pertanyaan orang-orang yang punya pekerjaan bagus. Biasanya mereka dulu yang mem-back-up untuk piodalan, kita yang tidak punya uang nanti akan bayar ke mereka dengan mencicil.*" Interview with Ibu Oka, on 25 July 2014.

who are not very fortunate within the glamour tourism industry in Pecatu. What her comments indicate is how tourism has influenced the way in which local people regard obligations to their ancestors and God in the socially defined terms of religious ceremonial commitments. It seems that the logic of the more income you receive the more you should spend for ceremonies prevails in many parts of Bali. This logic appears to serve the tourism industry where religious festivals are part of their 'package' of attractions subsidised through the free labour of local villagers.

Changing Meanings and Spatial Practices

The expansion of the tourism and real estate industries in Pecatu has indeed brought both positive and negative impacts. Many benefits are frequently argued, including providing new opportunities for jobs and income generation in the formal and informal sectors; improving infrastructure and access to public services (Adhika 2011b); and raising the economic value of relatively 'unproductive' dry land. Putu Yusa, the local dry *subak* leader, observed that due to tourism in Pecatu, unemployment is very low, because locals can increase their economic opportunities if not directly in the tourism industry, by providing services and accommodation to migrants who seek jobs in the area.[8] The massive growth in tourism is also argued to contribute to expanding art and cultural activities, for example, the establishment of *sekaha kecak* (*kecak* dance groups) (Adhika 2011b). Adhika (2011b, 213) sees the standardisation and even glamorisation of rituals and cultural activities, which has taken place in Pecatu as evidence of increasing religiosity. However, there is a longstanding critique that suggests that mass tourism has reoriented the local per-

[8] "*Masak orang luar saja datang ke sini [Pecatu] untuk cari kerja, sedangkan kita tidak kerja? Pendatang kerja di sini kan juga makan di sini, dan kita bisa menyiapkan makan untuk mereka sehingga masyarakat di sini bisa punya usaha kecil-kecilan, termasuk kos-kosan.*" Interview with Putu Yusa by Carol Warren, on 1 August, 2012. Similarly, Pak Baki, a private security guard (*satpam*) in Vila Dugong says that "this land [where Villa Dugong stands] was my father's land, but he sold it to a developer, Tropical Property, owned by a foreigner. This then was subdivided into several land plots to be sold to other foreigners. I have been employed as a *satpam* in this villa, [it is] better than being unemployed" (quoted by Adhika 2011a, 269).

ceptions of Balinese culture into a more instrumentally framed 'touristic culture'.[9]

Due to tourism expansion, infrastructure for these projects was also improved, making the connections between the village and the capital city of Denpasar, and other economically developed areas easier. Previously, being a '*Nak Bukit*' ('Bukit person')—a derogatory term referring to those from the hilly southern peninsula of Bali, including Pecatu—implied backwardness,[10] due to its remoteness and the poor conditions for agriculture and access to basic needs, especially water. Although water infrastructure from Perusahaan Daerah Air Minum (PDAM/Regional Water Drinking Company) has been developed, it is distributed to only 40% of the total households in the village, while the rest remain dependent on rainfall and buying water from private suppliers (Desa Pecatu 2007). For those connected through PDAM infrastructure, its water supply is rarely adequate because very often PDAM's water does not flow properly even to high-end users in the tourism industry. Ibu Oka buys water from a 5000-litre water tank truck that only lasts for four to five days.[11] For a family of five, Ibu Oka's family consumes 200 litres water/person daily, which is well below an average per capita water consumption in urban areas, that is, 300 litres/day, while a starred hotel room consumes 3000 litres/day (Kurnianingsih n.d). Hence, both public and commercial users increasingly depend upon private water suppliers. Nyoman Suardika, a local water supplier, has eight water tank trucks to supply water not only to households, but also to tourist accommodation in Pecatu, including the luxury Bulgari Hotel. He takes water from a water spring in Jimbaran and then transports it to his customers for US$ 12.6–U$ 15/tank, depending on the distance.[12]

[9] For discussion on the relationship between 'cultural tourism' and 'touristic culture' in Bali, see Picard (1996).

[10] Interview with Putu Yusa by Carol Warren, 1 August 2012. He mentioned that the image of '*nak bukit*' recently has improved due to the development of the tourism industry, and argued that the status of Pecatu should be considered as an urban rather than rural village area.

[11] Interview with Ibu Oka, on 25 July 2014.

[12] Interview with Nyoman Suardika, on 1 August 2014.

Tourism and Land Values

Tourism and real estate development have also had extreme impacts upon the value of land. In Lombok, as noted by Warren (2013), the development of tourism in Gili Trawangan Island on abandoned plantation land has transformed land values and led to severe conflicts between the companies who claim concession rights to these areas and the local fisherfolk and farmers who have occupied and spontaneously developed tourism on the island. Similarly, in Pecatu, before the tourism boom, land had been used for dry agriculture (*tegalan*) to grow corn, beans, and cassava.[13] Land at that time functioned largely in terms of its immediate use-value. Rapid commodification accompanied the dramatic rise in the price of land, as large-scale resort and residential developments drove up the market value. In 2013, it was recorded that a 0.01-hectare plot of land in Pecatu was worth around US$ 21,672–US$ 36,120,[14] much higher than the price of an equal size of agricultural land in other parts of Bali.

Consequently, the associated tax burden on land in the Pecatu tourism zone has also increased.[15] Pecatu farmers have experienced an increase of up to 400% in land taxes during 2011–2012. A five-*are* (0.05 hectare) plot of dryland, for example, in 2011 was taxed at US$ 17 per year, but in 2012, taxes more than doubled to US$ 46 (*Nusa Bali*, 22/05/2012). Renaya, for instance, a farmer from Banjar Suluban, Pecatu, explained that tax on his 46-*are* (0.46 hectare) plot of land was raised to US$ 2000 in 2012 (*Antara News*, 04/04/2011). The land tax was hardly affordable for small peasants, and at some point it became more economical to sell or to lease the land for commercial purposes, given the dramatic increase in land prices and the aggressiveness of land brokers (*calo tanah*).[16] Considering how much local people were forced to spend

[13] Interview with Ibu Mardi by Carol Warren, on 1 August, 2012.

[14] https://www.lpdpecatu.or.id/lpd/tentang_kami.php?idp=16.

[15] The market value (NJOP/*nilai jual obyek pajak*) is the basis of land tax under current tax law (Article 6 paragraph (1) of the Land and Building Tax Law No. 12/1994). The NJOP itself is calculated according to the location or condition (including the use and accessibility) of the land.

[16] Many of them sold their land and then bought a piece of land in other districts, for example Penebel (Tabanan), Klungkung or Negara; but, in a short period of time they resold it because the distance made it difficult for them to manage or monitor.

from their income on water as a basic necessity as well as on land taxes, both Ibu Oka and Nyoman Suardika agree that life has become very expensive in Pecatu due to tourism, and they express great concern over how long locals would be able to maintain their livelihoods there.[17] Ibu Oka admits that "[i]t seems that tourism has made everything becoming expensive. My [household] income of around [IDR] 15 million is not enough to live here every month. I must pay for our debt around [IDR] 5 million. In fact, our lives are not *boros* [extravagant] … we all spend money *ngirit* [economically]". Nyoman Suardika states,

> [l]ife in Bukit is *biaya tinggi* [high cost]. Perhaps, in the future local people could not live any longer here. If they are working as a labourer in tourism, they now may be *pas-pasan* [very tight on budget] and are able to survive because of low-interest debt from the koperasi [local cooperative] or LPD [*Lembaga Perkreditan Desa*/*desa adat*'s village credit institution]. *Lama kelamaan* [in a given time in the future], if we could not afford to pay the debt, we would go bankrupt and could not borrow money anymore. This possibility is very likely. Currently, we who live in Bukit have experienced the burden of everything becoming expensive. Even for me who have a business, I feel the same because our operational cost is quite expensive.[18]

Due to the increase in land value, the contestations over ownership of land have become more common and have wider impacts, including upon the economic and cultural 'resource' of Uluwatu Temple. The temple is not a single temple area, but a temple complex that includes the Luhur Uluwatu Temple and several smaller temples, each of which has its own assets including *tanah pelaba pura* (temple-owned land) and its own ritual cycle. The responsibility to manage and maintain the temple complex is shared amongst two noble families, Jero Kuta and Puri Celagi Gendong, assisted by the local customary village of Pecatu. Based on the Balinese concepts of inheritance, those stakeholders of the temple complex presume that responsibility is accompanied by entitlement. Thus,

[17] Interview with Ibu Oka on 25 July 2014.
[18] Interview with Nyoman Suardika on 1 August 2014.

conflict related to the ownership and access to the benefits of the temple's assets including *tanah pelaba pura* has frequently occurred between the noble families as trusties of the temple. Jero Kuta, the noble family serving as a trustee (*pengempon*) for Uluwatu Temple, established the Yayasan Uluwatu (Uluwatu Foundation) in 1992 to undertake inventory, registration, and certification of all temple assets in the name of the Foundation, ostensibly to protect them from expropriation. These attempts of the Uluwatu Foundation have several times brought it before the civil or administrative courts in relation to the conflicting claims of Puri Celagi Gendong and other parties.

Over the period 2007–2010, there have been at least three cases filed by the Uluwatu Foundation. The first case was heard before the Civil Court of Denpasar concerning two legal grounds: the first was the unlawful certification, undertaken by Puri Celagi Gendong, of a piece of land claimed by the Uluwatu Foundation as a Luhur Uluwatu Temple asset located in Labuan Sait, Pecatu. According to the Uluwatu Foundation, the land should be under the control of the Foundation. The second ground was based on an allegation that Puri Celagi Gendong had leased Luhur Uluwatu Temple's land to two companies—Nanno Bali and Dreamland Bali—for tourist accommodation developments. However, both plaintiffs' claims were dismissed by the civil court due to the plaintiff's inaccuracy in describing the object of dispute (location and legal status of the land). Unsatisfied by this verdict, the Uluwatu Foundation took another legal avenue by suing Puri Celagi Gendong together with the National Land Agency (BPN/Badan Pertahanan Nasional) before the Administrative Court of Denpasar. The Uluwatu Foundation asserted an unlawful land certification process undertaken by the National Land Agency (BPN) and Puri Celagi Gendong. The administrative court finally dismissed the lawsuit on the principle of *ne bis in idem* (one case should not be heard twice), because the case had already been heard by the Civil Court of Denpasar.

In 2007, the Foundation undertook another legal action before the Administrative Court of Denpasar against the Badung District Head for hindering the Foundation's efforts to obtain approval for temple land certification in its name. The Foundation wanted to certify a piece of land claimed as an asset of the Luhur Uluwatu Temple; in order to proceed, it required a statement letter (SK) from the head of the village where the land was located. In fact, the administrative head of the village of Pecatu refused to sign the letter, saying that according to the *Awig-Awig* (*adat* law) of Desa Pakraman Pecatu, the land is managed cooperatively between Jro Kuta, Puri Celagi Gendong, and Desa Pakraman Pecatu, and could not therefore be certified as private property. The Foundation demanded that the district head issue a letter of clarification for certification purposes, but the district head instead issued a letter stating that the required SK could not be issued on the basis that it would violate Desa Pakraman Pecatu's *Awig-Awig*.

The refusal letter itself became the object of dispute before the administrative court in legal proceedings, concerning whether or not the refusal letter constituted an object of administrative dispute. It was taken from the administrative courts, through the lower court and court of appeal, up to the Supreme Court. The administrative court of Denpasar decided to accept the letter as an object of administrative court jurisdiction and to accept the claim of the plaintiff, ordering the head of district to revoke the refusal letter, and to issue the SK required for certification. The court of appeal in Surabaya and the Supreme Court in Jakarta reversed this verdict, stating that the refusal letter was only a correspondence and should not be considered as an official administrative decision of the district head. Accordingly, the plaintiff's claims were dismissed. Hence, the land could not be certified under freehold title on behalf of the Foundation, leaving the land under the shared management of the Foundation and Desa Pakraman Pecatu. This collective management, albeit uncertain 'ownership', so far has been able to prevent the transfer of its ownership to third parties, especially investors, and in turn to postpone development on the land to date. This has been a consequence of the struggles to obtain ownership over the land from the three parties who equally claim to have legitimacy to control the land.

The high level of land transactions in the area has also concerned *dinas* and *adat* village leaders. Sukarno's populist land reform program in the early 1960s had been able to distribute land to its tillers (*petani penggarap*). In fact, until the mid-1990s, such distributed land in Pecatu was primarily registered on the village's Letter C Book or '*pipil*', a colonial model of land registration for taxation purposes. During the late-1990s to mid-2000s, with the state's mass land titling project (PRONA), villagers collectively certified their land to obtain a freehold certificate. In both registration and certification processes, the role of village chief (*perbekel*) and *bendesa* were important to prove the proponent's landholding in the village. However, once the certificate has been obtained, land transactions in the village more recently rarely involve local village officials and *adat* leaders; they are sometimes only informed after the transaction has been carried out before a notary and then to be certified by the national land agency (BPN/*Badan Pertanahan Nasional*), because the subsequent transaction no longer requires the village chief.[19] Therefore, the *Perbekel* and *Bendesa* are unaware whose land is sold within the village and by whom it was bought. However, if there is a dispute on land matters located within the village, they are the first party to be notified and asked to be involved in the settlement.

The PRONA land titling project was not unproblematic. From political economy perspectives, as many authors have observed, the program was driven by intent to put land on the commercial market (Fauzi 2009; Hirsch 2011; Warren and Lucas 2013). In the Pecatu context, land titling became a land accumulation process for local elites. Due to the poverty and illiteracy of many among the local farmers, they were unable to handle the land titling process themselves. Very often, they had to work collaboratively with well-off individuals either from the village or neighbouring villages acting as their 'broker' (*calo*) who funded the whole process on their behalf. Once the certificate of freehold was obtained, some proportion of the land would be transferred to the brokers in compensation, based on a mutually acceptable arrangement. Consequently, those brokers own disproportionate amounts of land in the village. In the village profile (Desa Pecatu 2007, 60), it is indicated that 2% of the total households from 1975 own up to 55% of the total 769.60 hectares of private land in the village. Broker practices in land titling also show how titling that is advocated by Hernando de Soto (2000) to transform 'dead

[19] Having said that, according to Government Regulation No. 24/1997 on land registration, a village chief's role in providing a statement of proof is still needed for registering land for the first time, and for the transfer of ownership right due to inheritance.

capital' into a farmer's 'live capital' is far more complex than he assumes, since the process very often involves capture by local elites acting as brokers in return for a land share or fees.

Tourism Development and Its Paradox

Tourist visits to Uluwatu Temple present opportunities for generating an income for the local community, which shares the responsibility for its upkeep and ceremonial obligations. Pecatu villagers responded to this opportunity by forming a *kecak* dance group to perform in the area of Uluwatu Temple as a tourist attraction. From the beginning, this project has led to disharmony between the two noble families (Jro Kuta and Puri Celagi Gendong) as *pengempon* and Pecatu villagers as *pengemong*. The villagers had built facilities for dance performances without asking for permission from the noble families beforehand, since they were concerned that their proposal would have been rejected (Adhika 2011b, 215). However, they did inform both families after the stage and other facilities had been built. It appears that the relationship between the families and Pecatu village is complicated largely due to the ongoing competition between the noble families. Villagers took no sides in this competition and found an opportunity to pursue their interests by circumventing the complicated relationship.

Due to the rapid development of tourism, an unnecessary tension between the *adat* and *dinas* village structures has arisen with regard to the division of labour for the operative management of tourism in Uluwatu Temple. In contrast to Adhika's (2012) observation that the tidily overlapping structure between administrative and *adat* village provides strategic opportunities to use each other's positions in better serving the needs of villagers and undertaking development within the village, competing interests emerged with lucrative opportunities. Adhika (2012) assumes that both institutions share similar normative orders and interests towards community development, but he overlooks how competition between them may arise, affected by changing power dynamics and resource distribution within the village. Yudasuara (2015, 143–144), for example, observed that on many occasions not a single parking officer showed up to manage tourist buses or cars in the parking lot of Uluwatu Temple Complex, because the parking fees go to the *dinas* village, while the officers are employed by the *adat* village. Pecatu villagers conceive Desa Pakraman Pecatu as the local institutional structure with the primary responsibility for local affairs. This is partly informed by the fact that the *desa adat* is more capable of organising collective action for economic, social, and religious/cultural purposes than its *dinas* counterpart. More importantly, this preference reflects a general sense of higher obligation towards the *desa adat* for its role in the religio-social domain.

The flood of investments in Pecatu since the New Order has not necessarily benefited villagers as a whole. This may be best represented by their experience with Bali Pecatu Graha (BPG), a company owned by Tommy Suharto, son of the President Suharto, since 1995. In fact, Ketut Sudikerta, a Pecatu-born Golkar politician and the former vice-district head of Badung (2005–2013) and former vice-governor of Bali (2013–2018), one of the well-known land brokers, was also involved as Tommy Suharto's locally trusted agent. In 1996, 200 local peasant households were forcibly displaced from 650 hectares of land they had been working on that was claimed by the Provincial Government of Bali as state land (*tanah negara*) to be made available to the company to build a luxury resort and real estate complex—including several golf courses. They were forced to sign a letter provided by the government stating that they were just tillers of state land (*petani penggarap tanah negara*) (Hasan 1998). Around 36 farmers refused to give up their land and resisted displacement. Two of their leaders, Wayan Rebo and I Made Dana, were detained and put in prison on the grounds of illegal occupation of state-owned land and provoking other farmers to reject a state development project.[20] To date, Wayan Rebo has never agreed to give up his land to the company. Consequently, his family (*dadia*) temple is located within the company's concession that now has been transformed into a golf course. After being postponed due to the economic crisis and the fall of Suharto in 1998, the project has now been resumed, still in Tommy Suharto's hands. The company also claims Dreamland Beach as part of its assets

[20] Interview with Wayan Rebo, on 5 August 2014.

and—to demonstrate its claim over what was once public space—has renamed the site New Kuta Beach.

The coercive character of the BPG has not ended with the post-Suharto 'Reform Era'. During the period 1998–2006 following the fall of Suharto, the beachfront areas and BPG's land had been occupied by local people from Pecatu to operate their food stalls. Made Putrawan, BPG's new director, claims that the company lost around 250 hectares of land from these unilateral occupations (*Bisnis Indonesia*, 04/11/2006). In 2009, around 37 small food stalls (*warung*) owned by Pecatu Villagers on the shore of Dreamland Beach were forced to relocate in the name of *penataan pantai* (beach improvement) to 'clean up' the company's tourist site. This agenda was also part of the revival of the company. Made Jenar, coordinator of food stall owners and the owner of Boy's Warung, was disappointed with the relocation decision imposed by the BPG, arguing that tourists used to love spending their time there, rather than at the overpriced and stylish star hotels. He and the other stallholders would lose their customers with relocation away from the areas most visited by tourists (*Jakarta Post*, 10/02/2009). Many decided to resist and continued to open their *warungs* on the beachfront, but they finally were relocated because they were considered to have no legitimate justification to support their stance.

Access to the beach also became a livelihood issue for local people. Pak Sontar, for example, recounts that when it was proposed to open an access road to Suluban Beach, he and some other landowners gave up their land voluntarily, expecting that they would benefit from this infrastructure. Subsequently, conditions changed due to rapid tourist and villa development along this road. Feeling marginalised and seeking a fair share from the development, Pak Sontar and other ex-landholders established a group to charge road access and parking fees from visitors passing along the road (Adhika 2011b, 217). The expansion of real estate and tourism accommodation in specific areas has also led to the relocation of communal temples or their inclusion within private property as 'local colour'. In Nusa Dua, Segara Temple had to be relocated due to the development of the Club Med Hotel, and in Kuta, Sanggaran Temple was relocated for the development of Kartika Plaza Resort (Suartika 2005, 147–166). Pecatu is not an exception. One of the temples in the Uluwatu Complex,

Batu Belah Temple, is now located within the area of Uluwatu Resort. While the locals may still conduct rituals and ceremonies in the temple, permission is required from the resort beforehand (Adhika 2011b, 216). From the viewpoint of the tourist accommodation owners, keeping this temple within their private commercial areas would mean a free cultural attraction for tourists who stay at the hotel, and at the same time assures them of greater control over its use.

In summary, the local dynamics described above show how villagers' perception of space and place is continually reconstructed through accommodation, contestation, or negotiation with internal and external forces seeking expansion of the tourism and real estate industries. As a result, how the local community perceives threats and opportunities posed by tourist and real estate development in their local areas has been highly ambivalent. Indeed, they are clearly aware of how their livelihoods have been affected by the massive expansion of tourism in their village, but have come to believe that they have little choice except to advance it further in order to widen their economic opportunities so that they might catch up with the high cost of living that has resulted from tourism. This paradox is very important for understanding the controversies surrounding the Provincial Regulation on Spatial Planning for Bali Province (Perda RTRW Bali No. 16/2009), especially the provisions on the sphere of temple sanctity.

Sacred Space and Local Resistance in Spatial Planning

A critical human geographer, John Urry (1985, 30), once observed that the organisation and control over space is inevitably competitive and conflictual because of the limited nature of space itself. Sacred space, a specific spatial production, is even more subject to competition and conflict,[21] not only over the organisation and control of a scarce physical resource, but also over the abundant 'symbolic surpluses' that arise from

[21] "just as the sacred is a contested category" (Kong 2001, 213).

its appropriation (Chidester and Linenthal 1995, 18; Kong 2001). This is because a sacred space is an arena full of symbols and signs with multiple meanings, which are produced and reproduced through spatial practices of 'ritualisation', 'reinterpretation', and 'contests over legitimate ownership' (Chidester and Linenthal 1995, 9). Chidester and Linenthal (1995, 7–9) elaborate four political acts implicated in such production and displacement: (1) the politics of position, whereby "every establishment of a sacred place was a conquest of space"; (2) the politics of property, whereby sacred space may be "appropriated, possessed and owned"; (3) the politics of exclusion, whereby its sacredness is "certified by maintaining and reinforcing boundaries that kept certain persons [or things] outside the sacred place"; and (4) the politics of exile, "which takes the form of modern loss of or nostalgia for the sacred".

In this regard, sacred space is not only a social arena where 'profane forces' are brought to bear through existing power relations, but also an arena where those constructions are negotiated and resisted based on other 'profane' interests as well as the culturally constituted symbolic meanings of such space. Within a pluralistic legal and institutional setting, the ways in which sacred space is conceived may be different across scales, identities, and social positions. Thus, several acts of politics argued by Chidester and Linenthal appear to be yet more complicated. In such setting, the imposition of sacred space as a product of state power and the scientific knowledge of experts and planners may be adjusted, negotiated, or contested by local power holders utilising local knowledge to preserve or expand their own playing fields in the pursuit of interests and values that are not necessarily consistent or coherent.

In the context of Bali, the production of sacred space, as argued by Hauser-Schaublin (2004), is entangled with the contest over power by the strategic use of a geo-cosmological model underpinned by religious normative orderings.[22] Despite important insights, there are several limitations of Hauser-Schaublin's (2004) examination of the production of

---

[22] She classifies three models of such geo-cosmological concepts in Bali, which are: "(1) the compass rose, or rose of the winds, *nawa sanga*, (2) the microcosm/macrocosm (*buana alit*/*buana agung*), and (3) the model of the two axes, *kaja*/*kelo*d (mountainward/seaward) and *kangin*/*kauh* (east/west), that often crosscut each other" (Hauser-Schaublin 2004, 292).

sacred space in Bali. Firstly, she merely deals with the dynamics surrounding the hierarchy of space within the village scale. Thus, the questions of cross-scale implications are unattended. Secondly, she does not interrogate the changing values and meanings of space in the context of contemporary Bali since she only focuses on the production of sacred space for social status reproduction. Even a cultural and religious attempt to produce sacred space is often intertwined with other 'profane' motives beyond the narrow reproduction of social status, for example, property relations, conservation, tourism, and so forth. Thirdly, the production of sacred space in Bali is assumed to be a top-down and unidirectional process imposed by two dominants actors, the ruler and priest, upon the populace. Hence, this section aims to provide a wider picture of the contestations over the production of sacred space involving different social forces across scale.

Contestations in Governing Uluwatu Temple's Sacred Space

As discussed in Chap. 3, one policy strategy to address the negative impacts of regional autonomy at the district level, but also to respond to the political economy of overdevelopment from the perspective of public, NGO, and academic critics, has been through reorganising spatial governance through the Provincial Regulation on Spatial Planning (Perda RTRW Bali) No. 16/2009. This was possible after the enactment of National Law No. 26/2007 concerning Spatial Planning in which opportunities arose to designate provincial strategic areas within district territories. Indeed, in the Memorandum of Understanding (MoU) No. 075/06/KB/B.PEM/2008, signed by the governor of Bali and all district/municipal heads, agreement was reached regarding the designation of 'provincial strategic areas', one of which is the Uluwatu Temple Complex. This is based on the temple's status as a Sad Kahyangan, one of the six holiest Bali-wide temples to be protected by a sacred space designated according to the 1994 *Bhisama* ruling as five kilometres from the temple's centre. Within this area, buildings that have no spiritual connection to the temple are prohibited.

The *Bhisama* religious ruling was issued by the Parisada Hindu Dharma Indonesia (PHDI), a state-sponsored Hindu organisation, in response to the controversial megaproject development at Tanah Lot Temple by the Bakrie national conglomerate (see Warren 1998). It is derived from religious conceptions of sacred space, standardised and simplified to metric quantification informed by a 'seeing-like-a-state' logic (Scott 1998; Wardana 2015). The religious ruling converts a perceptual radius: (1) *apeneleng agung*, as far as the eye can see at a great distance, to a five-kilometre radius; (2) *apeneleng alit*, as far as the eye can see at a short distance, to a two-kilometre radius; and (3) *apenimpug*, a stone's throw, to a 5–25-metre radius. These apply depending on the hierarchical status of the temples according to province-wide, district-wide, or local significance.

At the village level, however, Desa Pakraman Pecatu as *pengemong* of Uluwatu Temple rejected the way in which sacred space had been designated by the *Bhisama* and adopted into state spatial planning regulations. This does not mean that the *adat* village denies the sanctity of Uluwatu temple, but that it uses a different concept for designating sacred space. Instead of metric quantification as formulated in the *Bhisama*, sacred space designated by Desa Pakraman Pecatu uses a different interpretation for designating the sanctity sphere, that is the village forest cover surrounding the temple known as *alas kekeran*.[23] Indeed, *alas kekeran* has no metric quantification but, if quantified in the context of Uluwatu Temple, is less than a five-kilometre radius, thus creating a conflicting normative ordering concerning the status of areas beyond *alas kekeran* that are within the *Bhisama* declared protected zone. Consequently, the land beyond *alas kekeran* but within the five kilometres officially declared sacred radius became a 'grey zone' due to the overlapping spatial concepts and functions.

[23] The *Awig-Awig* of Desa Pakraman Pecatu (1987: §27/6) stipulates that "the existence of *kekeran* is designated to reinforce the sanctity and sacredness of Ulutwatu temple and should not be used for farming or building … It should only be used for growing trees which function as *alas peneduh jagat* (the forest shading the domain)". This is based on local custom that then has been codified into a written *adat* rule since 1987.

This conflict is not only between interpretations of religious law (the *Bhisama* on the sacred sphere of temples) and *adat* law (the *Awig-Awig* of Desa Pakraman Pecatu), but also within state law itself. While Perda RTRW Bali No. 3/2005 stipulated sacred space based on the *Bhisama* in which there should be no buildings within a five-kilometre sacred space, a *Surat Keputusan Bupati Badung* (Decision of Badung District Head) No. 79/2000 concerning Detailed Plans for the Arrangement of the Uluwatu Temple Complex, classified the sacred space of Uluwatu Temple into three sacred rings in which different rules apply.[24] Ring one is the *alas kekeran* surrounding Luhur Uluwatu Temple, where building is prohibited akin to the stipulation in the *Awig-Awig* of Desa Pakraman Pecatu. Ring two is the area between *alas kekeran* and Batu Belah and Kulat Temples, the two nearest temples from the core Luhur Uluwatu Temple and Nyang-Nyang Beach, which can be utilised as forest, *tegalan* (dry agricultural land) and tourist facilities, but no tourist accommodation. Ring three includes the areas beyond Ring two up to the border of Pecatu Village, which can be utilised as residential areas for local Pecatu villagers, and may include small-scale tourist accommodation, as well as locally owned restaurants and homestays. What the decree means by 'small scale tourist accommodation' was not clearly defined; thus, a 0.20-hectare villa might be considered by developers to fall within this category.

Since the era of regional autonomy began, desacralisation of areas within a five-kilometre provincially designated sacred space through land sale for villas/hotel construction and other 'profane' tourism facilities has been occurring regularly. This desacralisation (Chidester and Linenthal 1995, 2) of the sanctity sphere of Uluwatu Temple as a *Sad Kahyangan* is widely regarded as desecration by Balinese Hindus across the island. For Pecatu Village, however, land conversion for developing tourist facilities outside the *alas kekeran* has been legally justified by Awig-Awig Desa Pakraman Pecatu and the Badung District Head Decision No. 79/2000. Although in theory this should not be the case because a lower decree

[24] Until the new Perda RTRW Badung No. 26/2013 was finally enacted after a long period of deferral, the District Government of Badung, using regional autonomy as the justification, had resisted applying the decree as a legal condition in granting development permits in Pecatu Village.

could not overturn higher legislation, on the ground, the Perda was never enforced by the provincial government itself, making it a '*macan kertas*' ('paper tiger'). Consequently, violations of the *Bhisama* and Perda RTRW Bali No. 3/2005 continue to occur across Bali.

The adoption of Perda RTWR Bali No. 16/2009 and the outcomes of the *Bhisama* provisions in the regulation did not mean the end of the controversy. Another concern for Pecatu Village with the regulation opened up when the newly elected members of the DPRD Bali began their term in office. Disel Astawa, a PDI-P politician from South Kuta, for instance, was among a number of DPRD members who were opponents of Perda No. 16/2009. The position of Pecatu Village was supported by Badung District government officials, especially I Ketut Sudikerta, serving as the Vice District Head of Badung, who was also a public figure (*tokoh masyarakat*) of Pecatu Village. Besides Sudikerta, several other district officials who occupied strategic positions in the District Government of Badung—such as the Chairs of *Dinas Pendapatan Daerah* (Dispenda/Regional Revenues Bureau) and *Dinas Perizinan Daerah* (Bureau for Regional Licences), as well as two DPRD Badung members, one of whom was serving as the Vice Chair of DPRD Badung—were also from Pecatu Village. Hence, despite utilising different (and ultimately conflicting) idioms derived from their different institutional positions, an alliance between Badung District government officials, DPRD Badung, and DPRD Bali members was informally formed to oppose the newly promulgated provincial spatial planning regulation.

While the district government officials based their arguments on the state regional autonomy regime, which gives them authority to manage their territory,[25] Pecatu Village placed Balinese *adat* principles of '*otonomi*

[25] Bayu Kumara, the Chair of the Development Administration Division of Badung, quoted by Ardika (2011a, 296), says that "according to the Detailed Plan for Badung Dictrict, Pecatu is designated as a tourism area. However, the Provincial Government designates it as sacred space … If someone proposes a development in Pecatu, but the District Government refuses to grant a permit, we will be brought to court because the district spatial planning is for tourism and permits are under the authority of the District Government. This is like colonialism in an independent era. If the provincial regulation on spatial planning will be implemented, people simply cannot live here." The District Government official's argument is based on the weak legal reasoning that denying a permit proposed by a citizen could be brought on legal grounds before the administrative court

desa pakraman' (*adat* village autonomy) and '*desa-kala-patra*' (according to place-time-circumstances) at the centre of their argument. These principles have been used to justify the changing spatial practices in the village. I Made Sumerta, the former Chief of Pecatu Administrative Village, complains that "our people are confused. In the past, when land here was valueless, we lived in poverty, and no one cared [about us]. Now, with the development of tourism, our lives become much better, then there is the *Bhisama* that indirectly *memasung* (restrains) our lives. Not to mention, other people outside our village protest to prohibit development although it takes place on our land and property" (quoted by Adhika 2011a, 218).

Several informants during interviews mentioned that their stance against the *Bhisama* was also due to personal circumstances. Many of them have sold their land since the late 1990s to investors and other external actors, but the land could not be built on due to the *Bhisama* restriction, and the promised employment has not ensued. Komang Sunia, a Pecatu Villager, mentions that he sold his land in Labuan Sait in early 2000, before the controversy over Uluwatu Temple's sacred space arose, to a Jakarta-based businessman who intended to build a luxury villa. Not so long after the transaction, the controversy emerged and the land itself was located within the five-kilometre sacred space; to date, the buyer has not built the villa.[26] Moreover, many land transactions have also been cancelled after learning of the future likelihood of sanctions stipulated in the *Bhisama* if adopted and enforced by the new spatial planning regulation. Ibu Oka, for instance, says that in 2009 her 20-*are* (0.2 hectare) plot of land was about to be sold to an Australian for constructing a villa near Uluwatu Temple, but the day before the transaction, the buyer cancelled it saying that he received information on the prohibition to build within the sacred zone where the land is located.[27] Since the land transaction contract also contained an entitlement for the former landowner to be employed when the development project is implemented, such delays

(PTUN). To the contrary, the district government could be taken to court if it gives a permit that violates higher regulations.

[26] Interview with Komang Sunia, on 4 August 2014.

[27] Interview with Ibu Oka, on 25 July 2014.

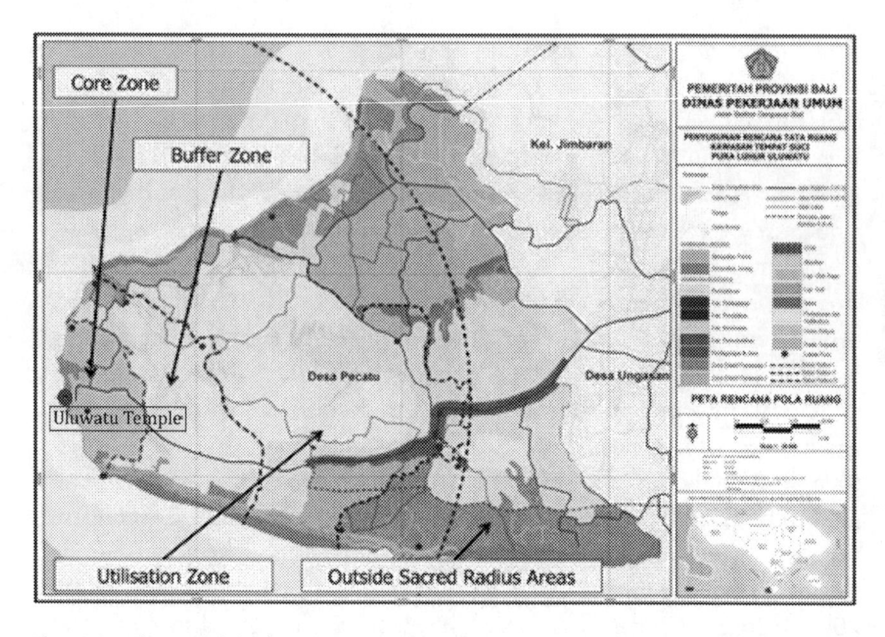

Fig. 4.2 The spatial planning map for Uluwatu temple's sacred space. Source: Wartha Bakti Mandala (2012)

and cancellations in turn mean a loss of work opportunity in the tourism sector. With little or no land remaining to work on, these Pecatu villagers face economic uncertainty (Fig. 4.2).

In this complex legal setting, 'forum-shopping' (von Benda-Beckmann 1981) has also been used by Pecatu Village for scaling up their opposition beyond the local *adat* sphere. With prompting from those local figures above, especially Sudikerta, Pecatu Village filed at least eight judicial reviews concerning the new spatial planning regulation before the Supreme Court in Jakarta, represented by prominent Jakarta-based law firms. They included two on behalf of local institutions, *Desa Pakraman Pecatu* and *Badan Permusyawaratan Desa* (Village Consultative Assembly) of Pecatu,[28] and six individual cases submitted by several landowners within the five-kilometre temple sphere of sanctity, including I Made

[28] Registered as Case No. 34 P/HUM/2010 and Case No. 35 P/HUM/2010. See Arya Utama and Sudiarta (2011).

Deg from Banjar Karang Bomo and I Wayan Puja from Banjar Tengah. Ketut Murdana, the *Bendesa* of Desa Pakraman Pecatu, vaguely admitted that it was Sudikerta who suggested they take their objections to the Supreme Court and facilitated the proceedings using his resources and national network. Murdana said, "before the judicial review process he [Sudikerta] gave ... '*adalah*' ['something']. [He suggested that] because we are in a tourism area so that we do not *merusak citra pariwisata* [disturb the image of tourism—due to demonstrations], let's try to bring this to *ranah hukum* [the legal sphere] to show that we are not arrogant".[29]

The legal grounds concerned the additional category of in-situ protected areas (*kawasan perlindungan setempat*) in Perda RTRW Bali No. 16/2009. The category is the temple's sphere of sanctity (*radius kesucian pura*) as specified in the *Bhisama* (Article 44). According to Law No. 26/2007 on Spatial Planning, the plaintiffs argued, there is no such category as '*radius kesucian pura*' specified in the national legislation; therefore, there was no legal ground to regulate space by incorporating it in the Provincial Regulation. Moreover, they argue that the religious ruling (*Bhisama*) is not officially recognised as a source of law by national laws, although, in fact, there are provisions for cultural considerations in many local regulations.[30] Their primary concern was actually the anticipated consequences of the in-situ protected area designation over their land. Physical and commercial developments within these designated areas would be restricted, depriving local interests of the economic advantages from such developments. The landowners are prevented from utilising their land for building tourism accommodation, decreasing the value of this land on the market. This is because the plaintiffs argue that 60% of Pecatu village territory falls within the five-kilometre temple sanctity

[29] Interview with Ketut Murdana, *Bendesa* of Pecatu, on 18 July 2014.

[30] The acknowledgement of distinctive *karakteristik daerah* (regional characteristics) in regional legislation is affirmed by the establishment of Legislation Law No. 10/2004. Article 12 of the Law states that "The substances of Regional Regulations are the whole materials in the framework of regional autonomy and duty of assistance, and to accommodate special local conditions as well as further elaboration of the higher Regulations." The *Bhisama* religious ruling was incorporated in the state-legal system for the first time, through the 2005 Provincial Spatial Planning Regulation for Bali Province.

sphere of Uluwatu Temple.[31] Since the protected zones cover a significant area of the village, this policy would have a severe impact on landowning villagers and on the village economy.

After hearing both plaintiffs and defendants' claims, the Supreme Court finally rejected the claims, stating that Perda RTRW Bali No. 16/2009 is legitimate and does not violate any national law on these matters. The court considered that the protection of sacred areas is an attempt to preserve the uniqueness of Balinese culture and environment as the basis of 'cultural tourism', guaranteed under the Indonesian Constitution and the regional autonomy legislation. The stipulation on the sacred sphere of temples should not be interpreted as neglecting the rights of landowners to utilise their land, but as an attempt to regulate the kinds of activities allowed or disallowed within that sphere based on its zones (core, buffer, and utilisation). On the issue of property rights, the Supreme Court states that the regulation should not be interpreted as denying the right of local people to become involved in tourism businesses because the land may still be utilised for agricultural and religious activities that also support cultural tourism, and that the government, in fact, could provide an incentive for the landowners in the form of, among other things, tax reduction and compensation.[32] The court concluded by rejecting all of the plaintiffs' claims.

This decision reveals formal state recognition of the religious ruling (*Bhisama*) at the national level under the provincial government's authority to protect the cultural uniqueness of the region. However, the Supreme Court appears to avoid the slippery question of the complex legal constellation in contemporary Bali, although the relationship between customary and state jurisdiction was implicitly raised by the plaintiffs. In the positivistic logic of the Indonesian legal system, customary law has been considered subordinate to state law, and therefore, the extent to which the autonomy of the customary community is recognised by the state would depend on the extent to which its customary law is consistent with state law and regulations. This is because lawyers assume

---

[31] *Made Deg v. Governor of Bali* [2010] Supreme Court of Indonesia, No. 30 P/HUM/2010, at 40.

[32] This is based on Perda RTRW Bali No. 16/2009, Articles 96, 127, 128.

that the existence of unofficial or non-state law should be regulated by the state-legal system; put differently, "state law is rightfully the dominant set of rules" (van Rossum and Taekema 2013, 157). The use of legal mechanisms in this conflict is partly explained by their attempt to avoid the use of confrontative strategies, such as demonstrations, that may affect the image of tourism and, in turn, worsen the village's tourism economy.

Uncertainty and Ambivalence

These complex legal and institutional structures produce legal 'uncertainty' and 'grey areas' that may provide spaces for either resisting or facilitating investments. In Pecatu, in fact, tourist infrastructure and luxury real estate developments have continued unabated by channelling them through local institutions captured by elite interests. The most recent developments involved the construction of restaurants and food stalls (*warung*) by several villagers within Uluwatu Temple's sacred space in both the utilisation and buffer zones without any impediment. This was a form of local disobedience and simultaneously an attempt at 'testing the water' to see whether Perda RTRW Bali No. 16/2009 is really enforced. To date, there has been no enforcement conducted by the provincial government, and this in turn has triggered more construction within the area. Politically, the non-enforcement of Perda RTRW Bali No. 16/2009 is partly explained by the fact that Ketut Sudikerta, a Pecatu elite figure, occupied a strategic position in the provincial government's structure as vice-governor of Bali, with a direct influence over the politics of law enforcement in the province. Moreover, Governor Pastika (2008–2013 & 2013–2018) never intended to implement the regulation, but rather that the regulation itself gave provincial authorities a strategic opportunity to pursue their own rent-seeking agendas.

As development continued, 'hidden transcripts'—speeches, gestures, and practices taking place 'offstage' or 'beyond direct observation by powerholders' that may be regarded as a confirmation, contradiction, or inflection to the mainstream discourse (Scott 1990, 4)—nonetheless, have in fact also emerged. Despite the dependence on tourism, like most

Balinese who have been polled on the subject (Warren 2012), there is opposition to the ongoing unregulated development among Pecatu villagers. Ibu Mardi, a local Pecatu masseuse at Dreamland Beach, for instance, believes that spatial planning regulations should be more stringent and that buildings that violate the regulations should be demolished. She is also opposed to the high level of land transfers from locals to outsiders, and the uncontrolled development in her area that has had negative impacts on her livelihood. Although she as a woman is excluded from a direct role in decision making on the spatial planning controversy because both local customary institutions as well as official village councils are dominated by men, Ibu Mardi was able to keep her husband from selling their inherited land, in the face of intense pressure from middlemen (*calo*) to do so.[33] Ibu Oka also agrees that development in Pecatu should be controlled to prevent Pecatu from chaos (*semrawut*). In 2014, a similar concern was clearly articulated by the first edition of *Majalah Catu*, an annual local magazine owned by Desa Pakraman Pecatu. In the headline, it is stated that

> Pariwisata Pecatu kini berkembang pesat. Kemakmuran pun perlahan dirasakan masyarakat Pecatu. Tapi diam-diam membiak rasa khawatir, Pecatu bakal mengulang sejarah Kuta: industri wisata maju di satu sisi, tetapi kawasan menjadi semrawut dan masyarakat lokal tersisih karena kalah bersaing.
>
> [Pecatu's tourism has nowadays rapidly developed. Prosperity has been gradually experienced by villagers. However, there is a silent concern, [that] Pecatu would repeat Kuta's history: on the one hand the tourism industry progresses, but on the other hand the area becomes chaotic and local people are marginalised because of inability to compete]". (*Catu Magazine*, 01/2014, 3)

It appears that this concern has become a growing public concern. Meanwhile, Putu Yusa, chair of the *subak* association in Pecatu, agrees that the sacred sphere around temples should be protected and that agri-

---

[33] Interview with Ibu Mardi by Carol Warren, 1 August 2012.

cultural land should be preserved, but he is not prepared to give up his rights over his own land through designation as protected areas, when other landowners are not required to do so.[34] Yasa's statement raises an important issue about the ultimate unfairness of all zoning arrangements that impact upon market values. It illustrates how inequity is inherent in planning processes unless redistributive and progressive taxation regimes dampen excesses and eliminate the disproportionate consequences.

Conclusion

Pecatu Village once was regarded as a backward village due to its lack of resources, especially agricultural land and water. As the Uluwatu Temple, an iconic temple situated on the top of a cliff, has developed since the New Order era to be one of the most popular tourist destinations in the island, Pecatu Village has also been affected by tourism. As a result, the value of land in the village has increased dramatically, making every space in the village a valuable asset of its owner to be sold or rented to build tourism accommodation and other facilities. In turn, the village's economy has been put in a single basket of tourism due to its heavy dependency on the tourism industry. Meanwhile, local institutions through which collective interests supposed to be pursued have been captured by local elites. As tourism entrepreneurs or middlemen for investors, those elites are the main beneficiary of the further expansion of tourism industry in the village. Hence, the ways in which villagers responded to the Bhisama and the Provincial Spatial Planning Regulation concerning sacred radius of the Uluwatu Temple were to a larger extent influenced by these structural conditions. They seem to have little choice to adapt with the rapid changing of their livelihood and at the same time to catch up with the increase in the costs of living except by submitting themselves to local elites' interests and expecting the trickle-down effects.

Moreover, the case study also shows how sacred space is never fixed, as the structural conditions that produce its meanings and people's interests

[34] Interview with Putu Yusa by Carol Warren, 1 August 2012.

over it constantly change. Accordingly, the re-production of sacred space through spatial planning undertaken by the state is far from technocratic tasks to conserve particular areas having ecological and cultural significances for a collective good. In fact, it is necessarily an exercise of power which implicates power relations that are embedded in the existing configuration of space. In this regard, the several acts of politics in the production and reproduction of sacred space, argued by Chidester and Linenthal (1995) mentioned above, appear to be yet more complicated. Within a pluralistic legal and institutional setting, the imposition of sacred space as a product of state power and the scientific knowledge of experts and planners may be adjusted, negotiated, or contested by local power holders utilising local knowledge to preserve or expand their own playing fields in pursuit of interests and values that are not necessarily consistent or coherent.

5

The Making of World Heritage Landscape

This chapter demonstrates how the reconfiguration of space has been undertaken in the making of the World Heritage landscape in a highland community of Bali. The process for developing heritage tourism was undertaken without carefully considering the complex institutional and legal constellation and the social dynamics within which the landscape is produced. As we shall see, what has been assumed to be a technocratic task in engineering socio-spatial relations and establishing an adequate management plan and institutional arrangement to govern the landscape has been navigated and transformed by social actors utilising the complex legal and institutional setting in the pursuit of different interests. In contrast to Vickers (2012 [1990], 299), who regards the World Heritage making in Bali as merely about enhancing the Balinese cultural identity or, in his own words, as 'a way of keeping out Islam' from the island, I argue that the making is exactly about creating a new space for tourism capital expansion by scaling-up the previous village tourism project to the global level using a World Heritage Site as a label for competitiveness.

A. Wardana, *Contemporary Bali*, https://doi.org/10.1007/978-981-13-2478-9_5

Jatiluwih and the Village Tourism Project

The Village of Jatiluwih

In public policy circles, the Subak Landscape of Catur Angga is typically identified with Jatiluwih, a village located within the upland landscape of north-central Bali. Historically, the development of Catur Angga as a World Heritage Site has been centred in this village. Thus, examining the politics of World Heritage Listing upon the wider Catur Angga landscape should start from here. This is because the landscape is partially the product of a scaling up of the previous Jatiluwih village tourism project for the global market, using the World Heritage brand to enhance its competitiveness. In fact, the designation of core/buffer zone within the landscape, which privileges Jatiluwih as the core zone, has been the main issue in the debate on how the landscape should be governed and how the benefits from tourism should be distributed (see MacRae 2016).

Jatiluwih, a 2233-hectare village, is located about 800 metres above sea level in Penebel Sub-District of Tabanan, a two-hour drive from Denpasar, the capital city of Bali Province, to the north. Jatiluwih village is bordered by Batukaru Nature Reserve in the north, Babahan Village in the south, Wongaya Gede Village in the west, and Senganan Village in the east. It has a population of 2675 people, and they depend on farming as their major source of livelihood (BPS Tabanan 2014).

Institutionally, like other villages in Bali, Jatiluwih is governed by two different and overlapping administrative (*dinas*) and customary (*adat*/*pakraman*) village institutions (Table 5.1). The administrative village (*desa dinas*) of Jatiluwih is composed of two customary villages (*desa adat*), namely Desa Pakraman Jatiluwih and Desa Pakraman Gunungsari. While the administrative village of Jatiluwih is under the leadership of a village head (*Perbekel*) who is elected by all *dinas* village members, the *adat* villages are each under the separate leadership of a *Bendesa*, who is elected through a *sangkepan* (meeting) of *adat* village members. Below the village structures, there are seven hamlets that institutionally are also divided by tasks: administrative affairs managed by *dusun*, under the

Table 5.1 Institutional structure of Jatiluwih

Administrative village	Customary village	Hamlets
Desa Dinas Jatiluwih	Desa Pakraman Jatiluwih	1. Banjar/Dusun Jatiluwih Kangin 2. Banjar/Dusun Jatiluwih Kawan 3. Banjar/Dusun Kesambahan Kaja 4. Banjar/Dusun Kesambahan Kelod 5. Banjar/Dusun Kesambi
	Desa Pakraman Gunungsari	1. Banjar/Dusun Gunungsari Desa 2. Banjar/Dusun Gunungsari Umakayu

leadership of a *kepala dusun*; and customary affairs managed by *banjar*, under the leadership of a *kelihan banjar*.[1]

The other vital local institution, of central importance to this case, is the *subak*, which is the core institution for managing the wet-rice landscape. The *subak*, as a customary and officially recognised institution, and as a landscape, are together the focus of the World Heritage Listing. Subak Jatiluwih is a *subak gede* (a federal-like overarching institution) covering 303 hectares of wet-rice agricultural land. It is composed of seven *tempekan subak*s (smaller sub-units of the *subak gede*), namely: (1) Tempek Telabah Gede; (2) Tempek Besi Kalung; (3) Tempek Kedamaian; (4) Tempek Uma Dui; (5) Tempek Uma Kayu; (6) Tempek Kesambih; (7) Tempek Gunungsari. Membership of *tempekan subak* does not necessarily coincide with *banjar* membership because the former is defined by the location of his/her agricultural land, regardless of his/her *banjar*, which is normally determined by residence. In fact, in the *subak* sphere, there is no differential treatment whether a member originates from the village or not.

Subak Jatiluwih is under the leadership of a *Pekaseh*, and each *tempekan subak* is under the leadership of a *Kelihan Subak*, although both are elected by their *subak* members through *paruman* (assembly). Unlike the *desa dinas* mode of leadership, which follows the Western concept of

[1] Except in Banjar Jatiluwih Kangin, where the positions of *Kelihan Banjar* (*adat* hamlet chief) and *Kepala Dusun* (*dinas* hamlet chief) are held by one person, in the other *banjars*, the two positions are separated and occupied by different persons.

elected authority, in *subak* (as in *banjar* and *desa adat*) important decisions remain based on the consensus of members rather than on the *Pekaseh*'s discretion. In most parts of Bali, the principle of consensus-based decision making prevails across *adat* institutions (*desa, banjar, subak*) in theory, if not always in practice. The concept of '*pakraman*' rests authority in the *krama*, the collective membership of customary institutions. Thus, as Warren (1993, 127) notes regarding Bali's customary institutions, traditional leaders are in 'constant negotiation' with their members.

The relationship between *subak gede* and *tempekan subak* is also analogous to that of *desa pakraman* and *banjar*. Daily interaction and direct participation in decision making takes place both formally and informally at the lower levels, namely, the *tempekan subak*. At the *subak gede* level, day-to-day decision making typically involves the committee members of *subak gede*[2] and *tempekan subak*, except for essential matters beyond the *tempekan* level, such as adopting *awig-awig* (customary rules), building a *subak* hall or temple, where an assembly of the whole membership is required.

Officially in the state record, members registered in Subak Jatiluwih are the landowners located within the *subak* landscape. However, actual rights and duties are referred to the land users, the owner himself or the tenant (a sharecropper) or a combination of the two. According to Nyoman Sutama, *Pekaseh* of Subak Gede Jatiluwih, roughly 5% of its 562 members are sharecroppers, and at the *subak tempekan* level, that percentage varies considerably. This figure is however unreliable since there is no data available to verify it because the member registered is the landowner, while the numbers of sharecroppers may change every season according to the availability of land and labour.[3] In terms of landownership in Subak Jatiluwih, the average registered landholding is around 0.5

[2] In Jatiluwih, committee membership of Subak Gede Jatiluwih comprises elected persons representing each *subak tempek*, who are typically, but not necessarily, the *kelihan tempek*.

[3] The Kelian Subak relies on the information provided by the sharecroppers for whom they work. The only available data on officially registered landownership is the Definitive Plan for the Needs of Subsidised Fertiliser Groups (Rencana Definitif Kebutuhan Kelompok Pupuk Bersubsisi/RDKK). According to Agus Palguna, a district government official at the Penebel Technical Unit of Bureau of Agriculture (interview on 21 February 2015), the RDKK data is far from the reality on the ground.

hectares, ranging from 2 hectares (6 landholders) to 0.10 hectare (13 landholders). The size of landownership, especially wet-rice agricultural land (*sawah*), in an agricultural society remains the symbol of a person's social-economic status (Parker 2003, 51). In Jatiluwih, where 63.10% of the population are farmers (BPS Tabanan 2014, 27), the gap in *sawah* ownership is fairly limited, and the socio-economic hierarchy is relatively flat compared to lowland Bali, for example, in Pecatu Village (Chap. 4). The data also shows that there is no concentration of landownership in a small group of powerful elites who may determine the mode of agricultural activities in the village.

In terms of sharecropping practices, Geertz (1980, 66) once argued that the relationship between landowner and sharecropper in Bali is 'autonomous'. Parker (2003, 61) similarly asserts that sharecropping arrangements rely solely on the two parties involved, the land owner and its sharecropper, "without the regulation of a group or organisation". Geertz and Parker overlook the fact that as a 'semi-autonomous social field' (Moore 1973) *subak* affairs are also informed by the wider legal structure, whether local customary law or state law. Customarily, the landowner-sharecropper relationship is defined by an agreement on the sharing of the harvest.[4] Both landowner and sharecropper are not absolutely free to decide which model they choose to adopt, but to some extent they should consider the custom, very often the unwritten convention and most popular model used within the *subak* where the land is located. Thus, local custom frames whether a sharecropping practice is socially and culturally acceptable in a given historical and temporal space. In Jatiluwih, *subak* may also interfere with landholding relationships based on whether sharecroppers are able to participate in *subak* activities and to comply with the *subak* rules (*awig-awig* or *perarem*). *Subak* may demand that the landowner replace a recalcitrant sharecropper on the grounds of violating such rules that may jeopardise the integrity of the

[4] Such as *ngapit* (75% for landowner and 25% for sharecropper), *petelon* (60% for landowner and 40% for sharecropper), and *nandu* (50% for each landowner and sharecropper) by which a different set of obligations are attached based on the negotiations between both parties.

subak system. At some point, if the demand is not satisfied, the *subak* may appoint another person to be the new sharecropper.[5]

Every society has some form of social differentiation, and kinship is one such form that may be used to justify access to power and resources. In contrast to Geertz and Geertz's (1975) distinction between gentries and commoners and the dynamics of the Balinese caste system in Brassika observed by Parker (1989, 2003), social stratification in Jatiluwih is neither based on a simple gentry-commoner polarisation akin to Javanese society nor based on the Indic-inspired caste system. Jatiluwih villagers are mostly members of the Pasek clan; in other parts of Bali, they would be considered as commoners and simultaneously *sudra* caste. Although a status hierarchy does not exist in relation to other clans[6] or ruling 'castes', status is instead derived from temporal distinctions between the 'firstcomers' and 'latecomers' in founding the Jatiluwih Village settlement. Thus, the social division in this village, and Catur Angga in general, is closer to a system of rank based on 'precedence' in Austronesian societies (see Reuter 2009; Fox 2009).

In this regard, the Pasek Badak sub-clan was the 'firstcomer', as it founded and first inhabited Jatiluwih. Afterwards, other sub-clans arrived as the 'latercomers' and were permitted to reside in the village provided that they were willing to comply with the firstcomer's rulings (*Bhisama Pasek Badak*). Until recently, those who are descendants of the Pasek Badak sub-clan may informally be regarded as having more power at the

[5] Putu Duta, *Kelihan* of Subak Tempek Kedamaian, recounts his experiences accompanying the *Pekaseh* to meet a landowner in Denpasar regarding a sharecropper who did not want to be involved in *subak* activities and who had failed to pay the requisite fines for dereliction of duty. He warned the landowner to pay the fine and to ask the sharecropper to follow the *perarem* (*subak* assembly decision); otherwise, no water would be supplied to the rice-field and he would replace the sharecropper with another person. Finally, the landowner paid the fine and asked the sharecropper to be active in *subak* activities. As water supply is the most essential resource for agriculture, under *subak* control, until recently, no replacement of sharecroppers had occurred, since both landowner and sharecropper are obliged to comply with the *subak* demands. Interview with Putu Duta, *Kelihan* of Subak Tempek Kedamaian, on 20 January 2014.

[6] The sub-clans are Pasek Badak, Pasek Gobleg, Pasek Tangkas, Pasek Beratan, Pasek Sekalan, and Pasek Manikan.

expense of other sub-clan descendants.[7] All *pemangku* (priests) in Jatiluwih temples are from the Pasek Badak sub-clan, except the one for the Pura Dalem, where a *pemangku* from Pasek Gobleg was appointed through a village meeting since a Pasek Badak candidate was not prepared to become *pemangku*.[8] Most local leaders have been from the Pasek Badak clan, including the recent *Perbekel* and *Bendesa*, but in *subak* leadership, this is less frequent. Even the current *Pekaseh* is not from Pasek Badak showing how charismatic individuals can transcend rank and other structural impediments to exert power and influence in Balinese culture. Clan affiliation is also far from homogenous, and it is not neatly paralleled to local political and economic alliances.

Since the mode of production in the village has always been based on agriculture, Subak Jatiluwih has played an essential role in shaping the hilly landscape of Jatiluwih for centuries. Lefebvre (1991, 31) notes that "every society—and hence every mode of production with its subvariants ...—produces a space, its own space". However, this production of 'space', particularly in the case of the rice terraces in Jatiluwih, is not only an economic activity to transform nature through human labour in order optimise rice production. It is also a cultural activity to create a 'place', both in the sense of "geographical space" and "social position and value"

---

[7] According to Pan Suka (interview on 3 March 2015), almost three-fourths of the 350 households in Jatiluwih are from Pasek Badak. He believes that there is a Pasek Badak's *Bhisama* (religious ruling) which rules that priests serving at *Tri Kahyangan* (three village temples) and Petali should be from Pasek Badak. Although the position of *Bendesa* (and *Perbekel* as it later came to be) is not mentioned in the *Bhisama*, there is a common aspiration that a leader of Pasek Badak is preferable to maintain the stability and security of the village. He mentioned that there were several moments when a person from a different Pasek clan served as *Bendesa* and during their term violated the *Bhisama*. When Nang Kajin, from Pasek Manikan, served as *Bendesa* in the 1970s, he changed the religious festival (*odalan*) at Pura Dalem. The festival used to be on the same day as similar festivals at Pura Puseh. Nyoman Murtika, from Pasek Gobleg, served as *Bendesa* during 1999–2003, coincidently, in tandem with Sumarjaya, from Pasek Manikan, who served as the *Perbekel*. Murtika changed the traditions where the position of priest at Pura Dalem was allowed to be held by other clans, in particular Pasek Gobleg. It is commonly believed (by Pasek Badak) that those changes have created an imbalance and led to many incidences of suicide, family division, financial issues, and social conflicts, including the controversy over Villa Petali. Recently, the *Bendesa* and *Perbekel* positions have been held by Pasak Badak, who have attempted to reintegrate the festival and follow the Pasak Badak *Bhisama* consistently with little dissent.

[8] Interview with Nengah Kartika, Administrative Village Chief (*Perbekel*) of Desa Jatiluwih, on 21 January 2014.

that links to the construction of identity (Smith 2006, 75–76). For Pan Suka, a farmer and local artist, for example, the landscape also creates spiritual meaning and sense of enjoyment, "Let alone the foreigners, even for myself who was born and have lived for my whole life in this village, it is a great pleasure enjoying the rice fields here".[9] He stresses that foreigners may find the rice terrace landscape interesting because it is different from their daily environment. For him, although the landscape is a part of his everyday rhythm, he still feels amazed by what he has inherited from the ancestors, and this creates his strong sense of identity as a Jatiluwih farmer.

The Village Tourism Project

In the early 1990s, faced with the public criticism of emerging mega-tourism developments perceived as marginalising the Balinese public, the Governor of Bali Ida Bagus Oka (1988–1998) turned to 'village tourism' as a potential new product for the tourist market on the island. Under the auspices of the Ministry of Tourism and Gadjah Mada University, a village tourism project was planned for three remote villages over the period 1988–1994, namely, Penglipuran (Bangli), Sebatu (Gianyar), and Jatiluwih (Tabanan). While Penglipuran represents a traditional village with unique architecture and Sebatu represents a village of artisans, Jatiluwih was chosen because of its impressive rice terraces managed by the *subak* (see Yamashita 2003; Prasiasa 2010; Wardana 2014a). Typical of the top-down model of development projects at the time, participation of the local community in village tourism development was also artificial. In Jatiluwih, the project was managed by the District Government of Tabanan. Since the initiation of the Village Tourism Project, the rice terraces of Jatiluwih have been put on Bali's tourist map as an alternative tourism package.

Considering tourist revenue allocation (Fig. 5.1), however, it is apparent that the *subak* institution has been excluded as beneficiary despite the fact that its rice terraces had become the main object of the

[9] Interviewed with Pan Suka, a farmer, on 21 January 2014.

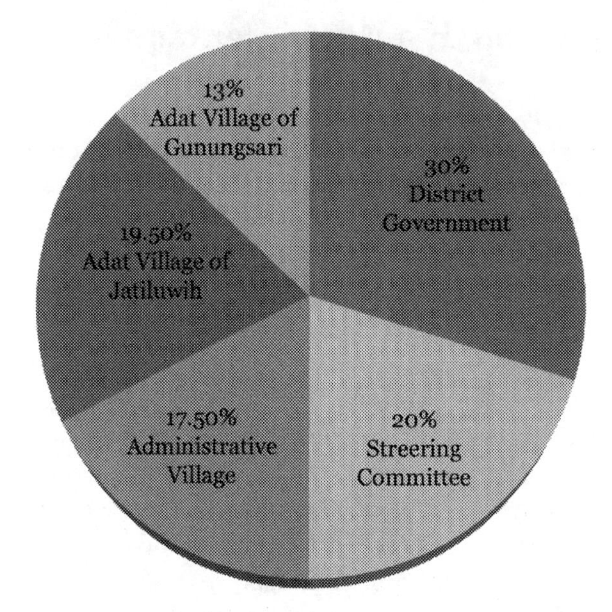

Fig. 5.1 Allocation of revenues in the Jatiluwih Village Tourism. Source: the District Head of Tabanan Decree No. 6/2001

'tourist gaze' (Urry 2002). The district government assumed that *subak* members are also members of *desa adat* and *desa dinas*, which receive half the tourist revenues; therefore, *subak* would benefit only indirectly from the percentages allocated to the village institutions. Although it is true that almost all *subak* members in Jatiluwih are also members of *desa adat* (either *Desa Pakraman* Gunungsari or Jatiluwih) and *desa dinas*, the *subak* as a socio-ecological institution has no direct structural relation with *adat* and *dinas* village institutions (see Geertz 1959). There is no reason to assume that the share provided would work to preserve either the *subak* system or the livelihoods of the farmers who depend upon it. The conflation of relationships between *desa adat, desa dinas*, and *subak* has created a more difficult tension, especially in addressing the slippery question of into which village institution's domain the tourism project falls, that in turn would determine its governance and revenue allocations.

The Production of a World Heritage Site

Following the ratification of the 1972 World Heritage Convention in 1989, the state of Indonesia has been eager to nominate properties to be listed under the convention. It is required that the properties should have 'outstanding universal value'.[10] Eight properties located in Indonesia have been listed by the Convention as World Heritage Sites under the natural, cultural, or cultural landscape categories.[11] The most recent is 'the Cultural Landscape of Bali Province: The Subak System as Manifestation of the Tri Hita Karana Philosophy' representing the only 'cultural landscape' or living heritage among Indonesian sites. This cultural landscape consists of four clusters across five districts: (1) Supreme Water Temple of Pura Ulun Danu Batur and Lake Batur in Bangli District; (2) Subak Landscape of Pakerisan Watershed in Gianyar District; and (3) Royal Temple of Pura Taman Ayun in Badung District; and (4) Subak Landscape of Catur Angga Batukaru (Catur Angga thereafter) in Tabanan and Buleleng Districts, the particular focus for this chapter.

According to the nomination dossier, the main objective of nominating the cultural landscape has been to support the preservation of the *subak* system. Previously, the national government attempted to nominate Pura Besakih, Bali's largest and holiest temple, in 1990, 1992, and 2001, but such attempts received a hostile reaction from the public, concerned with losing control of its management and religious significance (see Darma Putra and Hitchcock 2005). Following these failures, the national government under the Ministry of Culture and Tourism (MCT) and the Provincial Government of Bali continually searched for other potential sites of parallel tourism significance to the temple of Pura

[10] Paragraph 49 of the 2005 Operational Guidelines of the Convention defines the 'outstanding universal value' as "cultural and/or natural significance, which is so exceptional as to transcend national boundaries and to be of common importance for present and future generations of all humanity. As such, the permanent protection of this heritage is of the highest importance to the international community as a whole."

[11] Borobudur Temple Compounds (adopted in 1991), Prambanan Temple Compounds (in 1991), Komodo National Park (1991), Ujung Kulon National Park (1991), Sangiran Early Man Site (in 1996), Lorentz National Park (in 1999), Tropical Rainforest Heritage of Sumatera (in 2004; later listed as 'world heritage in danger' in 2011), and cultural landscape of Bali Province (in 2012).

Besakih. Learning from past experiences, to ensure public support and based on the ICOMOS suggestion (Dharmiasih and Lansing 2014), the nomination committee changed its strategy by putting the *subak* system at the forefront of disseminated information, despite the fact that several temples, including the Pura Ulun Danu Batur,[12] were included. It was hoped that by making the *subak* the focal point of the nomination, no controversy would be raised since the future of the *subak* system and its rice terraces had become a matter of public concern, expressed widely in the mass media and daily conversation (Warren 2012; see Chap. 3). Thus, the *subak* nomination was convenient for both parties, the Government of Indonesia and the UNESCO.

It took almost 12 years before the Cultural Landscape of Bali Province was finally listed in June 2012. It started in the early 2000s when the Government of Indonesia nominated two sites to the World Heritage Committee in the province of Bali, consisting of the archaeological sites of the Pakerisan Watershed representing cultural heritage, and the rice terraces of Jatiluwih Village representing natural heritage. In 2004, a revised dossier entitled 'Sites of Balinese Cosmologies' was submitted, incorporating the rice terraces of Jatiluwih Village, the Royal Temple of Taman Ayun, and a series of archaeological sites along Pakerisan River valley (Fox 2012, 110). In 2008, the World Heritage Committee (WHC), based on an advisory body's evaluation, deferred the examination of the dossier and recommended that Indonesia re-nominate "a site or sites that display the close link between rice terraces, water temples, villages and forest catchment areas, and where the traditional *subak* system is still functioning in its entirety and managed by local communities" (ICOMOS 2012, 170). Based on this recommendation, the reconfiguration and rescaling process of the rice terraces of Jatiluwih Village began to incorporate "all interconnected natural, religious, and cultural components that encompass the entire extent of the traditional *subak*" (ICOMOS 2012, 171).

In the process of revision, the 'rice terrace of Jatiluwih Village' had been rescaled upward to cover a vast area, including two mountain lakes

[12] Besides being regarded as the supreme water temple for the *subak* in Bangli and Gianyar (Indonesia. MCT 2011), Pura Ulun Danu Batur is also one of the six most sacred temples in Bali (Sad Kahyangan), representing the Lord Wisnu or the god of water.

(Tamblingan and Buyan), a large protected forest, local institutions of the *subak* and villages, five water temples (Pura Luhur Batukaru, Pura Luhur Puncak Petali, Pura Luhur Tamba Waras, Pura Luhur Besikalung, and Pura Luhur Muncaksari), springs, and sections of several rivers situated across two districts of Tabanan and Buleleng (Indonesia. MCT 2011, II-10). This was later labelled in the dossier as the Subak Landscape of Catur Angga Batukaru in which Jatiluwih is just a small part of the landscape. This rescaling of the Jatiluwih site recommended by ICOMOS for the purpose of World Heritage Listing has created a new configuration of space, which consequently could not be governed by the existing district administration. On the basis of the 2008 Governor-District Heads' MoU and Perda RTRW Bali No. 16/2009, the landscape's governance has subsequently been transferred to the provincial government as a provincial strategic area.

The process of rescaling itself is not unproblematic, however, since the politics of inclusion and exclusion are inevitably involved. There are only 17 *subaks*, 12 *dinas* villages, and 14 *adat* villages named in the dossier, while on the ground those local institutions are both greater in number and overlapping. The number of *subaks* included is confusing due to inconsistencies between those named in the dossier submitted to the WHC, those included in government regulations, and the actual *subak* arrangements in Catur Angga.[13] In the government regulation, especially Perda RTRW Bali No. 16/2009, there is confusion between *subak gede* and *subak tempekan*.[14] However, in Tabanan District Regulation No. 6/2014 on Green Zones (*Jalur Hijau*), Subak Soka is not included.[15]

[13]The dossier includes 17 *subaks* but only 15 of them are mentioned, which are the *subaks* of: (1) Bedugul; (2) Jatiluwih; (3) Kedampal; (4) Keloncing; (5) Penatahan; (6) Pesagi; (7) Piak; (8) Piling; (9) Puakan; (10) Rajasa; (11) Sangketan; (12) Soka; (13) Tenggalinggah; (14) Tengkudak; and (15) Wongaya Betan. Recently, four more *subaks* were newly established during the nomination as a result of subdivision (*pemekaran*), that is, Subak Tingkihkerep, Subak Dalem, Subak Pancoran Sari, and Subak Sri Gumana.

[14]For example, it mentions Subak Jatiluwih, Subak Gunungsari, Subak Umadui, and Subak Kusambi. In fact, the last three *subaks* mentioned are *subak tempekan* under Subak Jatiluwih as the *subak gede*.

[15]According to the *Pekaseh* of Subak Senganan, during an interview on 28 September 2014, and *Pekaseh* of Subak Jatiluwih, in an interview on 7 November 2013. This exclusion has caused com-

When the names are collated, there are actually 21 *subak* institutions in Catur Angga, with numbers to increase with the continuing subdivision of *subaks* triggered by the potential benefits arising from the World Heritage Listing.[16] Every *subak* in Bali receives a Provincial Government grant of US$ 2167 annually, regardless of its size or membership. In addition, it is planned that each *subak* within the World Heritage Site will receive an extra grant of US$ 7224 annually (*Antara News*, 03/01/2014).

With regards to the relation between *dinas* and *adat* institutions, the dossier is no less confusing.[17] It reflects a simplification of the relationship between *subak* and *desa adat*, in which a *subak* is assumed to relate only to a single *adat* village on the basis of where the majority of *subak* members live or where the water temple is located. In reality, however, the picture is more complex. There are several geographical typologies of the overlapping *desa dinas—desa adat—subak* institutional arrangements in the Subak Landscape of Catur Angga Batukaru based on its physical landscape: (1) *subak* located across *desa adat* but still within the territory of a single *desa dinas*; (2) *subak* located across several *desa adat* and *desa dinas*; (3) *subak* located within a single *desa adat* and a single *desa dinas*. In terms of membership, the institutional overlap is even more complex since *subak* members may be residents of a village that is located beyond the *subak's* geographical landscape.

This is a matter of not only correcting details, but also questioning the underlying assumption of the dossier, reflected in how boundaries are constructed. Scrutinising the map of Catur Angga,[18] it is apparent that

---

plaints from members of Subak Soka, who demand to be included as a part of the Catur Angga (*Bali Post* 22/06/2012).

[16] Interview with Made Suwitra, *Pekaseh* of Subak Penatahan, on 28 November 2014. He says that Subak Penatahan will be subdivided shortly into Subak Penatahan and Subak Catur Nadi.

[17] It mentions *dinas* villages within Catur Angga as follows: Jatiluwih, Mengesta, Kelocing, Penatahan, Pesagi, Wongaya Gede, Puakan, Rajasa, Sengketan, Tegallingah, Tengkudak. In fact, Kelocing and Puakan are not *dinas* villages, but are *adat* villages that come under Desa Dinas Wongaya Gede and Desa Dinas Tengkudak, respectively. Moreover, there are 16 *adat* villages stated in the dossier, namely, Wangaya Gede, Jatiluwih, Gunungsari, Mengesta, Penatahan, Pesagi, Piling, Puluk-Puluk, Rejasa, Sangketan, Soka, Tegallinggah, Tengkudak, Wongaya Betan, Babahan, and Utu.

[18] Map of Subak Landscape of Catur Angga Batukaru. https://anthropology.arizona.edu/sites/anthropology.arizona.edu/files/u298/Bali%20Partnership%20for%20Governance%20Transition101027small.pdf. Source: Indonesia. MCT (2011).

mapmaking is a part of this political exercise of spatial reconfiguration. The mapmakers deliberately include and exclude features within the borders of the proposed landscape, to become what Harley (1988) calls mapped 'silences'. This exercise may have important practical consequences, where the excluded features are assumed to be 'non-existent' or irrelevant to the desirable objectives. For example, it treats the Lakes Buyan-Tamblingan and their surrounding forests as an empty space, a blank slate for non-heritage area exploitation, despite the fact that they are ecologically essential to the water supply for the *subak* in Catur Angga (and Bali more widely). In fact, around 44 lake-fisherman families of *Astiti Amerta* and members of Banjar Tamblingan who have inhabited forest lands near Lake Tamblingan for decades have repeatedly been silenced by the state-led project, not only due to their problematic status since the Department of Forestry considers them to be illegal forest occupants, but also because of their resistance to tourism developments in the area.[19] In addition, as the World Heritage consultation merely focused on Tabanan District, because only villages within Tabanan are included, the Four-Custom-Village Association (*Catur Desa Dalem Tamblingan*), the traditional guardian of lakes Buyan and Tamblingan located in Buleleng District, were not considered. Therefore, both the *Catur Desa Dalem Tamblingan* and the lake-fisherman group have not been involved in any consultations whatsoever.[20]

This exclusion reflects a 'seeing-like-a-state' pattern (Scott 1998), by which space is homogenised and what is included on the map depends on the interests of the mapmakers. The expansion of Catur Angga to include the forests and Lake Buyan and Tambilangan areas solely relies on the Department of Forestry's map of these areas. This is indicated by the dos-

[19] They are originally people from villages surrounding the lake, who moved from their congested family compounds, and many of whom were also refugees from Karangasem due to the Mount Agung eruption in 1963. As they have no land to live and work on, fishing is their main economic activity, and building a settlement within the lake area that is designated by the Bureau of Forestry as a protected forest where no human settlement is permitted, their status is unrecognised. They have continued to settle in the area, arguing that they play a significant role in maintaining temples and protecting the lake and forest areas.

[20] Interview with Ketut Artina, Secretary of Catur Desa Dalam Tamblingan, on 6 February 2014.

sier that states: "The lakes and forests are already managed as conservation areas by the Department of Forestry" (Indonesia. MTC 2011, II-49). As a sectoral map that only deals with homogenised 'nature', it does not include cultural and religious interrelations between nearby villages and the forest and lake areas that shape the wider landscape. Acknowledging such interrelations would mean including those communities as a part of the landscape and recognising their shared customary tenure. The exclusion ignores the long struggles of these communities to protect the forests and lakes against development projects proposed for the Buyan—Tamblingan areas.[21] It is very likely that those who are excluded as stakeholders would have limited opportunities to negotiate their interests or to utilise mechanisms provided for challenging decisions taken under the World Heritage Management Regime.

Besides the exclusion of several local groups from early consultations, the subsequent participation process was also inadequate. Even in Catur Angga, although some informants point out that the World Heritage nomination was discussed in the *banjar* or *subak tempekan* meetings, insufficient information was provided and no consultation was conducted regarding the rights and responsibilities of local people at these levels.[22] The participation process was treated as merely 'functional' (Blackstock 2005) in terms of fulfilling stipulated requirements in Chapter III.A 123 of the 2011 Operational Guidelines of the 1972 World Heritage Convention and identifying potential problems to be overcome in supporting the nomination and maintenance of the sites. No claim could be made that 'free prior and informed consent' was obtained through the consultation process.

As a typical top-down state project, it was assumed by the planners that local leadership models akin to the Western-style elected leadership

[21] They raised their voices against the Nusa Bali Abadi (NBA) projects on the basis that the forests and lakes are sacred sites (see Strauss 2015). Moreover, the lake fishermen group have been strong local opponents of the development of the Geothermal project at Bedugul in the middle of the protected forests near their villages. They were concerned by the environmental impacts of the power plant on the lake's water and the sulphur gas emitted with the steam.

[22] Interview with Putu Armini, on 24 March 2014; and interviews with Kadek Jaya; Putu Suciwati; Putu Demen; Andalina Tari, on 25 March 2014.

constituted appropriate representation; local leaders at the village level were assumed to represent the voices of the whole.[23] In fact, except for the *Perbekel* who is a part of the state structure, local leadership in Catur Angga is based on collective decision making through assembly. This is the model of participation in large villages such as Jatiluwih, which typically takes place at the *banjar* (hamlet) and *subak tempekan* (*subak* subunit) levels rather than at the village (*desa*) and *subak gede* levels. Unlike at the higher village levels, in which the division between customary (*adat*/*pakraman*) and administrative (*dinas*) domain is formally demarcated (Warren 1993), 'free prior and informed consent' at the *banjar* and *subak tempekan* would have been more likely to have answered the question of whether they need tourism through World Heritage branding in order to preserve their landscape and, if so, whether World Heritage governance should be placed within *desa adat* or *dinas* or, more appropriately, in the *subak* domain for effective preservation.[24]

As mentioned earlier in Chap. 3, the nomination of the Cultural Landscape of Bali Province is based the fact that the *subak* system is in crisis (Lorenzen and Lorenzen 2005; Indonesia. MCT 2011; Fox 2012). Despite being widely recognised as the cause of the current crisis, it becomes more apparent that tourism has been also seen as its 'salvation'. This view is widely shared not only among policymakers, but also among academics. Pitana and Adi Putra (2013), among others, claim that tourism could also offer a basis for the conservation of Balinese agriculture and the *subak* system. World Heritage Listing was meant to deploy 'cultural heritage' to marry sustainability and development. It was also an attempt to expand Bali's 'products' to meet the increased demand for different forms of tourism (Subadra and Nadra 2006), among others—ecotourism, as well as heritage tourism. These scholars and policymakers assume that the revenues from tourism visits to the *subak* landscape would generate income for local people and make them realise the eco-

[23] This is what Timothy (2007) terms 'tokenistic involvement', by which local people are not empowered to be critical of the nomination or to reject the top-down process.

[24] Despite many weaknesses in international law, the right to 'free prior and informed consent' (FPIC) at least provides a 'wider set of tactics' for local communities to engage in open debates and to defer imposed projects until a consensus is reached (Colchester and Farhan Ferrari 2007).

nomic value of their heritage so that it would be worth preserving (Windia 2013; Pitana and Adi Putra 2013; *Antara News*, 25/09/2015). Cok Ace, a noble figure of Ubud Palace, serving as the district head of Gianyar to get involved in the nomination process, mentions:

> [d]espite about heritage, it [World Heritage List] has a bargaining position for [tourism] promotion. When subak is scaled up to the international level and recognised by UNESCO as a World Heritage site, it means that *subak* is the only one on earth. This is about [creating] differentiation [to be outstanding within tourism markets]. It is expected to be a strong *modal* (capital) for promoting Bali.[25]

Indeed, as many scholars have observed, the listing provides 'world branding' for a site as having 'universal outstanding value' to stand firmly and competitively on the global tourism market (Li et al. 2008; Kough 2011). However, in reality, whether the market would deliver its promises to small farmers and *subak* institutions is far from straightforward.

Governing Heritage Space in a Complex Setting

The encounter between 'global' and 'local' through the UNESCO World Heritage Regime has brought a relatively rural area in Tabanan into a more complex legal and institutional situation. Put simply, this complex legal setting consists of a range of legal orders: international law governing the protection of heritage, both intangible and tangible; state law at every government tier from national, provincial, and district to village laws and regulations dealing with spatial planning, heritage conservation, and tourism; as well as the customary law of 41 customary villages and 21 *subak* associations. Consequently, local communities and other concerned groups must interact with one another through institutions and agencies at different scales to advance their preferred outcomes, which are sometimes in conflict.

[25] Interview with Tjokorda Oka Artha Ardhana Sukawati (Tjok Ace) on 24 January 2014.

Given the conditions of this complex institutional and legal setting, the attempt to reconfigure and rescale Jatiluwih and its surrounding areas into the Catur Angga heritage site does not automatically lead to an integration or unification of people's conceptions of space and place. The contested cognitive and normative conceptions of space and place that have been manifested through heritage discourse can be represented in the use of daily vocabularies—referring to 'Jatiluwih' or 'Catur Angga', for example. Both point to a dynamic and contested conception of space and place before and after the UNESCO World Heritage Listing. On the one hand, 'Jatiluwih' reflects a village-based spatial scale and construction of identity for securing access to economic and symbolic capital of the rice terraces of Jatiluwih, justified by local customary law and district regulations. On the other hand, 'Catur Angga' is a conceived space constructed through international law, central and provincial law, and regulations aimed at reconfiguring the *subak* landscape for both conservation and commodification.[26] As shown below, this discourse is not something independent from reality, but is generated by concrete social relations and has material implications (Smith 2006, 15).

The national state works through the provincial government in rescaling Jatiluwih into Catur Angga by designating it as a provincial strategic area to facilitate a new space for the tourism industry, regulated by a competing authority. Because Catur Angga is located within two districts, the provincial government claims authority for governing the area. The district of Tabanan, in fact, treats Jatiluwih separately from Catur Angga in its new spatial planning regulation by designating Jatiluwih, which lies within its borders as a 'district strategic area'. By separating this area out, the district government may develop village tourism projects similar to Jatiluwih in each village within its jurisdiction of the Catur Angga heritage site.[27] If the projects work properly in every village, it

[26] Prior to the World Heritage nomination, Catur Angga referred solely to the four water temples in the highland of Tabanan (Temples of Besi Kalung, Petali, Tamba Waras, and Batukaru) which play essential ritual roles for *subak* associations in the district.

[27] The prerogatives associated with this separation are a consequence of Indonesian legislation, especially the regional autonomy regime, which gives authorities to district governments to find their own sources of district revenue. Influenced by the demonstration effect of heavily developed

expects to receive tourist revenues from different sources while overlooking the 'unintended consequences' of these projects resulting from competition amongst those villages. In contrast, the provincial government aims to design an integrated tourism project for the whole Cultural Landscape of Bali Province under the management of a Governing Assembly at the provincial level. Bypassing the districts, the revenues would be distributed directly to all *subaks* and villages included in the cultural landscape. Thus, in turn, the contestation within the state structures would inform how agencies at the local level see the World Heritage Listing and, more importantly, with whom they ally themselves in order to advance their perceived interests.

Institutional Arrangements

The nomination dossier provides a 'political pledge' from the state of Indonesia to the UNESCO WHC to establish a management plan for the cultural landscape. In the dossier, it is stated that a management plan has been adopted by the province of Bali, "using principles of adaptive co-management by diverse stakeholders … This system of adaptive governance will connect individuals, organizations, agencies, and institutions at multiple organizational levels by means of a democratic Governing Assembly" (Indonesia. MCT 2011, V-1). Governor's Regulation (*Peraturan Gubernur*) No. 32/2010 was enacted for establishing the Governing Assembly for Bali's Cultural Heritage (*Dewan Pengelola Warisan Budaya*, thereafter the Governing Assembly) two years before the World Heritage Listing. This is further enhanced by Governor's Decision (*Keputusan Gubernur*) No. 281/03-H/HK/2012 on its organisational structure and membership consisting of appointed representatives from government bureaus at the provincial and district levels, *subaks* and customary villages, and academics and NGOs. The regulation does not specify the numbers and method of selection for each of these categories but instead justifies the individuals appointed by the provincial government

Badung District, the District Government of Tabanan is also very keen to develop its own tourist objects as a development priority.

to serve the structure. At the district level, a Governing Body of Cultural Heritage (*Badan Pengelola Warisan Budaya*, hereafter the District Governing Body) should also be established simultaneously to be the subordinate of the Provincial Governing Assembly.

From the dossier and literature supporting the management plan, it appears that the Provincial Governing Assembly is constituted as a multi-stakeholder governance model (e.g. Indonesia. MCT 2011; Fox 2012). The policymakers assumed that the assembly would be a technocratic and managerial institution rather than a political one in which every individual involved in the institution would have an equal and representative position. When the assembly is problematised as a 'field of power', where power is distributed unevenly within society (Hall 2007; Grenfell 2008), serious questions arise with respect to the principles of local participation and informed consent under international law. The adaptive co-management approach proposed in the management plan for the Assembly fails to acknowledge the importance of power relations that would inform its operations and effectiveness, and determine how the Provincial Governing Assembly and District Governing Body would be adjusted, manipulated, or even hijacked by particular interests through power exercised at different scales.

In mid-2013, the District Government of Tabanan was warned by the central government to establish a district governing body to manage the World Heritage Site immediately. The pressure arose from concerns that Indonesia as a state party to the World Heritage Convention might find itself shamed if the site were put under an 'in danger' listing due to the lack of an effective management regime at the local level. A series of meetings were conducted to discuss these matters. At every meeting, the *Pekaseh* of Subak Jatiluwih stressed that the *subak* should be the leading institution within the District Governing Body, as the preservation of the *subak* is the main goal of the World Heritage Listing. He also suggested the need to involve *Sabhantara Subak* (the *subak* federation at the district level) as well as the traditional ruler (*cokorda*) from Puri (*palace*) Tabanan, considering that historical and ritual connections between the *subak* and the palace should be represented in the body.

After a period of delays, the District Government of Tabanan finally established a management structure at the site level in late 2013. A joint agreement between the district head of Tabanan, the administrative village head (*Perbekel*) of Jatiluwih, the chiefs of *Adat* Village (*Bendesa*) of Jatiluwih and Gunungsari, and the *subak* leader (*Pekaseh*) of Jatiluwih was also signed on 27 December 2013 to legitimise such an establishment. But instead of focusing on World Heritage management, what has been established is a village-based institution dealing with tourism management, known as the Governing Body for the Tourist Attraction Area of Jatiluwih (*Badan Pengelola Daya Tarik Wisata Jatiluwih*, thereafter the Jatiluwih Tourism Governing Body).

Following the joint agreement, the district head of Tabanan, Eka Wiryastuti, enacted a District Head Regulation (*Peraturan Bupati*) No. 84/2013 concerning the organisational structure, membership, and job description of the Jatiluwih Tourism Governing Body and appointed herself to serve as the chairwoman of the body. Besides this governing body, the regulation also establishes another institution for daily management named the Operational Management (*manajemen operasional*) Committee. Structurally, however, the relationship between the Jatiluwih Tourism Governing Body and the Operational Management Committee is unclear. The district head as the chairwoman of the governing body enacts decisions regarding the organisational structure, membership, job descriptions, and standard operational procedures for the committee.

Based on the joint agreement between the District Government of Tabanan and local institutions in Jatiluwih, members of the management committee were appointed rather than nominated and elected by local community members. This reveals how the district government exercises its power supported by local elites, namely, the *Perbekel* and *Bendesa*, in deploying their loyalists in the committee. The joint agreement clearly shows how the World Heritage Listing has been used strategically for boosting the pre-existing village tourism project and in turn for accessing benefits arising from it. Those two institutions established by the district government are resulted from higher-scale pressures (from the international community, national and provincial governments that require the establishment of a management regime for the World Heritage Site) and lower-scale aspirations (from village institutions which demand the reinvention of an operational management committee to manage tourism exclusively in Jatiluwih). Between these scales of pressure, the District

Government of Tabanan manipulates the institutional arrangements to pursue its interests in tourist revenues and to facilitate access to power and resources for favoured district and local elites by capturing both institutions.

Members of the committee are nominated by the *Perbekel* together with the District Governing Body. Every local institution—*adat* village, *subak*, and *banjar*—is represented by one person, respectively, through the appointment of the *Perbekel*, the chief of *dusun* (instead of *kelian banjar*), and *Pekaseh*. However, the representatives of local institutions occupy only middle-lower positions in the management structure, while the manager and secretary are appointed by the *Perbekel* based on their political and personal ties to district government officials, albeit all of whom originate from Jatiluwih. The manager is Putu Purnama, a Denpasar-based businessman owning a travel agency and known to be close to the secretary of the regional government (*Sekretaris Daerah*/Sekda) of Tabanan District. His secretary is Kadek Suryasa, a young property entrepreneur in Tabanan serving as a committee member in the Indonesian Democratic Party of Struggle (PDI-Perjuangan Party), the ruling party in Tabanan. In fact, *subak* interests remain marginalised from both institutions.

On the ground the *subak* landscape of Jatiluwih is now under threats even greater than before being listed as a World Heritage Site. Although the *Perbekel* and *Bendesa* claim to be committed to preserving the rice terraces of Jatiluwih, they have opened up the opportunity for dry agricultural land to be developed, including for tourism facilities and animal husbandry. Consequently, the *Pekaseh* of Subak Jatiluwih observes that at least five new restaurants and villas have been constructed on dry agricultural land within the World Heritage Site since the nomination process. These were granted permits by the District Government of Tabanan, disregarding objections from the *Pekaseh* of Subak Jatiluwih who stresses the ecological connection between dry agricultural land and wet agricultural land, especially in terms of water supply. The newest villa is Sang Giri Villas and Restaurant, located in the water catchment area and the buffer zones of the Batukaru Nature Reserve. Using World Heritage Listing for marketing purposes, this development is described on its website as a "Tented Rainforest Resort in the Mountains of Jatiluwih—a World

Heritage Site". The *subak*, in fact, gains no contribution whatsoever from this development.[28] However, *Pekaseh* also uses World Heritage discourse as a means of resisting activities that may undermine the *subak* system. In other contexts, it is also used as a claim for a better policy framework from the government to empower farmers.

Incentives and Benefit Sharing

The reconfiguration of space for pursuing global recognition as a World Heritage Site by which Jatiluwih has been conflated with and at the same time privileged over its neighbouring villages is a political process, with conflicting objectives at every scale. For the effective management of the site, a hierarchy of space is created, which engenders social, political, and legal implications not only within Jatiluwih, but also in its relationship to the wider Catur Angga heritage space. Most informants from Jatiluwih, including the *Perbekel* and *Bendesa*, mention that Jatiluwih is the icon of the Subak Landscape of Catur Angga Batukaru, while the other villages and *subak* are just the 'buffer zone', designated to protect and enhance the value of Jatiluwih as the core zone. For them, the governing body established should be a Jatiluwih-based institution, and its employees should originate from the village. A greater share of incentives and benefits from the listing, according to them, should go to Jatiluwih Village.

During the fieldwork (2013–2014), it appeared that opinions on incentives and benefit sharing depend on informants' social positions, in terms of class, institutional affiliation, and geographical location (either centre or periphery). Brenner (2004, 13) argues that "inequalities are not only expressed socially, in the form of class and income stratification, but also spatially, through the polarization of development among different territories, regions, places, and scales" (Brenner 2004, 13). In other words, social inequalities may be materialised in spatial inequalities, and vice versa. In producing the heritage space of Catur Angga, it is 'spatial inequality' initially shaped by geography, law, and markets that produce

[28] Interview with Nyoman Sutama, *Pekaseh* of Subak Jatiluwih, on 3 March 2015.

'social inequality', which in turn reproduces intensified spatial inequality. In this regard, the centre-periphery polarisation is considered necessary for the sustainable commodification of the core zone through supporting environmental and cultural services from the buffer zone.

The benefits arising from commodification of the centre, however, do not distribute evenly, creating social inequalities and tensions within the centre as well as between the centre and the periphery. The revenue from tourist visits managed by the operational management committee is to be distributed based on the joint agreement between the District Government of Tabanan and Jatiluwih's local institutions. The gross revenue is split into operational costs (40%, including for the management committee and the governing body's expenditure on development and promotional programs) and net revenue. This net revenue is then divided according to the formula set out in Fig. 5.2, with 45% to the District Government of Tabanan and 55% to Jatiluwih Village.

At the village level, the benefit component is distributed further among the local institutions. This allocation is as follows: 25% for the Administrative Village of Jatiluwih, 30% for the Adat Village of Jatiluwih, 20% for the Adat Village of Gunungsari, 21% for Subak Jatiluwih (wet *subak*), and 4% for Subak Abian Jatiluwih and Gunungsari (dry *subak*). According to the monthly report of the Operational Management

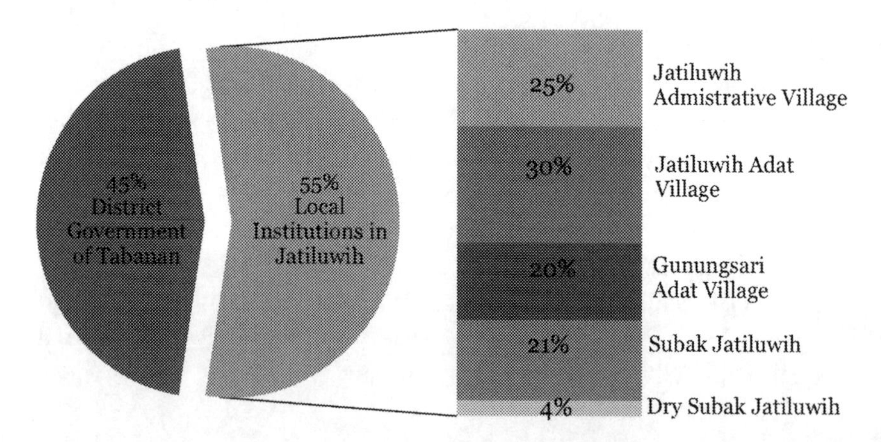

Fig. 5.2 Allocation of net revenue from Jatiluwih tourism. Source: the joint agreement between the District Government of Tabanan and Jatiluwih village

Committee (2014) in July 2014, the gross revenues from tourist visits were US$ 26,874 and the operational costs for the committee and the Jatiluwih Tourism Governing Body were US$ 9391, which was divided into US$ 1878 for the District Governing Body, and the rest was managed by the Committee. The net revenue was US$ 17,482, out of which US$ 8596 went to the District Government and US$ 8885 went to the village institutions. At the village level, Subak Jatiluwih (wet *subak*) itself received US$ 1878, Subak Abian Jatiluwih and Gunungsari (dry *subak*) only received US$ 144, respectively. Meanwhile, the Administrative Village of Jatiluwih received US$ 2240, the Customary Village of Jatiluwih received US$ 2672, and the Customary Village of Gunungsari received US$ 1806. Although the above data is rather outdated, it gives us a sense of how the revenues were distributed based on the allocation scheme made by the district government and the village institutions. In fact, the scheme remains in place to date.

The unequal allocation of benefits arising from tourist visits were rationalised differently by the local actors involved in the negotiations. Wayan Yasa, *Bendesa* of Desa Pakraman Jatiluwih, states that the 55% distribution for Jatiluwih village is the negotiated outcome between the village and district government after an objection was raised against the district government's proposal for an equal profit share.[29] The village representatives stressed that the cultural responsibilities that fall upon the local people in Jatiluwih justified receiving the higher proportion of the shares. The *Bendesa* mentions that the local share will be used for renovating temples in Jatiluwih and also for conducting regular temple festivals. Although the amount of its share would be sufficient for freeing *adat* members (*krama*) from *pepeson* (financial contribution), he plans only to reduce the amount of contribution, but not make it free because the *pepeson* is a proof of commitment to the temples.[30]

[29] Interview with Wayan Yasa, the *Bendesa* of Desa Pakraman Jatiluwih, on 21 January 2014.

[30] Although in theory it is the *krama* that has the authority to make this determination, the *Bendesa*'s statement is indicative of his claim to authority over how the benefits should be spent. In contrast, most informants during fieldwork expected that they would be free from *pepeson* by allocating the benefits to fund regular festivals and temple renovations so that they would focus solely on the customary services (*ayahan-ayahan*) through labour (interviews with Putu Armini, Putu

Meanwhile, the smaller share for Subak Jatiluwih has been questioned by its members. For them, since it is the *subak* that is the focal point of the World Heritage Listing and that most needs material support for its preservation, the largest share should go to Subak Jatiluwih rather than other institutions. Larger shares for the administrative village and custom villages are justified by the claim that they provide public infrastructure and conduct rituals and customary festivals regularly for the village temples. This spending, however, is not directly related to *subak* preservation objectives, as articulated in the dossier (see Fox 2012; Indonesia. MCT 2011).

Although the *subak*'s members are in most cases also members of the customary and administrative villages, they assert that the division of responsibilities among these institutions should be reflected in the benefit distribution. Otherwise, *subak* members are not supported to undertake the required efforts to preserve the *subak* landscape in their roles as farmers.[31] Being a farmer in the village involves a double obligation of time and resource commitments to both the custom village and the *subak* simultaneously. In the context of the World Heritage status, it also would mean having a double cultural responsibility—both preserving the intangible heritage (including rituals and festivals in both custom village and *subak* association contexts) as well as the tangible heritage of the rice terrace landscape (most of which is family-owned property) and the irrigation network that belongs to the *subak*.

Those who are located on the periphery or 'outsiders' to Jatiluwih express similar dissatisfactions. For them, the allocation of tourist revenues which are not at all shared with them is seen as denying the contribution of other villages in the making of the World Heritage 'brand', which in turn brings tourist flocks to Jatiluwih. In fact, all listed sites are

---

Kembariani, Putu Demen, & Putu Suciwati, on 25 March 2014; Ketut Nuraja & Kaka, on 6 February 2014).

[31] Interview with Nyoman Sutama, *Pekaseh* of Subak Jatiluwih, on 7 November 2013. He states that although one farmer may also be a member of those three institutions [*subak, desa adat,* and *desa dinas*], his individual role [within each of those institutional structures] is different. As a *Pekaseh*, representing the *subak* and its members, he is dedicated to pursuing the interests of the *subak* and its members.

actually under the provincial banner of the Cultural Landscape of Bali Province. In response, the managers of the Operational Management Committee, *Perbekel* of Desa Jatiluwih and *Bendesa* of Desa Pakraman Jatiluwih, as well as those who are in favour of locating World Heritage management and benefits in Jatiluwih Village, argue that tourists visit the heritage site to experience its iconic feature, that is, the rice terraces of Jatiluwih. In terms of the benefits for other villages, they suggest that it should be the district's responsibility to share its revenues with those villages and *subak*s outside Jatiluwih.[32]

As the governing body is located in and specifically for Jatiluwih, villagers outside Jatiluwih have no channel to express their concerns and expectations regarding heritage management. Nengah Sudarma, *Pekaseh* of Subak Kedampal, and Made Sudira, *Bendesa* of Desa Pakraman Wongaya Betan, argue that *subak* and *desa adat* beyond Jatiluwih have been neglected so far and demand equal treatment and equal benefit shares for the whole of Catur Angga.[33] Made Sudira criticises the World Heritage designation for treating his village as only a '*pelengkap*' (complement) in order to enable Jatiluwih to meet the minimum scale requested by the ICOMOS back in 2008. Not benefiting from the tourist visits that are concentrated in Jatiluwih Village, Mengesta Village, where Subak Kedampal and Desa Pakraman Wongaya Betan are situated, has started to develop a village tourism project akin to that of Jatiluwih. This tourism economic model is spreading across Catur Angga, in which 10 out of 12 administrative villages have now been designated under the district spatial planning regulation as village tourism 'objects' with relatively similar attractions to compete for tourist visits.[34]

Opinions also differ on the issue of incentives, especially concerning the land tax subsidy. This reflects assumptions of a common social posi-

---

[32] Interviews with Nengah Kartika, the Administrative Village Head (*Perbekel*) of Desa Jatiluwih, on 21 January 2014; Putu Purnama, the manager of the Operational Management Committee, on 27 January 2014; and Nengah Tirtatayasa, the secretary of the Operational Management Committee, on 23 March 2014.

[33] Interviews with Nengah Sudarma, *Pekaseh* of Subak Kedampal, and Made Sudira, the *Bendesa* of Desa Pakraman Wongaya Betan, on 23 March 2014.

[34] Jatiluwih, Mengesta, Penatahan, Tegallinggah, Rejasa, Pesagi, Wongaya Gede, Tengkudak, Babahan, Sangketan.

tion of the farmers, whether they are landed farmers, smallholders, or sharecroppers. Although many informants mention that the state pledged to assist farmers when asking for their support for the World Heritage nomination, how this commitment would be implemented remains unclear.[35] Ketut Duita, Kelian Tempek Subak Kedamaian, is sceptical towards the effectiveness of a land tax subsidy, considering the fact that 10 out of 60 members of Tempek Subak Kedamaian are sharecroppers.[36] For them, the subsidy for land tax would disproportionately benefit landed farmers and landlords, rather than sharecroppers and small land-holding farmers who most need economic support. Instead, the *subak tempekan* members are more in favour of subsidising fertilisers and seeds as well as improving markets for their produce. Subsidising fertilisers and seeds would help to reduce the operational costs for sharecroppers since costs for fertilisers are usually shared between the sharecropper and landlord. The land tax, instead, is the responsibility of the landlord alone.

Farmers and sharecroppers articulate their sense of 'fairness', not as equal treatment to all ('*iustitia commutativa*') but rather as proportional to socio-economic conditions ('*iustitia distributive*') in which relative need determines distribution.[37] This demand appears to be off the District Governing Body and Provincial Governing Assembly's priority agenda. This was the reason the WHC in its Decision No. 38 COM 7B.14 regrets

[35] KD, a staff of the District Planning Bureau of Tabanan, says that the land tax subsidy would be derived from a cross-subsidy. This would mean either that the government budget would be cut to subsidise tax relief, or increasing land taxes would be imposed upon areas outside Catur Angga to provide the subsidies within the heritage-declared area. The latter is very likely to raise controversy from farmers outside Catur Angga. It would hardly serve the conservation goals of the World Heritage framework if support policies increased the burdens on farmers outside the site. Despite facing similar threats, farmers located outside Catur Angga are treated as 'second class' only because their *subak* landscape is less aesthetically appealing to international tourists. From the government policy perspective, this has more to do with the 'exchange' value of the landscape for tourism that has the potential to be exploited for purely economic rather than protected for cultural and ecological reasons.

[36] According to Putu Duta, Subak Tempek Kedamaian has the largest percentage of sharecroppers within Subak Jatiluwih. Overall sharecropping in Subak Jatiluwih is around 5% according to the *Pekaseh* but in Tempek Subak Kedamaian it is up to 16% (interview on 20 January 2014).

[37] This reflects a principle of 'generalised reciprocity' in anthropological terms (see Sahlins 1974, 193–194), although perceptions of bounded rights nonetheless lead them to exclude outside farmers.

among other things that "incentives and subsidies to support prosperous rural livelihood and strong *subak* institutions ... have so far not been delivered as envisaged" in the management plan and urges the government to implement the plan as soon as possible. In fact, the committee has no authority to force a state party to comply with its recommendation. In an extreme case, it may make a decision to put a World Heritage Site on the List of World Heritage in Danger. In the contexts of the Cultural Landscape of Bali Province, this would be unlikely, given the recent position of Indonesia as one of the 21 WHC members.

Alliances and Contestation for Resources and Power

As mentioned above, there are at least three types of local institutions that are fundamental to the context of the Subak Landscape of Catur Angga Batukaru: the *adat* village, the *dinas* village, and the *subak*. They serve as a negotiating ground for their members and as vehicles to contest or engage with other institutions. Individuals within this complex institutional setting are typically members of several of these overlapping local institutions (Geertz 1959). Which institution they chose to deploy is, to a large extent, the one that is in a position to articulate their values and expectations best. Those values cannot be understood only in a narrow material or economic sense, but also in the context of wider non-material values, such as identity, spirituality, and social as well as environmental values. Like Pan Suka quoted above, Ketut Duita, the *Kelian* of Subak Tempek Kedamaian and also *juru arah* (messenger) for the custom village of Jatiluwih showed great pride in identifying himself as a *subak* member during the interview. He was particularly animated when explaining the *subak*'s expectations after the inscription of Catur Angga as a World Heritage Site.

In practice, the extent to which the institution is able to advance its collective interests is dependent upon the extent to which its agents as representatives of the collective interest are able to articulate and defend those interests in a wider social context. In Jatiluwih, the *Pekaseh* was not able to persuade the local meeting to grant more shares to the *subak* institution, since the *Bendesa* and *Perbekel* were the better 'orators' during the village meeting. They were able to counter the *Pekaseh*'s argument on the grounds that the *subak* primarily serves private landowner's/user's interests mediated through water irrigation; giving more shares to the *subak* would mean facilitating individual wealth rather than pursuing the general welfare. Their position is that most shares should go to subsidise public expenses that affect all villagers, whether farmers or not, through the customary and administrative villages. Money for the custom village could be spent for religious ceremonies and festivals to relieve villagers of some of these costs. Money for the administrative village would support local infrastructure or development initiatives.

Far from giving up, in the context of a socially unacceptable direct confrontation, everyday forms of resistance to express unsatisfactory conditions come into play. For example, the *Pekaseh*, supported by several *kelian tempek subak*, eventually refused to attend any invitation from the District Governing Body when guests visit the rice terrace and need explanations about the *subak* system. This 'soft boycott' (*ngambul*) is commonly used to show that without their involvement the body could not work properly. Moreover, 'hidden transcripts' are also brought into play, although they are not clearly demarcated from the 'public transcripts' (Scott 1990). To some extent, people who are not able to advance their interests in a public forum employ 'hidden transcripts' as a vehicle to get their messages across to their opponents. In Jatiluwih, the *Pekaseh* uses these strategies mediated by a 'messenger' in order to influence power relationships, since he has difficulty in articulating his opinion directly in the local setting due to family ties. It is expected that the messenger would transmit his opinion to the contestants without acknowledging its source.

In this context, those who are considered as 'outsiders' to the local dynamics of everyday affairs might be the best messengers to inform the contestants. During a meeting of Forum *Pekaseh* Catur Angga in late 2014, an issue regarding stone mining on the upper side of Catur Angga was brought into discussion. Nyoman Sutama, *Pekaseh* of Subak Jatiluwih, who also serves as the coordinator of the Forum, asked the outside observers of the meeting, such as the NGO activists and researchers, to investigate and report it to UNESCO. The participants of the meeting, who were *pekasehs* from all *subak gede* within Catur Angga, agreed with his proposition and one of them commented: "it is better to have someone from outside rather than us [*subak*] do so to avoid personal conflicts [with those who are benefiting from the mining activities]". The effectiveness of these everyday forms of resistance may be ignored, but there is high sensitivity to these signals in Balinese culture, and they at least indicate to contestants and powerholders that something problematic is going on and warn of the potential for latent conflict arising from unsatisfactory decisions. The difficulty faced by concerned social agents to confront contentious issues directly in the local setting illustrates the failure of the top-down World Heritage designation and local distrust of the management bodies that should be responsible to protect the landscape in the first place.

Within the framework of this complex legal setting, competing perspectives should be able to find alternative sources of legitimacy for claim making. The notion of *subak* 'autonomy' has been used as one ground for 'breaking the silence' (Scott 1990) after more than 10 years, having received little benefit from the village tourism project. Tempek Subak Besi Kalung eventually established an entrance guard to charge every tourist for using their *subak*'s path to enjoy direct access to the *subak* landscape. Ketut Suci, the *Kelian* of Subak Tempek Besi Kalung says, "our *subak* decided in a *subak* meeting (*sangkep*) to charge a fee from tourists for using our path because we had been neglected. The *subak* has been used as an attraction for ten years since tourism has been managed by the administrative village and the district government".[38] He said that the revenues received from the entrance fee were spent to support *subak* activities, in particular, for improving its irrigation infrastructure. More recently, a number of *subak* members decided to build bamboo fences to guard their rice fields from tourists entering, which is very often damaging.

The tension between the provincial and district governments has become another resort to be exploited for alliance building by local actors.

[38] Interview with Ketut Suci, *Kelian* of Subak Tempek Besi Kalung, on 23 March 2014. Similar attitudes are also expressed by Putu Ardana, member of Subak Tempek Besi Kalung, interview on 21 January 2014, and Made Buana, the former *Bendesa* of Desa Pakraman Jatiluwih and member of Subak Tempek Besi Kalung, interview on 7 November 2013.

When the district government chose to channel its influence at the local level through the *Perbekel*, the *Bendesa* as well as the Jatiluwih Tourism Governing Body, during the nomination process, the *Pekaseh* became closely allied with the provincial government. The difficulty of influencing local dynamics after the World Heritage listing inclined him to inform authorities of 'off track' situations on the ground either through the Provincial Governing Assembly or through its international consultant, expecting that the assembly would step in to deal with his concerns. For example, the *Pekaseh* claims that the Jatiluwih Tourism Governing Body is far from the design envisaged in the management plan dossier. As he could not confront village officials directly during the meeting establishing the body due to complex personal and institutional relationships with the other local institutions and their officials, the *Pekaseh* finally reported this situation personally to a trusted member of the Provincial Governing Assembly. However, no measure has been taken because the district government argues that Jatiluwih—not Catur Angga—has been designated a district strategic area for tourism and specifically established the governing body to manage tourism in Jatiluwih.

Given the complex and difficult constellations that influence local decision making, the *Pekaseh* of Jatiluwih has moved to widen the *subak* alliance by establishing a Communication Forum for *Pekaseh* of Catur Angga (*Forum Komunikasi Pekaseh Catur Angga*). The forum is an effort to consolidate all the *subaks* within Catur Angga, as a vehicle for conducting communication, disseminating information, and negotiating the interests of the *subak* with external parties, including government and village institutions. The *Pekaseh* of Subak Jatiluwih was elected as the chairman of the forum, considering his knowledge and experience on the issues of World Heritage informed by Jatiluwih's position at the centre of Catur Angga. Since the suggestion of the *subak* to include the traditional ruler, the *Cokorda* (King) of Tabanan in the Provincial Governing Assembly and the Jatiluwih Tourism Governing Body has not been taken seriously, the forum turns to the *Cokorda* as its traditional patron in acknowledgement of his cultural and spiritual power traditionally needed by a *subak* in its rituals, especially for control of rat plagues. This resorting to traditional 'authority' can also be interpreted as an attempt by disenfranchised *subaks* to find alternative political and cultural alliances in navigating provincial-district contestations.

Conclusion

As the *subak* system has been threatened by multiple challenging pressures, UNESCO World Heritage designation represents a new approach to address such threats. In the view of some policymakers, the *subak* landscape has been granted a World Heritage label to expand the tourism market and in turn to provide incentives for local farmers to maintain their *subak* landscape. For effective and efficient conservation—as well as 'commodification'—of the *subak* landscape, a reconfiguration of space has been undertaken in the process of designing the World Heritage Site in the Subak Landscape of Catur Angga, as suggested by ICOMOS. However, the process did not carefully assess the pluralistic legal and institutional configuration, and the power dynamics that operate at every scale.

As a result, although the role of provincial government has been overemphasised by the management plan, in reality, the district government appears to be dominant as a consequence of designating Jatiluwih, the core zone of the Subak Landscape of Catur Angga Batukaru, as a district strategic area for tourism to extract revenues from tourism visits. Hence, the establishment of both the Jatiluwih Tourism Governing Body and the Operational Management Committee in Jatiluwih shows how existing power relations transplant themselves within new institutional structures (Mosse 1997). Nonetheless, these complex legal and institutional constellations also enable the marginalised *subak* communities to make use of different repertoires in challenging the dominant power structure. In this regard, alliances and contestations in governing the *subak* landscape have been shaped and are being reshaped through these complex legal-institutional constellations.

6

Reclaiming the Common of Benoa Bay

This chapter examines a large-scale development project in Benoa Bay, Bali. It demonstrates how the severely degraded condition of the Bay, caused by rapid and collusive development since the New Order, has been used by the post-authoritarian government as an excuse to transfer authority over its conservation and development to private enterprise. The complex legal and institutional configurations that are the product of decentralisation policies and neoliberal rationalisation provide a convenient opportunity for power play between private interests and government officials at every tier of state institutions to promote the massive reclamation project proposed by the politically influential owner of the Tirta Wahana Bali International (TWBI) project. The chapter also analyses how this complex configuration informs the ways in which the targets and strategies of resistance, challenging the project, are defined.

A. Wardana, *Contemporary Bali*, https://doi.org/10.1007/978-981-13-2478-9_6

Benoa Bay: Geography, Institutions, and Development

Geography and the Values of Benoa Bay

Benoa Bay is located between Denpasar Municipality and Badung District and cuts across the three sub-districts of Kuta, South Kuta, and South Denpasar (see Table 6.1). Situated in the middle of Bali's 'golden triangle' of tourism (Nusa Dua, Kuta, and Sanur), Benoa Bay and its environs have been a Mecca for migrants seeking jobs in the tourism industry, making this the most densely populated area on the island. At the same time, thousands of people are directly dependent on the bay

Table 6.1 Basic statistics for the Benoa Bay area

No	District/sub-district/ Kelurahan			*Adat* village	Population (in 2013)	Land area (Ha)	Area within the bay (Ha)
I	Badung district						
	A	Kuta					
		1	Tuban	Kelan Tuban	13,979	268	8.70
		2	Kuta	Kuta	13,389	782	9.20
		3	Kedonganan	Kedonganan	5809	191	17.40
	B	South Kuta					
		4	Jimbaran	Jimbaran	37,499	2050	96.00
		5	Benoa	Bualu	26,752	2828	113.80
		6	Tanjung Benoa	Tanjung Benoa Tengkulung	5242	239	23.80
II	Denpasar municipality						
	C	South Denpasar					
		7	Sanur Kauh	Intaran	15,942	386	19.30
		8	Serangan	Serangan	3986	481	608.00
		9	Sidakarya	Sidakarya	22,243	389	126.30
		10	Sesetan	Sesetan	54,692	739	77.60
		11	Pedungan	Pedungan	34,008	749	304.90
		12	Pamogan	Kepaon	50,122	971	314.70
			Total		283,663	10,073	1719.70

Adapted from: Dharma Putra (2009), LPPM Unud (2013), BPS Denpasar (2014), BPS Badung (2014)

itself for their sources of income or means of subsistence, including fishermen, seaweed farmers, and marine tourism operators.

The Bay is a semi-enclosed harbour with seven canals ranging from 100 to 150 metres in width (Hendrawan et al. 2005; Dharma Putra 2009, 63). It is also an estuary fed by two major rivers, Tukad Badung and Tukad Mati, which flow in all seasons (Sudiarta et al. 2013), and five other smaller and seasonal rivers which are Tukad Sama, Tukad Bualu, Tukad Loloan, Tukad Punggawa, and Tukad Buaji. Those rivers flow through densely populated, industrial, as well as agricultural areas of Denpasar and Badung (PEMSEA and Bali PMO 2004; Sudiarta et al. 2013), carrying organic and chemical effluents as well as solid wastes into the bay due to the lack of upstream management and the location of the Suwung Dumpsite at the estuary. The bay is surrounded by an ecologically important 1374-hectare mangrove forest known as the Great Forest Park (Taman Hutan Raya/Tahura) of Ngurah Rai.

Due to the common image of swamps, wetlands, and mangroves as dirty breeding grounds of mosquitoes, and thus a source of disease (Bowman 2002), the ecological functions of Benoa Bay have been overlooked. Traditionally, the north side of the bay area is called '*suwung*' which means 'empty', indicating a local conception of place that should be left empty without any human activities. However, as land becomes increasingly scarce and costly, Benoa Bay is seen as a free space with potential for expanding human use. Thus, the bay in recent decades has become the centre for several activities that in turn have significantly changed its natural characteristics (see Table 6.2). It became the site for a rubbish dump serving Denpasar, Badung, Gianyar, and Tabanan (Sarbagita), a sewage management installation, a power generating plant, as well as a site for marine tourism, fishery industries, residential and retail construction, and most importantly, Ngurah Rai International Airport and Benoa Port, the biggest port in Bali. Together, these have contributed to a decline in the mangrove forest surrounding Benoa Bay of 314.46 hectares (23%) during the period 1977–2000 (PEMSEA and Bali PMO 2004).

Many studies have been conducted in the area, concluding that Benoa Bay is the most heavily polluted area in Bali (Dharma Putra 2009; Bapedalda Bali 2006; PEMSEA and Bali PMO 2004). A study on initial

Table 6.2 Recorded mangrove forest conversion in the Benoa Bay area to 2013

	Area (Ha)	
Conversion to:	Actual	Licensed
Shrimp ponds	62.42	62.42
Rice fields	13.00	–
Suwung garbage dumpsite	38.00	10.00
Residential	7.50	7.50
Sewage treatment plan (BTDC Nusa Dua)	30.00	30.00
High intensity approach light system	0.50	0.50
Jalan bypass Nusa Dua	7.60	7.60
Ceramic research Centre and development	4.00	4.00
Fuel pipeline (Avtur)	0.40	0.40
SUTT 70 KV power installation	14.34	14.34
SUTT 150 KV power installation Pesanggaran-Kuta and Kuta-Nusa Dua	30.00	30.00
Toll road of Bali Mandara	2.40	2.40
Estuary dam	30.00	30.00
Denpasar sewerage development project (DSDP)	10.00	10.00
Expansion of Ngurah Rai Airport	15.00	15.00
Shortcut Mumbul-Tanjung Benoa	3.03	–
Serangan Island reclamation	103	103
Total	371.19	327.16

Adapted from: PEMSEA and Bali PMO 2004; Dharma Putra 2009; *Bali Post*, 30 March 2012; *Berita Bali*, 26 June 2013

risk assessment (IRS) conducted by PEMSEA and Bali PMO (2004) found that water quality of Benoa Bay is so polluted with high concentrations of nutrients and total suspended solids (TSS) that it poses high risk for human health and ecology.[1] These problems have been attributed to "the lack of waste management" in densely populated, industrial and agricultural areas that the rivers pass through (PEMSEA and Bali PMO 2004, 4–8). It also found that "sedimentation resulting from land reclamation in Serangan Island, which is located at the mouth of Benoa Bay, was also identified as an agent for mangrove decline" (PEMSEA and Bali PMO 2004, 4–5). Similarly, Dharma Putra, an environmental scien-

[1] The study, methodologically, uses a risk assessment approach and presents its results based on a quantitative model in which an area is defined as having high ecological and human health risk due to excessive amounts of PO4-P RQ, NO3-N RQs, and total suspended solids (TSS), which "may increase turbidity, reduce light penetration into water and potentially adversely affect photosynthetic activities" (PEMSEA and Bali PMO 2004, 52–58; see also TWBI 2014a).

tist from Bali's Udayana University, argues in his PhD thesis (2009) that Benoa Bay is 'the most polluted area' on the island due to the combination of geographical conditions as a semi-enclosed body of water, demographic factors produced by densely populated surrounding villages, and commercial activities, as well as cultural factors, namely, the lack of environmental awareness to protect the bay and rivers that feed into it.

In recent decades, disaster or potential disaster for an ecologically fragile area has been turned into an opportunity to accumulate profit by engaging conservation rhetoric with market forces (Igoe and Brockington 2007; Heynen et al. 2007b). The condition of Benoa Bay as a heavily polluted area with the most fragile mangrove ecosystem in Bali has been used by policymakers to justify the need for a capitalist intervention for more efficient and profitable investment in 'conserving' this area. In 2012, for instance, the governor, Mangku Pastika, issued a permit for the Tirta Rahmat Bahari (TRB) to manage 102.2 hectares of mangrove forest in Tahura Ngurah Rai for eco-tourism and its facilities, including accommodation. He justified it by saying:

> we [the government] have been overwhelmed to solve the problems of plastic rubbish [in Tahura Ngurah Rai]. Everyday we transport up to 4 trucks [of rubbish] from the area. But, the problem has not been resolved because we have limited personnel and budget … The permit granted by me [for the TRB] is to save our mangrove forest, since when it is managed by public servants, I believe that will be difficult. We need professionals to manage the mangrove so that the result will be maximal. (quoted in Erviani 2012)

This implies the need to involve private enterprise to "enable public sector organizations to get goods, services, and expertise that government in-house staff cannot provide" (Bevir 2011, 9) in governing the commons. However, local environmental organisations, such as the Indonesian Forum for the Environment (WALHI), have been concerned with the permit that provides a legal ground for the company to degrade the mangrove forest by building accommodations in the forest area. In the current Benoa Bay case, as discussed below, similar arguments and concerns have been raised in facilitating and constraining TWBI's project on a monumentally greater scale of environmental disturbance and risk.

Institutions and Representations of Space

In the Benoa Bay area, as shown in the Table 6.1, there are 12 administrative villages (*desa dinas*) and 14 customary villages (*desa pakraman*), with 29 hamlets (*banjar/dusun*) surrounding Benoa Bay. Besides those local institutions, there are several government agencies and state-owned enterprises that would claim to have some rights or authority, in different degrees to govern or use space in Benoa Bay. Among these, the most important are the Technical Management Unit (*Unit Pengelola Teknis*/UPT) of Tahura Ngurah Rai Mangrove Forest under the Ministry of the Environment and Forestry, and the Pelabuhan Indonesia (Pelindo/Indonesian Port Authority), a state-owned enterprise focusing on the management of Benoa Port, both of which are under national government's jurisdiction. There are also community-based groups, including business associations that are highly dependent on the bay, such as marine tourism entrepreneurs located in Tanjung Benoa and traditional fishery groups. Consequently, there will inevitably be contestation over space that reflect these diverse interests.

The representations of space in Benoa Bay as reflected through the spatial planning laws and regulations since the New Order have been under constant adjustment. In particular, these representations shape and are shaped by the rapidly changing conditions of the bay. The 1995 Spatial Plan for Bali Province, for instance, endorsed the supporting policy to develop tourism in the area by establishing a partnership between the provincial government and private sector to develop the marine tourist potential of the bay. The politics behind this endorsement was to provide a legal ground for the Bali Turtle Island Development (BTID) and the Bali Benoa Marina (BBM), both owned by Suharto family members, to develop tourist enclaves in the area. Responding to the severe environmental impacts of tourism development, especially BTID's Serangan Island Reclamation project, the Provincial Regulation on Spatial Planning for Bali No.3/2005 (Perda RTRW Bali 3/2005) in Article 30 acknowledges the need to rehabilitate Serangan-Benoa water areas.

In the era of decentralisation, when the dominant power to govern space was relocated to district-level governments, specifying the authority for governing space and resource use in Benoa Bay has become increasingly complicated. This is due to its division between two district-level governments (Badung and Denpasar) as well as due to its economic significance at all scales of governance. As a cross-district area, the Provincial Government of Bali regards Benoa Bay as falling under its authority, while the national government designates the bay as a vital area of economic significance for national development. For this reason, the representation of Benoa Bay's space in state regulations has become fragmented and conflicting, as shown in Table 6.3. Seemingly, Benoa Bay is a hyper-regulated space, but empirically it is unregulated since every institution

Table 6.3 Benoa Bay's status in spatial planning regulations

Regulations	The Status of Benoa Bay
National Regulation: Presidential Decree 45/2011 on Spatial Planning for Sarbagita Metropolitan Areas (Perpres 45/2011)	Designation of Sarbagita as the centre for national economic activities based on international-quality tourism. Specifically, Benoa Bay is designated as a coastal and small island conservation area due to its unique functions (Perpres 45/2011: §55(5b)). In addition, it can also be utilised for science and education, tourism, and recreation. Perpres no. 45/2011 directs the Bay's governance through the establishment of a special body that is not necessarily under the state structure to govern Benoa Bay areas in maximising their economic potential
Provincial Spatial Planning Regulation No. 16/2009 (Perda RTRW Bali 16/2009)	Benoa Bay is included within the newly designated pan-district metropolitan area known as Sarbagita (Denpasar, Badung, Gianyar, and Tabanan), which is a provincial strategic area with national economic significance
District/Municipal Spatial Planning Regulations: (Perda RTRW Denpasar no. 27/2011 and Perda RTRW Badung no. 26/2013)	The functions of Benoa Bay are designated as a conservation area, and simultaneously as effective tourism zones (*kawasan efektif pariwisata*) (Perda Denpasar no. 27/2011: §11(2) (f)) and Perda RTRW Badung 26/2013: §59(6))

The explanatory note to Article 16 paragraph 2 stipulates that "the development of the Sarbagita Metropolitan Area is not governed as a common metropolitan city, but in this regional regulation, it is treated as a partnership between central government, provincial government, and district-level governments of Denpasar, Badung, Gianyar and Tabanan, toward efficient and effective integrated urban ... infrastructure development cooperation" in the area claims to have authority to govern all or part of it. This fragmented administrative condition is in turn used strategically by various economic actors to pursue their interests over the bay's space.

In brief, Benoa Bay conditions nowadays partly reflect a modern version of the 'tragedy of the commons' allegory (Hardin 1968). The difference with Hardin's original allegory, however, is the cause of the tragedy. In Hardin's allegory, the destruction of a common resource is caused by the absence of institutions to manage it. In fact, the environmental crisis in Benoa Bay as a common pool resource is, to a large extent, perpetuated by the complexity of the institutional and legal configuration which in turn provides a different, sometimes conflicting, set of institutional platforms for economic actors to advance their interests by colluding with government officials.

The Political Economy of Development in Benoa Bay

Since the recent New Order, Benoa Bay has been targeted as a new 'hotspot' for the expansion of the tourism industry in Bali. There were at least two mega-projects proposed for the area that were facilitated by the national government, namely, the resort development by the Bali Turtle Island Development (BTID) project at Serangan Island and the marina development by the Bali Benoa Marina (BBM) consortium, both involving massive expansion of land to be dredged from the bay. Suharto's family circle had primary interests in both projects: BTID is a consortium led by the Bimantara Group, owned by Suharto's son, Bambang Suharto (together with Gajah Tunggal Group under control of his daughter, Tutut Suharto, and the Pembangunan Kartika Udayana, an Udayana Army Division Company); the BBM was a joint venture between the Hampuss Group, owned by Tommy Suharto, and the Mandira Erajasa Wahana Transportation Aerowisata, a division of Garuda Indonesia Airways (Aditjondro 1995). Due to the 1997–1998 economic and political crisis, which forced Suharto to step down from the presidency, both projects collapsed. The BTID project had already carried out the reclamation of Serangan Island, expanding its size fourfold; the BBM project was halted before works began, although its environmental impact assessment (ANDAL) had been approved by the government. Interestingly, each of their respective ANDAL documents ignored the existence and impacts of the other project, despite the fact that the two studies were conducted by Udayana University research teams.[2] This supports widespread criticism of 'engineered' impact assessments and the role of some academics in furthering vested interests by ignoring the cumulative impacts of the two projects and underestimating the severity of their effects on environment and socio-culture.

After two decades, and despite the ongoing impacts of dredging on the aborted Serangan Island project, Benoa Bay continues to attract investors. Since 2000, at least six different proposals were put on the government table to develop Benoa Bay as a new tourism enclave.[3] Pelindo, the management authority for Benoa Port, in its Port Master Plan (*Rencana Induk Pelabuhan*) No. 552/237/DPIK also plans to expand port territory by land reclamation of up to 143 hectares (*Radar Bali*, 6/9/2013). Before the Tirta Wahana Bali International (TWBI) was granted a recommendation for their proposed project by the Provincial House of Representatives (DPRD) of Bali, followed by a permit from the governor of Bali on 26 December 2012, the Bali Benoa International (BBI) had been granted a recommendation from the Regional House of Representatives (DPRD) of Badung on 19 January 2007, renewed on 28 December 2012. Both companies were competing for political support toward their projects from different tiers of government to access the bay, which was made possible by the complex institutional configuration of decentralisation. The TWBI, owned by Tomy Winata, a national tycoon who was known to be close to Megawati's husband, Taufik Kiemas, the patron of the PDI-P, found his political alliance at the provincial level, then governed by PDI-P. Meanwhile, the BBI, owned by I Gusti Putu Wijaya, who is the Vice Chairman of Golkar Party at the provincial level, chose to make its alliance with the Badung district administration that was under Golkar. Due to its national networks and financial resources, Tomy Winata's TWBI finally gained preferred status.

---

[2] I am indebted for this argument to Warren's (unpublished) manuscript on Serangan Project Reclamation.

[3] The Bangun Segitiga Emas, the Wijaya Property, the Bali Benoa Resort (BBR), the Garuda Jaya, the Bali Benoa International (BBI), and the Tirta Wahana Bali International (TWBI).

From the national policy perspective, there were at least three development projects to be located in Benoa Bay that were endorsed by the national government under the banner of President Yudhyono's *Master Plan untuk Percepatan dan Perluasan Pembangunan Ekonomi Indonesia* (MP3EI/ Masterplan for the Acceleration and Expansion of Indonesia Economic Development). These projects include the development of a worldclass resort by Bambang Suharto's BTID that had been halted since the 1997 economic and political crisis, and the Revitalisation of Benoa Bay project proposed by Winata's TWBI. As Yudhoyono's term came to an end, Tomy Winata appeared to support Jokowi's presidential campaign by, among others, providing Trans Wisata's private jet for Jokowi to meet his constituents and supporters across the archipelago. Although the Yudhoyono's banner of MP3EI was officially no longer used, the contents and projects, including the TWBI, have remained incorporated under Jokowi's National Mid-Term Development Plan.

The TWBI Project

Reclamation and Development of a New 'Exotic' Enclave

The Tirta Wahana Bali International (TWBI) seeks to develop a new tourist enclave in Benoa Bay by reclaiming land from the bay and constructing a luxury resort, exclusive apartment complexes, a cultural centre, as well as marina on at least nine artificial islands. Regarding the size of the proposed reclamation sites, there have been several different figures circulated depending on the documents cited. The figure of 838 hectares is derived from the Governor's Decision (*Surat Keputusan*) No. 2138/02-C/HK/2012 on the Utilisation Permit for the TWBI in Benoa Bay. The second figure is 'up to 700 hectares', which derives from Presidential Regulation (Perpres) 51/2014 on the Revision of Perpres 45/2011 concerning Spatial Planning for Sarbagita Metropolitan Areas. The changes seem to result from a more exact study on the feasibility of undertaking reclamation in Benoa Bay, in which the maximum size planned was finally reduced to a maximum of 700 hectares. The third figure is 810 hectares, derived from the company's proposal which states, "We, the Tirta Wahana Bali International propose to undertake Revitalisation for Benoa Bay (approximately 1,400 hectares) in which 810 hectares are for reclamation and the rest is for deepening water flow to protect the existence of mangrove forests and accessibility for fishermen and water sport enterprises" (TWBI 2014a, 2). The fourth figure of 599.4 hectares is derived from the feasibility study conducted by LPPM Udayana University (see LPPM 2013).

Employing the rhetoric of 'green development', the company plans to designate 40% of its artificial islands as green open space, particularly a botanical garden, to enhance the ecological functions of the bay in absorbing CO_2 emissions called afforestation under the Kyoto Protocol's clean development mechanism (CDM) scheme.[4] As it will use the mangrove forest as their tourist attraction, it pledges to conserve the forest as part of its 'sustainable' business practice through the mangrove preservation projects managed by Winata's mangrove NGO, Forum Peduli Mangrove (FPM/Mangrove Care Forum).[5] The establishment of this NGO comes off the back of multiple charity events run by Artha Graha Peduli, a charity foundation of his conglomerate, in the area. A number of these events were extremely generous, such as a new community hall worth US$ 144,484 (*Radar Bali* 25/08/2013), food bazaars, and so on, as part of the foundation's corporate social responsibility (CSR) obligations. In a context of contested environmental politics, CSR activities of this kind are part of a wider strategy both to respond to the public pressure toward the company and to anticipate potential opposition against its

[4] Afforestation is defined as "the direct human-induced conversion of land that has not been forested for a period of at least 50 years to forested land through planting, seeding and/or the human-induced promotion of natural seed sources" (16/CMP, Annex, paragraph 1(b)). This aspiration was clearly articulated by Ketut Sukada, an Udayana University academic and the acting chair of Forum Peduli Mangrove from Tanjung Benoa, in an interview on 11 November 2013.

[5] In early 2013, Artha Graha Peduli, a charitable foundation of the Artha Graha Group, the holding company of the TWBI, established an institution called *Forum Peduli Mangrove* (FPM/Mangrove Care Forum) in collaboration with five *Lembaga Pemberdayaan Masyarakat* (LPM/Community Empowerment Institute), local government councils focusing on community development and empowerment, in Benoa Bay (Tanjung Benoa, Jimbaran, Benoa, Tuban, and Kedonganan). The programs of FPM are restoration of degraded land, preserving mangrove areas, replanting and rehabilitation of degraded mangroves, and undertaking mangrove development projects. FPM has recruited local people from the five villages in Benoa Bay—around 40 villagers from Tanjung Benoa alone—who are hired above district minimum wages, with flexible working hours, to carry out FPM projects.

projects (Utting & Zammit 2009, 47). In Tanjung Benoa, the company used this strategy to create a dependent relationship with the targeted community to broaden its coalition in order to gain support from the outset to ensure that its future businesses operate 'sustainably' within the community.

To greenwash the project for public consumption in Tanjung Benoa and beyond, the TWBI has used its holding company's (Artha Graha Group) track record in undertaking the Tambling Wildlife Nature Conservation (TWNC) project in Bukit Barisan National Park, Lampung. The project, managed since 1992 by one of Artha Graha's companies, the Adhiniaga Kreasinusa, is claimed to be successful in rehabilitating the previously degraded forests and coral reefs, and for preserving the endangered Sumatran Tiger and its habitat (Onishi 2010; Suksma 2015). In the *New York Times*, TWNC is reported as one of the only two tiger rehabilitation experiments in the world which has "successfully returned four Sumatran tigers to the wild, in what some experts describe as a promising strategy to help save the world's population of wild tigers" (Onishi 2010). Recently, the areas have been developed into eco-tourism sites and promoted to the global tourist market attracting representatives of many international organisations including UNESCO, the World Bank, IUCN, UNODC, as well as celebrities to visit. In the Benoa Bay project, the TWBI is projecting a similar approach to combine conservation of mangrove forests and eco-tourism. The 'success story' of TWNC projects is exploited as the biggest difference between the TWBI and the other competitors to justify access to Benoa Bay for a sustainable business practice.

When we look closely at its 'success story', the conservation of Tambling is not unproblematic. For example, deleterious environmental changes in Tambling are deflected to local inhabitants who live within and surrounding the national park. The conservation project is then used to justify limiting local inhabitants' access to the national park using armed guards. The most recent Sumatran Tiger breeding project is also seen by local environmental activists as another way to guard the company's concession from infringements by the locals (*Jakarta Post*, 31/07/2009; Onishi 2010). If the TWBI finds it useful to resort to similar repressive mechanisms to maintain the integrity and economic sustainability of its future assets and concessions in Benoa Bay, local fishermen who depend on the bay as their livelihood and *adat* communities who regard it as a sacred space would be the immediate victims of the company's actions. Moreover, as a tourism market-based mechanism, the conservation of Benoa Bay under the TWBI would heavily depend on its profits to fund the conservation agendas. Given that the market is uncertain and the environment remains externalised in the profit-making process, under conditions where profits decline, the conservation agendas are very likely to be abandoned, leaving the environment unattended, as occurred in the case of the BTID development at Serangan.[6]

For the TWBI, constructing artificial islands through reclamation is more economical than buying a comparable area of land in a similar location in Southern Bali. From the provincial government's perspective, besides providing jobs, the governor of Bali, Mangku Pastika (2013), argues that reclamation is preferable in order to avoid massive agricultural land conversion. Moreover, he also notes that reclamation would increase the size of Bali, not least attractive to the provincial government because the reclaimed land would be owned by the Provincial Government of Bali (Pastika 2013). In fact, there is no reasonable guarantee that the development of new enclaves through reclamation would reduce land conversion. As shown in Chap. 3, land conversion is a product of complex and interlocking structural conditions, including the ongoing expansion of tourism and the real estate industry, pressures from private property and land tax regimes, speculation and rent-seeking practices, environmental changes, and the poverty and marginalisation of farmers.

Although the reclaimed islands would legally be state land (*tanah negara*), the TWBI will have an exclusive right of management (*hak pengelolaan*), potentially without a specified period of time. Rather than a type of property right (*hak atas tanah*) under the Basic Agrarian Law No. 5/1960 (BAL), the right of management (*hak pengelolaan*) is a transfer of the state's authorities to manage reclaimed land, including undertaking land-use planning, utilising it for its profit-making objectives, transferring land use rights to third parties, and gaining revenues or compensa-

[6] For further discussions on the failures of market-based conservation see Heynen et al. (2007a); also Igoe and Brockington (2007).

tion without a specific time period.[7] This is why Fitzpatrick (2008, 239) argues that this type of right was part of the New Order's politics of development by manipulating the permit system and taking advantage of the BAL's dispossessory provisions to build its "corrupt public-private alliances". In the legal context applied to the TWBI, the right of management provides a wider entitlement than simple land rights. That is in the sense that although those rights have comparable exclusive economic benefits, the right of management may be extended over mangrove/water areas in the bay as well as a whole reclaimed island[8] for its speculative and profit-making purposes, including to designate its own land-use planning, development and utilisation, as well as to lease some parts of its concession to third parties. In contrast, the right of ownership cannot be held over an island, and the use of land legally should be in accordance with the designated functions stipulated by spatial planning regulations. Hence, based on the management rights, the TWBI would technically be able to act like a small state within the Benoa Bay area.

Besides the claim of becoming the future icon of Bali's tourism (Pastika 2013), the rhetoric of revitalisation and rehabilitation of the degraded Benoa Bay environment has been a specific feature of the TWBI project proposal to justify its involvement in providing market solutions through eco-tourism and enclave tourism (TWBI 2014a). The term *'revitalisasi'*

---

[7] Government Regulation (Peraturan Pemerintah) No. 40/1996 stipulates that "the right of management is the state right of avail in which certain of its management authorities are transferred to the right holder". This right would be granted based on the proposal submitted by the company after it obtains the environmental permit (*izin lingkungan*) covering a proposed part of the Benoa Bay area, including the reclaimed land for a yet unspecified period. The legal status of the 700 hectares of reclaimed land would need to be registered under the right to build (*Hak Guna Bangunan*/HGB), given that the land is located within a management rights area. In the case of the reclaimed land of the TWBI, there are three possibilities: (1) the TWBI obtains the right to build (HGB) from the government in its own name; (2) it transfers its right to third parties (other companies) in obtaining HGB—in this case, the third parties should obtain the right to build (HGB) from the government based on an agreement with the TWBI; (3) the combination of both (1) and (2)—in this case, the TWBI retains some part of the reclaimed land under its name in the HGB document and transfers the other parts of its authority to third parties. Whichever the case, the right to build (HGB) will be granted for 30 years, with a possible extension of 20 years.

[8] Site plan of the TWBI project. The green colour represents the Ngurah Rai Mangrove Forest while the white colour represents areas surrounding the bay that are under other parties' control or ownership. http://cdn.kaskus.com/images/2014/09/26/7049639_20140926075940.jpg. Sources: the TWBI Master Plan 2014.

(revitalisation) is used by the TWBI to neutralise the negative collective memory of the Balinese toward BTID's '*reklamasi*' (reclamation of) Serangan Island in the mid-1990s.[9] Contrary to Astarini's (2015) argument, the use of the term is not merely a New Order style euphemism, but is a strategic means to justify the project ecologically, economically, and legally. Legally, the term '*revitalisasi*' (revitalisation) is stipulated by Perpres Sarbagita No. 45/2011: Article 68 in which "rehabilitation, *revitalisation*, and improvement of protected functions of important areas within Sarbagita are given priority" [author's emphasis]. This is reaffirmed by Perpres Sarbagita No. 51/2014, the revised version of Perpres No. 45/2011, by stressing the need to undertake revitalisation in Benoa Bay.

Ecologically, the term 'revitalisation' is understood as the process to revive the ecological functions of the bay after decades of neglect and misuse due to pollution and sedimentation caused by human activities, as well as contaminants from inland waterways that drain into the bay and threaten the mangrove forest. Under the guise of restoration, mountains of mud and sediment will be dredged to construct nine artificial islands for a tourist resort (TWBI 2014b) that, it is claimed, will provide 200,000 jobs for local people (Pastika 2013). From an investment point of view, it will be much more efficient and cheaper to undertake reclamation instead of buying a 700-hectare plot of terrestrial land in southern Bali to build a new resort. As an illustration, in the southern part of Bali where the real estate industry has grown rapidly, a hectare of land may cost at least US$ 5 million. Thus, for a 700-hectare plot of land, it would cost up to US$ 3.5 billion. This amount of money excludes the costs of gaining permits and construction. In fact, given that southern Bali is the most densely populated area in Bali, it would be unlikely to find a consolidated 700-hectare landmass in the area. Through land reclamation, instead, the company estimates it would cost the company around US$ 2.1 billion including the costs of gaining permits and constructions (TWBI 2014a;

[9] A similar line of argument was also put forward by BTID in proposing to undertake reclamation of Serangan Island back in the mid-1990s in order to protect the island from erosion (Warren unpublished).

Suryani 2014). Thus, even prior to construction, the TWBI would be able to save almost a half of its total investment.

Risks and Opportunities: A Technocratic Framing

In recent decades of Indonesia's environmental law regime, the role of technocrats has become increasingly important. As will be shown below, those groups that are not able to refer their arguments to scientific data are more likely to be ignored and excluded in the technocratic processes of defining the risks and opportunities of a project. Claims that draw on collective notions of justice, or other non-scientific arguments such as the protection of sacred space, have little traction in the decision-making process. Consequently, this process tends to work in favour of powerful interests, especially for those who are able to deploy the quantifiable tools of science.

Indeed, the TWBI used its resources for gaining as much scientific data as possible to underpin its proposal. At first, Udayana University (Unud), Bali's most prominent state university, was the only institution contracted by the TWBI to conduct a feasibility study of the project in late 2012. Once the project became controversial, around mid-2013, the team members who had nearly finished the study, as well as Unud itself, were pressured by the mass media, particularly the *Bali Post*, questioning their lack of sensitivity to the likely cultural and environmental impacts for Bali. This was reasonable criticism considering the reputation of Unud for issuing favourable environmental impact assessments for many controversial projects in the past, including the reclamation of Serangan Island. Finally, in September 2013, through a university senate meeting, the study concluded that the Benoa Bay project was 'not feasible' (*tidak layak*), although the preliminary result before the controversy had been 'feasible with conditionality' (*layak bersyarat*).[10] However, the meeting

[10] The study was commissioned by *its Lembaga Penelitian dan Pengabdian Masyarakat* (LPPM/Research and Public Service Institute) to assess the revitalisation project proposed by the TWBI in terms of technical, environmental, socio-cultural, and economic-financial aspects. The final conclusion was drawn up after the controversy arose by reconstructing the concluding chapter only, without reviewing the previous chapters where the research evidence is presented. The conclusion

did not result in the revision of the consulting team's discussion chapters, which were very supportive of the project. Thus, for the governor and communities of scientists, the feasibility study of Udayana University is scientifically questionable for its inconsistency due to the internal contradictions between the analysis of the data provided and the conclusion (see LPPM Unud 2013).[11] A close look at this debate, however, suggests that the inconsistency in the document shows how politicised the process is, how much impact public pressure can have on this supposedly scientific assessment, and, more importantly, how much impact the company's interests in commissioning the assessment has on the 'science'.

Following Unud's study, the TWBI has since hired five different universities outside Bali to undertake a scientific study on the project. They were Hasanudin University of Makassar, Gadjah Mada University, Bandung Institute of Technology, Bogor Institute of Agriculture, Surabaya Institute of Technology—all of which conclude that Benoa Bay needs to be 'revitalised' (*Kompas*, 29/02/2016). In his study, Prof. Dietrich G. Bengen, an expert on marine and coastal areas from Bogor Institute of Agriculture, for instance, observes that partly due to the construction of the Bali Mandara Toll Road in 2012,[12] Benoa Bay has

---

and analysis chapters appear to be contradictory. For example, the study concludes that the project is not feasible in terms of its impacts on mangrove and biodiversity but, in the preceding Chapter III, it says that the project would increase the size of the mangrove forest and create new green open space in which biodiversity would be nurtured and enriched (LPPM Unud 2013, III-30–31). Similarly, on socio-cultural issues, it concludes that the project is not feasible; However, the analysis in Chapter III argues that the project is predicted to have important positive impacts, for example, creating an image of Bali as an eco-friendly tourist destination, improving social and public facilities for local communities, preserving and developing Balinese arts and culture, generating a new economy, as well as contributing to government revenues (LPPM Unud 2013, III-41). This is not to mention the other technical and economic-financial aspects of the project. Hence, the internal contradictions of Unud's study appear to be pervasive.

[11] This was also the case for Serangan Island Reclamation's Impact Assessment document, particularly with respect to the *Bhisama*, which was appended as if it were compatible with the proposed development, when it clearly was not because the development is within Sakenan Temple's sphere of sanctity, as Dhang Kahyangan, which is stipulated as having a 2-kilometre sacred radius in the 1994 *Bhisama* (Warren unpublished).

[12] From a public policy point of view, the construction of Bali Mandara Toll Road should be seen as integrally connected with the proposed TWBI and the stalled BTID projects because all three were part of Yudhoyono's MP3EI priorities in Bali. Politically and, more importantly, the impacts from the previous projects—the toll road construction and BTID's Serangan Island reclamation—are used to justify further exploitation of the bay by TWBI cloaked as 'revitalisation'.

changed significantly; hence, he argues that a '*revitalisasi berbasis reklamasi*' (reclamation-based revitalisation) is urgently needed, otherwise, erosion of Pulau Pudut and negative impacts of sedimentation on the mangrove ecosystem would be exacerbated in the future (*Kompas*, 02/10/2014).

Apparently, the impacts and unintended consequences of previous state-sponsored development projects, such as the Serangan Island Reclamation by BTID, the construction of a toll road, the expansion of Ngurah Rai Airport and Benoa Port, have been used to justify the need for the TWBI project. The governor argues that "there are many people asking the Provincial Government to dredge and rehabilitate [Benoa Bay], how much money would be needed? In fact, in Bali many people still live in poverty, roads are in bad condition, *desa pakraman* and *subak* ask for more [grant] money. So, where would the money [for dredging and rehabilitating Benoa Bay] come from?" (*Kabar Nusa*, 32/01/2016). The governor's statement is itself indication that tax revenues for what many Balinese consider to be an already overdeveloped tourist industry, especially in the southern part of Bali, have inadequately compensated for the pressures they have imposed. Such justification to endorse the TWBI project based on financial challenges seems to overlook the long-term social and environmental costs and unintended consequences of a project which would inevitably impact upon the livelihoods of local communities. As shown in the case study of Uluwatu Temple, local villagers in Pecatu have faced a rapid increase in the cost of living due to tourism, and pessimistically now question whether they can survive in the future.

Apart from the studies conducted by academic institutions, independent modelling also was undertaken by an international environmental organisation. Conservation International (CI) conducted their modelling study in order to predict the impacts of reclamation in Benoa Bay on the marine environment. The study shows that areas surrounding the bay including Sanur Kauh, Pamogan, and Tanjung Benoa will be severely flooded if the reclamation is conducted (Sudiarta et al. 2013, 2). However, in several public consultation forums the results of CI's study have been ignored by academics, government officials, and the proponents of the

TWBI project in order to prevent conflicting scientific opinion from being presented in the process.[13]

The project has been through the environmental impact assessment (AMDAL) stage.[14] Unlike in the New Order Regime, where AMDAL was treated only as a recommendation, in the decentralisation era, AMDAL becomes a compulsory requirement to obtain an environmental permit (*izin lingkungan*) (see Bedner 2010; Warren and Wardana 2018). In this process, the TWBI hired Widya Cipta Buana from Bandung, West Java, to conduct the official environmental impact assessment (ANDAL). The process itself has been conducted in Jakarta commissioned by the Ministry of Environment and Forestry instead of at the regional level where public participation would have been more meaningful. Scaling the process up to the national level has been undertaken on grounds of the status of Benoa Bay as a national strategic area and because the project is a cross-province development since the materials for reclamation will be taken from the neighbouring province of West Nusa Tenggara.[15] Politically, this was the strategy to drive the project away from the local political sphere, which is no longer supportive to the

---

[13] Iwan Dewantama, one of the team members for the CI modelling study, in an interview on 26 May 2015, explains that CI has never been invited to a public consultation or other event related to the TWBI project to present its study. He presumes that the project's proponents would claim that the CI findings have been considered and accommodated in the master plan.

[14] Under Indonesian environmental law, particularly Law No. 32/2009 concerning the Protection and the Management of the Environment, and Government Regulation No. 27/2012 concerning the Environmental Permit (*Izin Lingkungan*), an Environmental Impact Assessment (*Analisis Mengenai Dampak Lingkungan*/AMDAL) consists of four sets of documents at four stages of the process which are the 'Terms of Reference' (*Kerangka Acuan*/KA), 'Analysis of Environmental Impacts' (*Analisis Dampak Lingkungan*/ANDAL), 'Executive Summary' (*Ringkasan Eksekutif*/RE), and 'Environmental Management Plan and Environmental Monitoring Plan' (*Rencana Pengelolaan Lingkungan dan Rencana Pemantauan Lingkungan*/RKL dan RPL). For a detailed discussion on Environmental Impact Assessment (EIA) in Indonesia's decentralisation era, see (Bedner 2010).

[15] Reclamation materials needed for constructing nine artificial islands to create 700 hectares of land are 2.5 million cubic metres of stones which would be transported from East Lombok District in West Nusa Tenggara (NTB) Province, and 37.5 million cubic metres of sand comprising 26.6% from sediments after the dredging process, 45.4% from East Lombok District, and 26.6% from Karangasem District in eastern Bali (TWBI 2014b). It is reported that the Governor of NTB has rejected the proposal to mine sand and stones in that province (*Antara News*, 17/04/2015); however, the District Head of East Lombok claiming regional autonomy at the district level has approved it (*Antara News*, 25/04/2015).

company's interests. By conducting the process in Jakarta, local opponents would find difficulty in participating due to limited resources.

In the terms of the reference document (*Kerangka Acuan*) for the environmental impact assessment, the TWBI (2014b) is not only arguing the importance of the project in terms of conservation of the mangrove forest of Tahura Ngurah Rai, but also claims the project will contribute to disaster mitigation. Highlighting the vulnerability of southern Bali, the centre of the island's tourism economy and the most densely populated area in Bali, to the threat of tsunami, TWBI (2014b, II-100) argues two points to justify the reclamation of artificial islands. Firstly, the company will build new roads to connect the reclaimed islands, Tanjung Benoa and the mainland of Bali.[16] With these new roads, Tanjung Benoa will not rely on the single access road as the only evacuation route if a tsunami occurs in the village; hence, it is expected to reduce casualties from the disaster. Secondly, the artificial islands, with vegetation and buildings on them, will be functional as barriers to protect Tanjung Benoa against tsunami (if the tsunami occurs from the western side of Benoa Bay) or Kedongan, Kuta, Tuban, and other areas (if the tsunami occurs from eastern side of the bay).

Both justifications seem to be illogical. If it were true that the reclaimed islands and their access roads will reduce the impact of a tsunami, it is difficult to understand why they are built within the semi-enclosed waters of Benoa Bay rather than on the Indian Ocean seashores, where the waves are more powerful. Dharma Putra (2009, 70), an Unud academic with environmental chemistry expertise, who recently served as a member of the AMDAL impact assessment commission team, contradicted this statement in his dissertation, arguing that "Benoa Bay is a very secure bay

[16] Suweda (2013), an Unud academic, conducted a study on the impacts of the TWBI Project on the traffic in the southern peninsula of Bali. He argues that the project may be able to reduce traffic congestion in south Bali because it would construct new roads that connect the reclaimed islands and the mainland of Bali; thus in turn this would add to the length of roads available to prevent traffic deadlock in 2070 (Suweda 2013). However, as past experience from the Nusa Dua tourist enclave shows, it is also a valid concern that the new roads would be guarded and used exclusively for tourists or workers travelling to and from the reclaimed islands. Moreover, the study does not calculate the traffic impacts from the projected increase in tourist visits after the TWBI resort is in operation.

('*teluk yang sangat terlindung*') so that its waves are relatively small … [which are] caused by the relatively weak winds and ship traffic within the bay". Whether or not the development could perform such a function, it is obvious that fears of disaster have been used to convince the public that the project is urgently needed for the survival of local people in Benoa Bay. In fact, this is part of the strategy by which the company attempts to represent itself not merely as a capitalist economic venture, but as one that the literature on business ethics commonly calls a 'triple bottom line' project—profit-people-planet (Elkington 1997)—by putting a conservationist and a humanitarian face to its profit-oriented enterprise.

Technically, the terms of reference for the document represent a tool to undertake scoping for every phase of the development. In terms of reference for the reclamation process, the impacts are divided into three phases: pre-construction, construction, and post-construction. For every phase, potential impacts (*dampak potensial*) are listed and then identified as hypothetically significant (*dampak penting hipotetik*) or not. In this process, the technocratic exercise appears to become political as some potential impacts are included or excluded in the list of hypothetical significant impacts that will be studied closely in the next stage of Analysis of Environmental Impacts (*Analisis Dampak Lingkungan*/ANDAL). Coastal erosion and landslides, the decrease in water quality, and the increase of water run-off are listed in the potential impacts, but are not identified as hypothetical significant impacts in the post-construction phase. Cleverly, they are only identified as a hypothetical significant impact in the construction phase (TWBI 2014b, II-199). With this in mind, those impacts are assumed to be temporary and are implied to be 'insignificant' in the post-construction phase.

The hypothetical significant impacts identified in the post-construction phase by TWBI's document are limited specifically to social domains, including the changes in local people's livelihoods, the decrease in local people's income due to competition with the new resort, and negative perceptions and attitudes of the locals (TWBI 2014b, II-199). With the focus on these social impacts, the company (TWBI and Dinamika Atria Raya 2016) is able to argue that they would be resolved by providing jobs, capacity building to develop income generating and creative economy projects, as well as CSR activities. Given the wide opposition from local communities, these plans, in fact, are likely to precipitate horizontal conflicts within the communities. This is because the plans may primarily be directed to reward the project's supporters, while the project's opponents may be left aside. Even now, the relative social cohesion in those communities has been compromised due to conflicting interests and attitudes toward the project, which would need a long period of time to be redressed and could not be easily compensated in monetary form.

In many development projects, compulsory monitoring commitments from project proponents are very often not met. Dharma Putra (2009) admits that the project proponents often do not comply with their responsibility to report regularly on their monitoring and implementation activities in accordance with RKL/RPL. During 2009–2010, for instance, there were 98 AMDAL or environmental monitoring/management efforts (UKL/UPL) documents approved by the Provincial Government of Bali, but none of them had reported on their project implementation and none were monitored by the government agency in the implementation phases (see Bapedalda Bali 2010, III-6).

There is a long history of poor implementation of AMDAL in Bali (Warren and Wardana 2018). For example, Bambang Suharto's BTID in the reclamation of Serangan Island project ignored its ANDAL commitment regarding the construction of a bridge, instead building a causeway with only a 50-metre underpass, that limited water flow and radically altered current patterns in the bay causing serious erosion along the Sanur coast (Warren unpublished). The BTID was never penalised for this violation of ANDAL commitments and remediation had to be undertaken by government with international assistance (JICA) to deal with intensified coastal erosion. In the Bali Mandara Toll Road construction, the developers used limestone to reclaim water areas of Benoa Bay and to construct pillars for the road, which was not mentioned in the ANDAL (*Metro Bali*, 30/07/2012). Given the past experience of failure to undertake monitoring and enforcement against the violations of AMDAL documents, it cannot be assumed that the government would require the TWBI to comply with its obligations, all the more to impose sanctions for violating them.

In the scoping environmental impact assessment document, the cultural and religious aspects of the Benoa Bay areas were also given consideration. Dharma Putra raised the issue of the project's potential impact on Benoa Bay as a sacred space. As a longstanding consultant for megaprojects in Bali, he is very aware that sacredness can be used effectively to mobilise opposition to a development project (as the Pecatu case has shown). In fact, many observers have argued against the project based on the sacredness of the Benoa Bay area according to the religious ruling of the 1994 *Bhisama* (PHDI 1994) concerning the sacred space of temples, and other traditional texts (Lanus 2014; *Bali Post* 11/01/2014; *Kompas*, 27/02/2015). Interestingly, as a supporter of the project serving on the AMDAL Commission Team, Dharma Putra advised the TWBI to build a statue of Lord Baruna, the god of the oceans, on one of the reclaimed islands.[17] By design, the statue will serve two main purposes simultaneously: first, it will 'offset' the whole bay as a sacred space to be concentrated into a single designated island so that all related religious and spiritual activities could be redirected to that place; secondly, the statue will serve as the icon of the TWBI resort, and in general as the new icon of Balinese tourism akin to the Merlion on Sentosa Island, Singapore. Hence, the project is a 'disneyfication' of Benoa Bay *par excellence*, by which tradition will selectively be 'reinvented' and 'simulated' in the designated space to serve the tourism market (Baudrillard 1975; Hobsbawn 1983; Minca 2000; Springer 2010).

[17] In an interview with *Pos Bali* (08/06/2015), Dharma Putra says that "in a given location, say on one of islands [within the reclaimed areas], an icon like Garuda Wisnu Kencana should be built. I suggested the proponent build a statue of Lord Baruna. We [Balinese] believe that the lord of the ocean and water areas is the Lord Baruna according to Hindu belief. [It] should be a well-carved statue. There would be a park [that] could be used for praying, doing yoga, and so forth. All the sanctity [of the bay area] can be redirected and concentrated [in the place where the Lord Baruna statue is located] through a specific religious ceremony. It is better located within the reclaimed island. [It] should not be too tall as it is used as an icon."

The Dynamics of Resistance

Civil Society Advocacy and Fragmentation

Although the project is owned by one of the most powerful Indonesian oligarchs, it cannot be assumed that the TWBI proposal will be successful. In many controversial projects in Bali, including this case, civil society, especially through non-governmental organisations and other civic associations, plays an essential role either facilitating or constraining their outcomes (see Suasta and Connor 1999; Warren 1998; Strauss 2015). Supported by the mass media, competing civil society groups have raised their voices and rallied public opinion against the TWBI project. There are at least three major forces opposing the project: *Forum Rakyat Bali Tolak Reklamasi*/ForBali (Balinese People's Forum against Reclamation), which is a Denpasar-based coalition of NGO activists, musicians, and urban-middle class youth; *Nasional Koordinator Penolakan Reklamasi Teluk Benoa* (National Coordinating Forum for the Rejection of Benoa Bay Reclamation), which is a lobby task-force established by Unud academics, other prominent individuals, as well as NGO activists who distinguish their strategy from mobilisation and street demonstrations employed by ForBali; and *Tanjung Benoa Tolak Reklamasi* (TBTR/ Tanjung Benoa Against Reclamation), which is a more local grassroots organisation based in Tanjung Benoa village. Although the National Coordinating Forum and ForBali adopt different strategies, they focus more on the legal aspects and impacts of the TWBI project for Bali, targeting the general public and urban young people through social media and pop culture respectively. TBTR's resistance is mainly informed by local customs and interests, especially concerns about the impacts on local livelihoods and sacred space.

Knowing that there is widespread opposition towards the project, the provincial government has been engaged in 'noise reduction' and 'demobilising' strategies. In early August 2013, Governor Pastika invited concerned groups to attend a public consultation. At the consultation, ForBali and Ibrahim, an Unud law professor who later found the National Coordinating Forum, questioned the legal basis of the Governor's Decision (*Surat Keputusan*) No. 2138/02-C/HK/2012 (hereafter, SK I) to grant utilisation rights to the TWBI as a violation of numerous higher regulations. As a result of this input, the governor then revoked the SK I and issued a new Governor's Decision No. 1727/01-B/HK/2013 (SK II) accommodating several higher regulations raised by the opponents.[18] The public consultations provided a forum for opponents and proponents of the project to engage in a dialogue so that the legalistic and technical arguments raised by both could be absorbed as 'advice' by the government, who subsequently improved and justified the resultant policy as 'participatory', without necessarily changing the underlying logic or government support for the project.

Another strategy to reduce noise and demobilise public concerns has been to establish a speaker's corner, following the models of Singapore's Hong Lim Park or the UK's Hyde Park. The speaker's corner is named '*Podium Bali Bebas Bicara*' (Bali's Podium of Free Speech) where every citizen may speak individually and freely on a designated podium. It is held every Sunday morning during the Car Free Day at the Bajra Sandhi Park Monument in Denpasar. The audiences are government officials and the general public who participate in the Car Free Day. Considering several international events would take place during that period (APEC 2013 and Miss World also in 2013), it was expected that both strategies would redirect street demonstrations that might affect Bali's image negatively into in-house negotiations on atomistic concerns. It also enabled 'free' speeches to be heavily monitored in public space.

At the national level, the central government, through the Board for National Development Planning (*Badan Perencanaan Pembangunan Nasional*/Bappenas), since 2013, has given special attention to the controversy over the Benoa Bay project due to persistent debate at the regional level. On the one hand, ForBali continued to oppose the governor's revised SK II by arguing that it still violates another higher regulation, the Presidential Regulation (*Peraturan Presiden*/Perpres) No. 45/2011 concerning Spatial Planning for Sarbagita, which designates

---

[18] For example, Perpres No. 45/2011 concerning spatial planning for Sarbagita and Coastal Area and Small Island Management Law No. 27/2007 and Perpres 122/2012 concerning Reclamation in Coastal Areas and Small Islands did not take this issue into consideration.

Benoa Bay as a conservation area. According to Perpres No. 122/2012 concerning Reclamation in Coastal and Small Islands, reclamation is prohibited within a conservation area.

The proponents of the project, on the other hand, stressed the potential status of Benoa Bay for tourism development. Framing the debates on the Benoa Bay project in terms of competing regulations enabled the national government to respond to the controversy by identifying it as merely a 'conflict over spatial planning' (*konflik penataan ruang*). Hence, the national government covers up the vested interests in expanding tourism development in Bali, which lie at the centre of the controversy. In this circumstance, a dispute settlement mechanism or a special rule (*pengaturan khusus*) should be adopted (Bappenas 2013a, b). This approach was also partly informed by the special status of the TWBI together with the BTID as parts of MP3EI fast track economic development projects that are given priority attention (Bappenas 2013c, 6). A meeting involving relevant ministries and national departments for settling the conflict was conducted in March 2014, which agreed to conduct a review (*peninjuan kembali*) of Perpres 45/2011 on Spatial Planning for Sarbagita (Bappenas 2014a), and a roadmap was adopted for such a review process. The Secretary to the Coordinator of the Economic Ministry suggested that the process should be accelerated to be completed before the 2014 general election (Bappenas 2014b). After conducting a public consultation in Bali and being advised by Yusril Ihza Mahendra, a constitutional law professor and former Minister of Law, President Yudhyono finally enacted a new Presidential Regulation (Perpres) 51/2014 revising Perpes 45/2011, concerning Spatial Planning for Sarbagita, just before leaving office.

There were several basic revisions of the previous regulation that were clearly intended to provide legal grounds for the TWBI project. Perpres No. 51/2014 in its introductory considerations states that taking into account the progress of national strategic policies and internal dynamics in the Sarbagita region, especially the use of space in Benoa Bay, and noting that the bay may be developed as a potential area for economic activities by taking into consideration the preservation of ecological functions of Tahura Ngurah Rai Mangrove Forest and its surroundings, and the existence of infrastructure within the area, there is a need to undertake 'revitalisation'. As the main legal constraint to the reclamation, Article 55 of Perpres 45/2011 is revised by Perpres 51/2014 by reclassifying the status of Benoa Bay from a designated coastal and small island conservation area into 'Zona L3' protected zones for the mangrove forest of Tahura Ngurah Rai, 'Zona P' buffer zones encompassing the water areas in Benoa Bay that are not part of the Tahura Ngurah Rai, and 'Zona L3/P' as temporary status for Pulau Pudut because at the time Perpres 51/2014 was enacted the island was still designated as part of the Tahura Ngurah Rai Mangrove Forest.[19] Its status still needs to be revised by a Ministry of the Environment and Forestry Decision to exclude it from the Tahura Ngurah Rai Mangrove Forest.[20] Subsequently, a decree, as shown on a map in its appendix, has been issued to revise the L3/P zone classification of Pulau Pudut into a buffer zone so that the island can also be reclaimed for project purposes. With water areas of Benoa Bay reclassified as merely a buffer zone through a re-regulation of space, activities permitted in the bay are broadened to include the reclamation of up to 700 hectares.[21]

Following the enactment of Perpres 51/2014 by President Yudhoyono, civil society struggles have been directed at the national government. Attempting to scale up advocacy against the project at the national level was the primary objective of establishing the National Coordinating Forum led by Unud academics, among others, Prof. Bakta (the former rector), and Prof. Ibrahim of the Law Faculty. Many Unud academics became outspoken opponents of the project after social movement and

[19] Comparison maps of Benoa Bay's protected areas. The purple colour represents the protected areas that through Perpres 51/2014 are reduced significantly to accommodate the TWBI project. http://www.mongabay.co.id/2016/02/18/tolak-reklamasi-teluk-benoa-14-bendesa-adat-datangi-kantor-kepresidenan/. Source: Muhajir 2014.

[20] This explains why Perpres 51/2014 avoids mentioning the exact quantified size of the conservation area (L3) within the Tahura Ngurah Rai Mangrove Forest, unlike Perpres 45/2011, which clearly states that the Tahura Ngurah Rai is 1375 hectares. Consequently, the areas that are to be excluded from the size of Tahura Ngurah Rai, including Pulau Pudut, would no longer be designated as within the core zone of the Ngurah Rai conservation area and would become a utilisation zone legally managed by the company, which could then be legally subject to reclamation works.

[21] The rationale behind this is that the real condition of the bay is far from an ideal conservation area due to the extent and impact of human activities—the Serangan reclamation, construction of a toll road, port, marine sports, and so forth, that make it difficult to maintain a case based on its integrity as a conservation area.

media pressure on their institution questioned its integrity and cultural sensitivity should the outcome of the Unud study appear to justify the project. On the other hand, the decision of the TWBI to hire five other universities outside Bali challenged Unud's academic integrity in order to counter its 'unfeasible' conclusion in the feasibility study.[22] ForBali refused to join the National Coordinating Forum, which it considered would hamper its own strategy and tactics. It chose to use its NGO networks in Jakarta instead to support its campaigns and to prepare a judicial review request before the Supreme Court on grounds of lack of public participation.[23] However, to date, the request for a judicial review has not been filed, presumably to be reserved as the final strategy and due to the uncertainty of outcome, given the past weakness of the court in the area of environmental protection.[24]

The debate on the TWBI project also moved from legal toward technical and scientific issues. Ari Sudijanto, the chair of the Commission on EIA Assessment (*Komisi Penilai AMDAL*) of the Ministry of the Environment and Forestry, suggested that both proponents and opponents of the project should provide the commission with a scientific study to be considered in the EIA assessment process (*Pos Bali*, 05/06/2015). In this regard, not only are the quality of arguments counted, but the quantity of submissions is also important, in the sense that proponents or opponents have to mobilise as many institutions or associations on their side to send input to the EIA commission. From the beginning, the

[22] Interview with Luh Kartini, an Unud academic and member of the National Coordinating Forum, on 27 January 2014.

[23] Interview with Dewa Alit Sunarya, a member of the ForBali legal team and the chairman of the Bali chapter of the Indonesia Legal Aid and Human Rights Association (Perhimpunan Bantuan Hukum dan Hak Asasi Manusia Indonesia/PBH), on 22 July 2014; personal communication with Bangun Nusantara, the Secretary of the National Coordinating Forum, on 2 August 2014.

[24] In a notable example, the Bali chapter of Walhi (Indonesian Forum for the Environment) sued the Governor of Bali before the Administrative Court (PTUN) of Denpasar due to his issuance of a location permit (*izin lokasi*) for Tirta Rahmat Bahari to develop tourist facilities on 102 hectares in the Ngurah Rai Mangrove Forest, which was regarded as potentially degrading and destructive to the forest. After a long battle, the Supreme Court in Jakarta ruled to dismiss WALHI Bali's cassation on the grounds that the permit is still in a preliminary phase so that it could not be used to determine whether the forest would be destroyed. According to the court, the potential damages could only be predicted scientifically based on an AMDAL that had not yet been undertaken (see Putusan MA No. 151 K/TUN/2014 on 22 May, 2014).

TWBI has been aware of the importance of widening its coalition by establishing new institutions and associations or building networks with existing ones. A new mass media outlet, *Pos Bali*, has by no coincidence been established as the mouthpiece of the proponent, in particular to counter public opinion built especially by the *Bali Post*.[25] This attempt to counter the important role of the local mass media was specifically inspired by the strategy of the Bakrie Nirwana Resort (BNR) in taking control of a competing newspaper (*Nusa*) for the same purpose: to serve the investors' interests in the Tanah Lot case (see Warren 1998).

Furthermore, different civil society groups adopting different strategies to resist the project have created tensions and polarisation among themselves. Those strategies are to a large extent informed by complex institutional settings where authorities to constrain or to facilitate the project are not located within one particular tier of government. The complex institutional and legal configuration in Bali's spatial governance diffuses the target(s) for intervention, confounding mobilisation efforts. ForBali sees the governor of Bali, Made Mangku Pastika, as the central figure in facilitating the project by issuing the Governor's Decrees recommending the project in the first place. The National Coordination Forum, on the other hand, has focused on the central government as the main target to be lobbied. Redirecting the focus into the national domain is partly informed by the reluctance of its members, many of whom are Unud academics, to be in direct confrontation with the provincial government, for which they often serve as expert consultants or become involved in its development programs. A new loose network of individuals led by Dr. Luh Kartini, an Unud academic and the chairperson of the Bali Organic Association, has been focusing on engaging the local community where the project would be developed, especially in collaboration with the local group, Tanjung Benoa Against Reclamation (TBTR).

---

[25] *Pos Bali* is a newly established newspaper owned by I Gusti Ngurah Oka, the owner of Gema Merdeka Group, but operated by Made Nariana as the editor-in-chief. Nariana is a former journalist for the *Bali Post*, who resigned due to internal conflict, and has become a close ally of Governor Mangku Pastika. When the *Bali Post*, the oldest newspaper in Bali, started to put the Benoa project issue in the spotlight, *Pos Bali* took a different stance, supporting the project.

The local fragmentation toward the TWBI project became yet more escalated during the 2013 general election. Tanjung Benoa villagers became highly politicised, in the sense that they identified their political affiliations not only based on existing patronage relations in the village, but also particular interests with respect to the TWBI project.[26] Unlike in Jatiluwih, where informal power based on sub-clan relations has influenced leadership at the local level, in Tanjung Benoa, material wealth, especially the economic position in the context of local marine tourism, has had a greater influence on leadership dynamics in both state and customary local institutions.

The dynamics of advocacy in Tanjung Benoa has also been affected by strategies employed by other groups outside the village, especially at the provincial level, some of which were counter-productive for the locals. ForBali activists' electoral strategy endorsing Jokowi ignored the complex political affiliations in Tanjung Benoa, which did not tidily coincide with their positions toward the TWBI project.[27] Assertions that Jokowi would revoke Perpres 51/2014 if he won the election were treated sceptically by TBTR activists, many of whom were inclined toward Made Wijaya's political support for Prabowo. Made Wijaya recalled, "in the presidential campaign, Jokowi's volunteers (*relawan*) said that Jokowi rejected reclamation and his administration would be anti the reclamation in order to gain votes. Now, I'd love to see how they show their forces to demand that Jokowi revokes Perpres (51/2014). It should not have taken this long".[28] Wayan Kartika more emphatically stated that "now is the time

[26] There were two local elite candidates competing head-to-head for a seat in DPRD Badung: Wayan Dharma, the Chair of LPM Tanjung Benoa, who is also the Chair of PDI Perjuangan South Kuta Sub-District, and Made Wijaya from Gerindra Party, the coordinator of TBTR and soon to become *Bendesa* of Desa Pakraman Tanjung Benoa. As marine sport entrepreneurs in Tanjung Benoa, both are relatively well-off local figures compared to ordinary villagers, many of whom also work for them. Regarding the TWBI project, the two hold contrasting views that were clearly articulated during the general election campaign period, Wayan Dharma representing the supporters of the project and Made Wijaya representing the opponents. Made Wijaya won the election.

[27] Made Wijaya, the key figure of Tanjung Benoa against Reclamation (TBTR), as a DPRD Badung member from Gerindra Party, was a local campaigner for Probowo-Hatta Rajasa in Tanjung. In contrast, Wayan Dharma, the key figure in support of the project, due to his position as the chair of PDI Perjuangan South Kuta Sub-District, was the local campaigner for Jokowi-Jusuf Kalla.

[28] Interview with Made Wijaya, the *Bendesa* of Desa Pakraman Tanjung Benoa, on 29 May 2015.

for those who had used the reclamation issue to gain popularity, including *orang-orang Jokowi* (Jokowi's men—the volunteers), to be responsible ... Their movement is unclear and is not being transparent with us ... We in Tanjung Benoa need individuals or organisations that are really a *petarung* [fighter], without any agenda except to thwart the project".[29]

The Use of Adat in Tanjung Benoa

The impacts of the Serangan Island reclamation by BTID significantly changed the conditions of Benoa Bay, contributing to the TWBI's rhetorical claims of the need for its purported 'revitalisation' project. As evident from the experience of reclamation at Serangan Island, severe coastal erosion along the southern coast of Bali and sedimentation within the bay occurred in the post-construction phase. PEMSEA and Bali PMO (2004, 8) found that "the reclamation of Serangan Island, located at the mouth of Benoa Bay, to four times its original size has been attributed in this risk assessment as the cause of the seagrass disappearance around the island's coast; changes in the current pattern leading to increased sedimentation in some portions of the mangrove area in Benoa Bay, causing some mangrove species, such as *Sonneratia*, to die; wide coral damage arising from siltation and sedimentation".

The most severe impact from the Serangan reclamation has been suffered by Tanjung Benoa Village. The village used to be a fishing village but, as of 2014, its 5.24 square kilometres (Sukada and Mentra 2010, 7) were inhabited by 5577 people (Kelurahan Tanjung Benoa 2014, 15), 25% of whom are working directly in the tourism sectors, especially water-sports, with only 4% remaining as fishermen (Kelurahan Tanjung Benoa 2014, 16). Administratively, the status of Tanjung Benoa is as a *kelurahan* in which local institutions represent the district government's administrative authority at the village level, rather than a *desa*, which elects its village head and more or less has its own authority to govern its

[29] Personal communication with Wayan Kartika, the Coordinator of Tanjung Benoa Tolak Reklamasi (TBTR), on 9 October 2014.

internal affairs.[30] The reclamation of Serangan Island in the late 1990s and early 2000s has affected coastal erosion around its beaches, and more severely on Pulau Pudut, a small island near the western coast of the village (the red dot in the figure in the link below)[31] which was once eight hectares but, nowadays, it remains less than a hectare. Pulau Pudut is still regarded as an important common space, having cultural, economic, and social significance. Wayan Wana Putra, former *Bendesa* of Desa Pakraman Tanjung Benoa, described the impact of reclamation at Serangan Island:

> waves that hit Tanjung Benoa coast have been much stronger and eroded a large part of the beaches in Tanjung Benoa. Besides that, during the western wind season, ocean currents from Serangan Island and Benoa Port dump a big amount of rubbish on Tanjung Benoa beaches, [this is] greater than before the reclamation of Serangan Island and perhaps due to the constraint of water circulation around the northern end of Serangan Island. As a result, all the currents with rubbish are redirected to Tanjung Benoa. We as the Tanjung Benoa community who depend for our livelihood on water tourism and fisheries have been very distracted by these conditions. (quoted by Dharma Putra 2009, 248)

In responding to the severe condition of Pulau Pudut, the local community, through their customary village leaders and the head of the administrative village (*lurah*), sent a proposal letter twice in 2008 and 2011 to the district government of Badung asking for assistance to rehabilitate Pudut Island and protect it from severe erosion. Made Wijaya, one of the prominent figures in the village, explains[32]:

> … due to the reclamation of Serangan Island and dredging [of Benoa Bay] by Pelindo [Indonesian Harbour Authority], Pulau Pudut has become severely eroded. Ever since, we, together with local community leaders

[30] On the differences between *kelurahan* and *desa* since the New Order 1979 Village Government Law, and the paradox of reduced democratic participation in the presumptively more modern *kelurahan* structure, see Warren (1993).

[31] Aerial view of Tanjung Benoa (in Benoa Bay). https://www.google.com/maps/@-8.7585119,115.2137007,11466m/data=!3m1!1e3. Source: Google earth (2014).

[32] Interview with Made Wijaya, *Bendesa* of Desa Pakraman Tanjung Benoa, on 29 May 2015.

> [*tokoh masyarakat*] and *Pak Lurah* have proposed rehabilitation of Pulau Pudut [to the government]. This [proposal] was long before the reclamation plan of the TWBI was proposed. I, as a chair of a turtle conservation group, felt that Pulau Pudut has been neglected because of the severe erosion.

Following this long-awaited aspiration to rehabilitate Pulau Pudut, in early 2013, an Unud research team came to the village and conducted two focus group discussions in January and February 2013. According to Wayan Kembar, *Lurah* of Tanjung Benoa, the team only mentioned that they were conducting a study for the rehabilitation (*penataan*) and development (*pengembangan*) of the western coastal areas of Tanjung Benoa. The lurah claimed that the team did not explain that the project was related to TWBI's plan to reclaim up to 700 hectares of artificial islands in Benoa Bay in order to build a new tourist resort, and that the villagers only became aware of this when the controversy erupted.[33] For him and other local community leaders who participated, the focus group discussions were assumed to be the follow up to their requests to the government. After each discussion, the participants were asked to fill in a suggestion form regarding the project. Responses on these forms suggest that the team did not provide sufficient and honest information to the participants. More importantly, it shows how local participants were led to believe that the project discussed was a limited reclamation project to rehabilitate Pulau Pudut, a long-held aspiration of the local community itself.[34]

The TWBI Project soon became contentious in the *adat* institutional domain. This was because, following the focus group discussions, Wana Putra, the *Bendesa*, on behalf of Desa Pakraman Tanjung Benoa, signed a

---

[33] Interview with I Wayan Kembar, *Lurah* of Kelurahan Tanjung Benoa, on 1 June 2015. He said, "... in fact, at first the villagers sought to revitalise Pulau Pudut to return it to its original size. The purpose was to accommodate a parking lot, schools and hospital."

[34] Putu Suwitra's form asks, "*Berapa hektar luas Pudut (Teluk Benoa) yang akan dikrib?*" [How many hectares of Pulau Pudut (Teluk Benoa) will be surrounded by a seawall for protection (*krib*)?]. Another local participant, I Nyoman Oka Sudarsana, suggested that "after Pulau Pudut has been reclaimed it should be used for green zones, a parking lot, and a new icon for Tanjung Benoa Tourism".

legal contract with TWBI to support the project.[35] It was only later revealed that the agreement was completely different from what was locally understood as the 'rehabilitation' of Pulau Pudut. The agreement was between two parties—the investor, the TWBI, represented by its director, Hendi Lukman, and Desa Pakraman Tanjung Benoa represented by the *Bendesa*, Nyoman Wana Putra, and the Chair of the LPM, Wayan Dharma. It was witnessed by, among others, the Lurah of Tanjung Benoa, Wayan Kembar, the Chief of Traditional Security Guard (*Pecalang*), Ketut Jatha, and the *Kelihan Adat* of Banjar Tengah, Wayan Ganjreng. It is mentioned that the TWBI intends to undertake an 838-hectare reclamation project and to develop and manage it as a tourism site for 50 years, extendable for another 50 years. The agreement states that the TWBI is responsible to rehabilitate Pulau Pudut to its original eight-hectare size and is to be managed by the local community. The company also pledges to provide jobs for the local people; to contribute to Tanjung Benoa an amount to be decided by both parties; to provide public facilities and social services in order to rehabilitate the turtle conservation sites; to build a soccer field; a medical clinic, schools and multifunctional halls; and to build an accessible road from Bali Mandara Toll road to Tanjung Benoa through Pulau Pudut. Meanwhile, Desa Pakraman Tanjung Benoa will fully support the TBWI's development project and will assist and support the investor in obtaining permits to realise the project and in providing security services during the construction. Both parties consent to be bound by the agreement that all information either written or unwritten and other information related to this partnership is confidential and shall not be revealed for whatever reasons to third parties or other unauthenticated persons except when authorised in writing beforehand by both parties, and this stipulation will apply although the agreement is terminated. After the agreement has been signed, Desa Pakraman Tanjung Benoa is prohibited from conducting and/or signing any similar agreement with other parties without written consent from the TWBI.

[35] The agreement No. 45, 8 March 2013 was signed before a Public Notary, Evi Susanti Panjaitan, in Badung on 8 March 2013.

More importantly, there is a clause stating that the contract is to remain a secret between the parties involved, making the villagers very suspicious of the deal between the *Bendesa* and the investor. Unlike conventional models of elected leadership, *adat* leaders are regarded as representatives acting on behalf of the *adat* membership (*krama*), and are understood to exercise authority only on the explicit basis of *paruman* (assembly) of *krama* (Warren 1993). Hence, the *Bendesa*, in taking a crucial decision without a legitimate mandate from the *adat* community precipitated a serious question of legitimacy.[36] A challenge to the legitimacy of this decision started from the *banjar* (hamlet) levels where direct engagements of *adat* members take place, a widely supported challenge was circulated to remove Wana Putra from his position as *Bendesa*. All *banjars* took decisions through assembly and finally through a meeting at the *desa* level held by all *kelihan adat* and *Sabha Desa* (the *desa adat's* representative assembly) to remove Wana Putra and to elect Made Wijaya, the former coordinator of TBTR and elected local parliament (DPRD) member, as the new *Bendesa*.

In this case, local customary institutions played an essential role in local advocacy. Given that the sub-district (*kelurahan*) is compromised by its subordinate position to district government authority, the *adat* village or *desa pakraman* has been targeted by the proponents and opponents of the project because of its potentiality as the only local institution that can claim democratic representative status. With the new leadership, Desa Pakraman Tanjung Benoa through its assembly has decided to reject the TWBI project based on its *awig-awig* (*adat* law) that regards Benoa Bay as a sacred space. This also demonstrates local capacities to articulate public opinion and use local democratic processes strategically to determine and pursue their collective interests against (apparently) more powerful interests backed by the state and its legal embodiment.

[36] In the Padanggalak case during the late New Order, the signature of the *Bendesa* of Desa Pakraman Kesiman without *krama* approval was a front page issue in the mass media. Threats to remove him from office and to impose *adat* sanctions (*kasepekan*) on the governor who was a member of Desa Adat Kesiman and had signed permit approvals were sufficient to abort the project (see Warren 2007). Letters to the editor in the local press made it clear that the issue of *adat* leaders' responsibilities to the community were understood to be very different from those associated with the *dinas* government regime at that time.

Although vital institutions in the local context have joined forces against the TWBI project, as the decision making involves a complex institutional configuration, much of it beyond the local domain, the future of the project is still open. Undoubtedly, this complex configuration has also opened up important political spaces for 'participation' in decision making regarding development projects. In addition, the uses of other normative orders outside the state order—for example, the *adat* village institutional autonomy and *adat* concepts of authority expressed in the *desa-kala-patra* (according to place, time, and context) principle, and local conceptions of sacred space—to challenge the dominant order and interest have also proved possible in this complex configuration. To what extent these challenges could be powerful enough to prevent the project, however, is a political economic question which would be dependent on the power dynamics and resources available across geographical scales, as the project is global in its aim and nature, politically and economically endorsed by the state from different tiers of government. So far, the interests of the project's proponents appear to be dominant in deploying state institutions and manipulating state policies; on the other hand, assisted by the mass media, public opinion against the project has grown steadily at the local level. The state and private interest actors who are more powerful and well-equipped to build formal and informal alliances across scales could potentially prevail, unless less powerful groups widen their resistance on the ground and remain uncompromised in their fight against the Benoa reclamation project.

Conclusion

The complexity and uncertainty in the Benoa Bay case is a product of a complex relationship between the state's mode of development in the area, the fragmentation of state structures caused by decentralisation, as well as the ongoing rent-seeking tied to the operations of oligarchy in Indonesia. It seems clear that Tanjung Benoa villagers' initial support for the TWBI to rehabilitate Pulau Pudut, to build health and education facilities, was from the outset directly related to the failure of previous state-sponsored development projects and the inability, or reluctance, of the state to undertake its responsibilities and to be responsive to local aspirations in the first place. Unlike in the New Order period, where environmental discourse had been used to strengthen state's "interventionist role" and "bureaucratic expansion" (Warren 1998, 230), in the reform era, environmental matters have been used to justify the need for private enterprise to step in by undertaking the supposed state social and environmental services—constructing infrastructure, providing education and health services, and 'conserving' the environment.

Having said that, the alignment of political and economic forces and the use of the state apparatus to serve vested interests rather than public interests demonstrate a continuation of the New Order practices in a significantly different structural setting. It is not 'the absence of spatial plans' that has led to unconstrained government practices in favour of vested interests as argued by Moeliono (2011, 308) in the case of West Java. The Benoa Bay case, in fact, shows that although a set of spatial plans for governing the bay had been established, once a development project is proposed by an economically and politically powerful investor, the plans were revised and adjusted by the government to advance the interests of the project, against its own environmental and social commitments. Hence, the main issue is not whether or not a spatial plan exists in governing a particular space, but rather, whose interests are advanced in the planning. In brief, the problem appears to be less legal than political economic in natures.

In August 2018, it was reported by the media that the AMDAL process was stopped. This was due to the fact that since 25 August 2018 the location permit had been expired and the Ministry of Marine and Fisheries did not extend the permit. A relatively long period of time faced by the TWBI in finishing its AMDAL was caused by its difficulty dealing with socio-cultural impacts of the project of that the opponent groups rely their arguments upon. The opponent groups were very pleased to hear the news and they celebrated their victory by stating Balinese had won the cause against Tomy Winata. In addition, the newly elected governor and vice-governor of Bali, Wayan Koster-Cok Ace, has declared that their administration rejects the Benoa Bay project. However, this euphoria appeared to be temporary as it was a strategy of noise reduction because in October 2018, Bali would be the host of the 2018 Annual Meetings of the International Monetary Fund and the World Bank. By 'freezing' Winata's project, the national government expected there would be no demonstration and protest banners on the island which might affect the image of the Government of Indonesia before the international delegates. Indeed, the strategy worked as expected and after the meetings, in mid-December 2018, the Ministry of Marine Affairs and Fisheries finally issued a new location permit for the TWBI indicating the AMDAL process had been resumed. The struggles also continued.

7

Rescaling Space and Resistance

The case study chapters have discussed how the environmental and socio-cultural crisis have become public concerns in contemporary Bali and how policymakers have responded to these concerns. This chapter is devoted as a comparative chapter of the three case studies. In doing so, I examine at least three features shared across the case. The first one is the development of new modes of spatial governance which dominantly is influenced by the logic of instrumentalisation of space. The logic that operates on the use of economics as the ultimate measure of value—through which space is commercialised, commodified, and privatised to advance tourism investments and widen its global markets—has an inherent contradiction, in which it advances particular interests at the expense of other interests. The second feature is the use of law and institution as a resource in social conflicts. Here, as the relations of power are embedded in particular configurations of space, reorganising space necessarily involved contestations to capture and navigate law and institution in order to maintain and obtain control over space, people, and resources. The third feature is the character of power struggles that pose diverse meanings of space and place against narrow commercialisation and private interest. In this regard, it discusses how the attempts to reorganise spaces in contemporary Bali are pursued through a rescaling

A. Wardana, *Contemporary Bali*, https://doi.org/10.1007/978-981-13-2478-9_7

process and how this process is adjusted, manipulated, and resisted by social forces whose interests and visions of the social world are implicated by such process.

The chapter is divided into four sections. First, I will demonstrate the ways in which space is reorganised by policymakers in Bali through the politics of rescaling upward, downward, and outward. Secondly, I will discuss how law and institutional structures in Balinese society have been navigated to pursue vested interests. Thirdly, I will examine the implications of rescaling to resistance in contemporary Bali. Finally, I draw a short conclusion for the chapter.

Rescaling Spatial Configurations

In this section, I will assess contemporary modes of spatial governance by considering the interplay between the pluralistic legal and institutional structures and the experimentation with institutional hybrids to address the perceived crisis shaped by environmental and cultural tensions and conflicts. The politics of scale is an essential feature in this respect. Here, I conceive 'scale' as 'fluid and dynamic' because it is "produced, contested, and transformed through a range of socio-political and discursive processes, strategies and struggles over what that social space contains" (Robertson et al. 2002, 475). Since law and space interact in a mutually constitutive dynamic (Blomley 1994), reorganising space will necessarily require a new legal configuration in providing legitimacy for its institutional arrangement (Robertson et al. 2002). Thus, this section takes the 'rescaling' of spatial organisation, which is not a monolithic process, as a focus of analysis in order to provide an adequate understanding of how new institutions have emerged or pre-existing institutions have been transformed for the purpose of governing space, people, and resources in a rapidly changing social field.

Given the typologies of scale ranging from global to local, traditionally, there are two rescaling strategies to transform state functions, downward and upward. Rescaling down means shifting the scale of state functions from one tier of government to a lower level of government, for example, through decentralisation from the national government to subnational institutions (Reed and Bruyneel 2010; Cohen 2012). Rescaling up refers to transferring state functions from one particular scale to a wider one, for example, from the local or national to the global (Reed and Bruyneel 2010; Cohen 2012). Recently, another aspect of the transformation of state function has been through an 'outward' strategy involving new networks and social actors located within similar or cross-scale configurations, but institutionally outside the state, be it the market or civil society (Reed and Bruyneel 2010; Cohen 2012). In the 'outward' transformation, a given space is no longer solely governed by the state, but its governance may be transferred to non-state actors or state/non-state collaborations (co-governance or public-private partnerships) (see Jessop 1998; Bevir 2011).

In the Balinese cases, a combination of such rescaling process has been deployed involving a more complicated set of aims and outcomes than the prevailing neoliberal paradigm might suggest. In the case of the Sacred Space of Uluwatu Temple (Chap. 4), for instance, the temple has long been governed by *awig-awig* (*adat* law) of Desa Pakraman Pecatu based on their local conceptions of sacred space. The *awig-awig* then has been superimposed by a religious law of the 1994 PHDI *Bhisama* on sacred space, and complicated further by the adoption of the Bhisama into the state law dealing with spatial planning, the 2005 Spatial Planning Regulation for Bali Province. However, there was no manifested protest expressed over the adoption of *Bhisama* in the spatial planning regulation at that time due to no substantial effects to the village. Constructions of tourist accommodation were also massively taking place within the sacred radius in the early 2000s by disregarding the regulation. Protests from Pecatu Villagers openly emerged when external actors to the village, mass media, and civil societies groups exposed the violations to the Bhisama and the spatial planning regulation and demanded the provincial government to control rapid tourism development within the sacred radius. They were concerned with the fact that the temple that is provincially significant for Balinese Hindus has been spiritually 'polluted' by massive tourism facilities within its sacred radius, which was permitted by the District Government of Badung. As a response, the Uluwatu Temple is scaled upward by the provincial government to designate it as a 'provincial strategic area', of which its governance is located under provincial government's authority aiming at protecting its spiritual integrity.

As shown in the study case, Pecatu Villagers were not passive recipients of the decisions of the provincial government that may implicate their economic interests. Instead, they expressed their disagreement through series of struggles across scales, mobilising local institutions at the village level, protests and demonstrations at the district and provincial level targeting policymakers, as well as judicial reviews to the Supreme Court at the national level. They argue that such designation might affect them economically. Due to strong resources mobilisation and alliances to political elites and tourism industries across scales to influence the dynamics of decision making over the provincial zoning regulation, the provincial government and the Provincial House of People Representative (DPRD) eventually relax provisions on the *Bhisama* through subdivision to accommodate Pecatu's demands. The regulation also acknowledges the authority of the local customary village, Desa Pakraman Pecatu, to govern the sacred space based on its *adat* law (*awig-awig*). Hence the governance of the sacred radius of the Uluwatu Temple is pushed outward to the *adat* institutional structure. Having said this, it does not mean that the provincial government gives up their spatial governance authority solely to Desa Pakraman Pecatu, but rather, to situate local governance within a wider 'nested' institutional structure dealing with sacred space. In other words, the sacred space of Uluwatu Temple is now governed based on a complex configuration of institutional structures in which Desa Pakraman Pecatu, a non-state institution, becomes one of the governing institutions alongside district, provincial, and national governments. There are 10 Sad Kahyangan and 252 Dang Kahyangan temples across Bali, each of which has a designated sacred space surrounding it. The *Bhisama* religious ruling specifies the sphere of sanctity for Sad Kahyangan as five kilometres and for Dang Kahyangan as a two-kilometre radius. Hence, similar 'nested' spatial governance arrangements will also apply to those temples across the island in which the spatial implication would be that around 34.13% of Bali falls within this category of the sphere of sanctity (see Bappeda Bali 2009, V-68).

Similarly, an upward rescaling process is also undertaken by the provincial government to the Subak Landscape of Catur Angga Batukaru and Benoa Bay. In the 2009 Spatial Planning Regulation for Bali Province, both areas are designated as a 'provincial strategic area' respectively in terms of social-cultural importance (in the case of Subak Landscape) and in terms of economic importance (in the case of Benoa Bay). In the Subak Landscape of the Catur Angga Batukaru case (Chap. 5), rescaling governance upward has been the main logic of the inscription of the landscape to the UNESCO World Heritage Convention, a global regime dealing with the 'common heritage of humankind', in order to scale up Jatiluwih's village tourism to attract the global tourism market. Accordingly, as a World Heritage Site and a provincial strategic area, the Subak Landscape then would legally be managed by the provincial government, who attempts to push the management outward through the establishment of co-governing bodies involving government officials, representatives of NGOs, academics and private enterprises, and local communities.

The outward process brings into play a close interaction between global governance schemes such as the World Heritage Regime with its own institutional arrangements, rules and procedures, decision making and compliance mechanisms, and domestic local institutional settings, with their already complex legal and institutional configurations, both within the state structures (national, provincial, district, and village) and between state and non-state structures (*adat* village and *subak* association). This global-local interaction has given rise to a new mode of World Heritage Management based on a co-governance model between state and non-state institutions: the Governing Assembly of the World Heritage Sites at the provincial level and the Governing Body of Jatiluwih Tourist Attraction at the district level. The 'rules of the game' used by the governing institutions to a large extent are in the form of 'soft law'[1] derived from World Heritage guidance and operational procedures. The decision as to whether or not those hybrid institutions are able to comply with the 'soft law' required to govern a site having 'outstanding universal values', and to what extent the integrity of these environmental and cultural values may be compromised is decided by an international committee under the UNESCO World Heritage Regime.[2]

[1] Soft law, here, refers to a range of legal and non-legal instruments that provide a large degree of flexibility and discretion in undertaking obligations (Gruchalla-Wesierski 1984).

[2] Unlike other international environmental conventions in which decisions are made based on consensus of all their state parties, decisions under the World Heritage Convention are made by the 22 countries elected to the World Heritage Committee representing its 192 state parties. For further discussion on these matters, see Goodwin (2008).

However, this upward and outward rescaling process is in fact pulled downward by the District Government of Tabanan by designating Jatiluwih Village as its district strategic area in terms of tourism in order to extract revenues from heritage tourism. Therefore, the Subak Landscape is pulled by social and governmental actors to different scales, where their interests over the landscape and benefits arising from its status as a World Heritage Site are served at best. More recently, due to the inability of the provincial government to make the District Government of Tabanan comply with the management regime suggested by the World Heritage Committee (WHC), the national government takes over its governance by designating the landscape as the national strategic area, through which it may exercise a more powerful authority over the district government than that of the provincial government.

In the case of the Benoa Bay reclamation development, pushing outward spatial governance is relatively straightforward. Indeed, the outward rescaling process appears to be the dominant logic in this case, where a part of the state's authority to govern 'commons' space, to the extent of transforming the bay with the construction of artificial islands, would be delegated to TWBI, a private enterprise. In this case, this outward process is justified by the fragmentation of state institutional structures dealing with the bay areas, which leads to uncertainty due to the governance gap. On the one hand, decentralisation provides more roles to the regional government in governing water areas of Benoa Bay.[3] On the other hand, the designation of Benoa Bay as a national strategic area for international tourism and economic development, and simultaneously as a protected area, has brought governing authority back to the national government.

To address the governance gap, delineation is pursued by granting *hak pengelolaan* (the right to management) to a private enterprise owned by a national powerful tycoon. If the artificial islands planned by Winata's TWBI are built, the spatial and environmental governance of Benoa Bay

[3] Benoa Bay, as a coastal and water area, is regulated under Law No 27/2007 on Coastal Area and Small Island Management. Article 7 mandates the regional government in designating coastal and small island areas for strategic planning, zoning, management, and utilisation of the areas. However, this does not cover all water areas of Benoa Bay, since there have been pre-existing rights granted to several institutions either public or private over some part of this zone (see Chap. 6).

to a large extent will fall within the company's domain. This model of spatial governance would provide the legal basis for the TWBI to operate as a governing body within its special designated areas, making decisions on land use, and enforcing other public rules within this semi-private space, heavily policed by the company's security forces, alongside its primary profit-making enterprises. The manipulation of decentralised governance is apparently aimed at shifting scales in order to make project approvals possible to date involving collusion from all levels of government except the *adat* village sphere.

In brief, the cases of Bali illustrate how the spatial rescaling process has compounded existing institutional pluralism. This not only exacerbates overlapping institutional networks between state and non-state agencies at multiple levels, but also results in more fragmented and divergent competing interests over space and the environment. This pluralism does not imply a reduction in the role of the state because politically the state remains the primary locus of power play in defining institutional capacity, decision making, as well as the forms of empowerment, representation, and participation that are to be engaged or subverted (Reed and Bruyneel 2010).

In this model, state institutions play two roles at the same time. On the one hand, they are components of newly established governing institutions, for example, in the context of institutional hybrids in the case of the Subak Landscape of Catur Angga Batukaru. On the other hand, they become a meta-regulator through which these hybrid governing institutions and arrangements are established, transformed, and maintained. In this role, the different tiers of government act by regulating the ways in which sacred space should be governed using customary legal claims to constrain the implementation of state law in the case of Uluwatu Temple, or to impose state law in efforts to circumvent *adat* community resistance to the Benoa project. In the case of the Subak Landscape, the government plays its role as meta-regulator by establishing the Governing Assembly and the Governing Body, together with their different 'rules of the game' in managing the World Heritage Sites. The role of meta-regulator in the context of Benoa Bay could be exercised by granting a right of management (*hak pengelolaan*) to TWBI and setting up the conditionalities for the company to govern some part of the commons space of Benoa Bay as a mechanism for supposed coordination of integrated coastal management of the area.

Navigating Law and Institutions

As discussed above, spatial governance in contemporary Bali has been rescaled upward and downward to different tiers of government and transferred to non-state or hybrid institutions. These rescaling processes necessarily require reorganisation of institutionalised power. Agrawal (2003, 257) posits that "if institutions are the product of conscious decisions of specific individuals and groups…then it may also be reasonable to suppose that institutional choices by powerful groups deliberately aim to disadvantage marginal and less powerful groups". Similarly, the rescaling process, by its very nature, is also contested, since these processes are not only a discursive exercise by the state, but a political means to distribute power and resources to particular social interests (Cohen and Bakker 2014). In consequence, the rescaling process has attempted to reduce or redirect social conflicts towards more tolerable outcomes through a particular mode of participation, referring to "institutional structures and ideologies that shape the inclusion and exclusion of individuals and groups in the political process" (Jayasuriya and Rodan 2007, 774).

In this context, it is important to look at how development agencies justify exclusions and inclusions in their modes of public participation. Cohen's concepts of (2012) 'output' and 'input' legitimacy prove to be useful for this understanding. 'Input legitimacy' is achieved by the presence of certain groups at the decision-making stage of the process; while 'output legitimacy' depends upon whether or not the outcomes of participation reflect the common interest. The second type of legitimacy is very often used to justify the exclusion of certain groups in the decision-making process by claiming that it is practically impossible to include all community members in the process. In fact, what matters in this type is that all interests have been taken into account by some representational claim (Cohen 2012).

In Bali, such exclusionary justification has been used in the World Heritage nomination process for the Subak Landscape of Catur Angga Batukaru (Chap. 5), and also in the Environmental Impact Assessment (AMDAL) process of the TWBI Project in Benoa (Chap. 6). In both cases, critical voices were deliberately excluded from the decision-making process by employing a range of strategies. The obvious one was a scalar strategy of forum construction, where an arena of participation is structured in order to position favourable groups and individuals to be able to mobilise resources and strategically make use of existing structural opportunities (Reed and Bruyneel 2010). In the nomination of the Subak Landscape of Catur Angga Batukaru, the consultation process was only conducted in Jatiluwih Village, the core zone of the landscape. Only village (*desa*) level institutions were invited to be involved, leaving out the lower-level local institutions of *banjar* and *subak* where meaningful interactions between members are more likely to occur. Local communities outside the core zone have been left behind not only in terms of information and decision making, but also in terms of the material benefits arising from tourist visits to the site. In the Benoa Bay case, the shift in scale from regional government (Bali Province) to national government in Jakarta to process TWBI's environmental impact assessment (AMDAL) has distanced opponent groups from being able to meaningfully participate in and challenge the project directly through the decision-making processes. Due to a lack of resources, opponents have been unable to go back and forth between Bali and Jakarta to attend the AMDAL meetings and consultations. Thus, the scalar strategy determines which institutional structures are granted relevance or not in providing representation for assessing project impacts. Once again, this strategy does not only define the framework of participation but, in the process, the distribution of power and resources (cf. Hameiri and Jones 2014).

Given the essential role played by social institutions in Balinese society, social actors involved in conflict would attempt to navigate them for pursuing their interests. Both the Subak Landscape and Benoa Bay cases also demonstrate deliberation of powerful groups in crafting new institutions for their benefit, masked by the rhetoric of representing 'the people' and 'in the pursuit of common good' as moral 'input' and 'output' legitimacy claims. The institutional complexity in turn has complicated the ways in which conflicts and resistance are expressed or suppressed. The complex institutional and legal constellation in contemporary Bali has been shaped by social conflicts, but it also shapes how conflicts should be expressed. The case of the Subak Landscape shows how the constellation can be used tactically by local leaders such as the *pekaseh* to engage in upward rescaling, taking the unsatisfactory situation to the attention of higher (and outside) authorities in hopes of intervention that might circumvent intermediate power regimes. In the Benoa Bay case, the fragmented structures of the state in governing the bay have made possible a game of power play by hiding behind each other's putative authorities. Consequently, fragmentation among opponent groups—in targeting different institutions as the central focus for advocacy—became more apparent.

In the post-authoritarian period, local Balinese institutional structures, especially *adat* institutions, have often been sites for "contestation and engagement" in articulating local common interests. In general, it has been *adat* institutions and relationships that have proved most able to "produce solidarities that strengthen the community hand when negotiating with state and private interests" (Warren 2007, 182). Thus, engaging as well as negotiating with *adat* institutions, as legitimate representatives of local common interest, has become an important, if not required, strategy for the state and private entities to build alliances in undertaking a development project in a given locality. 'Common interest' cannot be assumed as a given feature of community deliberations because, of course, *adat* communities are not homogeneous, and their processes often generate internal contestation. Here, the common interest should be seen as one provisionally constructed within a particular temporal and spatial context articulated by an institutionalised authority that has a legitimate moral and political claim to representation. The construction of such interest may sometimes involve repression and exclusion, and it also may seal or mask the particular interests of a dominant group. To the extent that these institutions are able to build or claim representative status, they increasingly become objects of governmentality projects, which have particular consequences for internal friction, and especially for leadership.

In the Uluwatu case, the ability of local economic and political elites to navigate the *adat* village has made the use of it strategically against the state spatial planning regulation by employing a customary principle of *adat* autonomy. Desa Pakraman Pecatu and Badan Perwakilan Desa (BPD/Village Representative Council), representing customary and administrative villages respectively, were at the foreground in articulating local disappointment with the adoption of the *Bhisama* religious ruling imposing a fixed sacred space through the Provincial Regulation on Spatial Planning for Bali (Perda RTWR Bali No. 16/2009). Although not all customary village members own a plot of land within the five-kilometre designated sacred space of Uluwatu Temple, through the *sangkepan* (assembly), the interests of landholding villagers, local political elites, and tourism entrepreneurs have been articulated as encompassing a wider 'common' interest because the implementation of *Bhisama* in the village will affect not only the landowners, but also the local economy and livelihoods of ordinary villagers who heavily depend on tourism. Notably, the importance of local responsibility for supporting temple ritual has been an important argument recruiting villagers to the developmentalist cause.

In the case of Benoa Bay, on the other hand, local interests shifted from the desperate need to rehabilitate the common space of Pulau Pudut and to improve local infrastructure to concerns with the risks of the TWBI development for their economy, socio-cultural values, and environment. At first, villagers were supportive of the project, but after gaining sufficient information to make a determination, they finally decided to reject the project by articulating their newly evaluated common interest through the *adat* village (*banjar*/*desa pakraman*) institution. The process of building the perception of common interest to oppose Winata's project was essentially started by channelling aspirations at the *banjar* level where day-to-day interactions take place. Once all *banjar* agreed to reject the project, they then demanded a meeting at the *desa adat* level that has released the official decision of Desa Pakraman Tanjung Benoa to refuse the project based on *adat* members' consensus. This demonstrates that when the interests of outside forces are at odds with what is considered as a local common good, the *adat* institutional structure provides a better vehicle for such articulation and mobilisation than does the 'well-disciplined' administrative village (*desa dinas*) or *kelurahan* structures.

In a highly complex institutional configuration, such as in the case of the Subak Landscape of Catur Angga Batukaru, defining 'common interest' is far from straightforward. Each institution has its own understanding of the variety of frameworks of legitimacy and representation that exist, where one interest may overlap and sometimes become incompatible with another. As we saw in Chap. 5, participation in the nomination and implementation process establishing the UNESCO World Heritage Site was mostly conducted at the core zone, Jatiluwih Village, by channelling participation to local institutions at the village (*desa*) level rather than engaging the lower-level hamlets (*banjar*) and irrigation institutions (*subak tempek*) where a more meaningful participation process might take place. Beyond the core zone, a cherry-picking consultation appeared to occur, where who was invited, on what basis, and why were highly selective.

The issues that could be articulated in the consultation process were confined to expectations in relation to the World Heritage Listing, while oppositional voices against the nomination were overlooked. One important institution in this regard has been the Subak Gede of Jatiluwih that directly participated in the process, but faced difficulty in pursuing and defending its members' interests before the other local institutions which claim to represent wider constituencies, *desa pakraman* and *desa dinas*, and which include non-farming residents. This complex setting explains why a hybrid institution for governing the site has been proposed and established as a 'nested' institutional configuration to bring about better coordination and negotiation between those institutions. However, the hybrid structure of the Governing Assembly at the provincial level and Governing Body at the district level have been instrumentalised by those who are best equipped to hijack such institutions for extracting revenues and maintaining their power. This is exactly because the planners and policymakers behind this designation overlooked the legal and institutional complexities, local dynamics, imbalances of power, as well as values that underpin local norms and practices within the village and across scales.

Institution may have different faces defined by its leadership interests towards particular issues. The state institutions should not also be assumed to have uniform interests in every issue in concerned. In the case of the Subak Landscape of Catur Angga Batukaru, the Provincial Government of Bali has been the alliance of Jatiluwih *subak* communities in struggling for fairer benefit sharing from heritage tourism. It has been advocating the revenues gained from all heritage sites in Bali to be managed by the provincial governing body. The central government in these cases appears to be in favour of the provincial government in attempting to neutralise the district government's interests to extract district revenues. Similarly, in the case of Uluwatu Temple, the provincial government was also supported by the Agama-Adat-Akademisi (AAA/Religious, Adat and Academic leaders) groups and NGO activists in preserving Uluwatu's sacred radius. They argue that the governance of Uluwatu's scared space would be effective when it is under the authority of the provincial government, as the temple has a province-wide significance. The argument is based on a naïve assumption that the provincial government is immune from elite captures so that it might enforce the regulations consistently. As the case of Benoa Bay shows us, this is not the reality. In this case, the state institutions and officials, either at the central, provincial, and district levels, have been captured by Winata's company in facilitating the development of a resort enclave in the bay.

In the Benoa Bay case, however, the *adat* institution has been the most vital institution to articulate local dissent against the project. In addition, desa adat also managed to organise inter-*adat* village solidarity known as Pasubayan Desa Pakraman Tolak Reklamasi Teluk Benoa (Pasubayan). The cause that is shared by the adat villages joining the Pasubayan is that Benoa Bay is regarded as a sacred space where religious rituals take place. Hence, the argument against the project moves towards the protection of the sacred space of Benoa Bay from encroachment. In contrast, the cases of the Subak Landscape and the Uluwatu Temple demonstrate how adat villages have in fact been the power broker of vested interests.

Furthermore, the Indonesian Hindu Dharma Organisation (PHDI) was also a target to be captured in advancing the reclamation project in Benoa Bay. Within the religious organisation, there has been a friction on how PHDI should take their stance with regard to the Winata's project. Structurally, the PHDI consists of three internal structures, the *Sabha Panditha* (Priest Council) the highest body in which the daily management is conducted by the *Pengurus Harian* (Executive Committee), and supported by the *Sabha Walaka* (Expert Council) as an expert body to the priest assembly. Ketut Wiana, a high official in the Executive Committee, openly supported the reclamation project and argued that 'reclamation-based revitalisation' (*revitalisasi berbasis reklamasi*) does not violate the Bhisama of sacred space.[4] In fact, the project may revitalise the ecological and spiritual significance of the sacred space of Benoa Bay that has been

[4] Interview with Ketut Wiana, the chair of the Executive Committee of PHDI Pusat, 5 September 2014.

neglected for many years (*Berita Bali*, 26/10/2015). In contrast, Putu Wirata Dwikora, a member of the Expert Council confronted Wiana's argument by saying that it was not an official statement of the PHDI but Wiana's personal opinion. The conflict within the PHDI was escalated when both camps tried to pull the Priest Council to be on their side. Eventually, the council established a special team consisting of nine high priests known as the Team 9 in order to assess both positions and formulate recommendations for the PHDI's decision.

In April 2016, a *Pesamuhan Sabha Pandita* (the Assembly of Priest Council) was conducted to enact decisions on Benoa Bay and Besakih, two main issues that attracted controversy among the Balinese public. In public, however, two different decisions circulated. They were Decision No. 1/KEP/SP Parisada/IV/2016 concerning Benoa Bay Sacred Areas (Decision No. 1) circulated by the Expert Council that declared Benoa Bay as a sacred space and hence should be preserved, and Decision No. 3/ Sabha Pandita Parisada/IV/2016 concerning Recommendation on the Besakih National Tourism Strategic Areas and the Benoa Bay Areas (Decision No. 3) circulated by the Executive Committee. The general chairman of the committee announced that the correct decision was Decision No 3, and in fact, it was the only decision that was posted in the official website of PHDI (www.phdi.or.id), whereas Decision No 1 was fake (*Pos Bali*, 13/05/2016). Decision No 3 only managed to produce vague wordings on the status of Benoa Bay by affirming that "within the Benoa Bay areas[,] there are several sacred sites that have to be protected, managed, preserved their sacredness by all parties without exception" in accordance to the 1994 Bhisama PHDI and the laws and regulations in Indonesia.

In its recommendation, it urges "to unite to protect the sanctity of Bali Island through the protection of areas that have been designated as sacred areas, including sacred sites within Benoa Bay, and to enable its utilisation and management for people's welfare as long as it does not 'pollute' and degrade its sacred values". The wordings imply that not all the bay areas are sacred, but rather, some parts of it are sacred sites, meaning areas that are not designated as sacred sites could be utilised for development. In fact, two out of eight highest priests chairing the assembly refused to sign such a decision, since they seemed to support Decision No 1 circulated by the Expert Council. This shows how the foremost religious organisation that is supposed to enforce its religious ruling of the 1994 *Bhisama* appears to be divided in the contexts of the Benoa Bay reclamation project. Such division provides a basis for each group involved in the conflict to choose the decision that underpins its interests in the conflict.

In brief, the ability to capture institutions is important in conflicts. As we have seen in the case study chapters, not only do the state institutions become the source of power to be 'captured', but also Bali's traditional institutions are mobilised by social forces. This is exactly because both formal and informal institutions have the capacities to generate rules and orms through their legal embodiments. Austin Turk (1976) once noted that social actors involved in a social conflict would need to utilise the law for legally justifying their interests. Here, the law becomes a resource or a 'weapon in social conflicts' (Turk 1976). Unlike Turk's narrow conception of law being attributed only to state law, in the context of conflicts in contemporary Bali, the law should be conceived in a broader manner to encompass different forms of legal orders available in society, as advocated by legal pluralists. State institutions, as the supreme organised political power, through state law, may generate laws advancing particular interests at the expense of other interests. Similarly, the local institutions, as a 'semi-autonomous social field' (Moore 1973), may also generate rules and norms internally and may use state recognition to their autonomy to prevent the state law from intervening what is conceived as an internal affair.

Once social forces fail to capture state law on their side of a conflict, they turn to find alternative legitimate claims provided by non-state legal orders, be they the *bhisama* of sacred space in the case of Benoa Bay or customary rules of *desa-kala-patra* (place-time-circumstances) in the case of Uluwatu Temple, to challenge the rival's interests embodied in state law. How long the divergence of interests served by different legal orders can last will depend on how long the state may tolerate legal pluralism and its consequences without resorting it into the use of coercive power to bring the pluralism to an end. This is because from the logic of the state, state law should prevail above non-state legal orders whose legitimacy dependent on the state recognition. The recognition towards legal pluralism may be compromised when it contradicts the state interests for 'maintaining law and order' in society. In the end of the day, the use of force would define the winner and loser once a conflict is highly escalated towards a zero-sum condition.

Spaces of Resistance

In this section, I examine the nature of resistance in the three case studies and how the law plays its role to express or hinder dissent in Balinese society. The dominant picture of the island in this literature has been informed by the colonial construction of Bali as being a harmonious and peace-loving society, an imagery that has played a vital role in the early development of the tourism industry. Furthermore, when the tourism industry has penetrated Balinese society deeply as the overriding economic sector, any potential political and social disturbance should be prevented in order to protect the fragile economic sector (Lewis and Lewis 2009). Despite such prevention, following the rapid transformation towards industrial society, conflicts, resistance, and struggles to access and maintain power and resources have become more common. Hence, I attempt to show that Bali is far from harmonious and instead it should be seen as a site of struggles where different social forces get involved in power contests to control space, people, and resources.

Struggles in Balinese Society

In contrast to the romantic view of Bali introduced by the Dutch Colonial, the history of Bali has been full of conflicts and struggles. The Balinese has been familiar with the history of the invasion of Bali by the Majapahit Kingdom and the struggles of King Bedahulu against such invasion and other pre-colonial histories. The early establishment of the Dutch Colonial administration also triggered wars among the local rulers. Two most notorious wars against the Dutch were the *puputan* wars of Klungkung (1908) and Badung (1906). Moreover, under the indirect rule of the colonial administration, a group of peasants in Gianyar Regency protested against the heavy land tax imposed by the administration, and they eventually were executed by the king of Gianyar, who was in charge of maintaining law and order in the area (Robinson 1995). In the early 1900s, Balinese intellectuals trained by the Dutch under their ethical policy questioned the colonial policy of 'reinventing' the caste system, which hindered their social mobility to work within the colonial administration due to their background from lower caste ranks (Pringle 2004).

During the era of the independence movement, the Balinese was divided sharply in relation to the colonial administration. Two forces were involved: the colonial collaborators who supported the existence of the Dutch Colonial along with preserving Balinese 'culture' and 'tradition'; and the Republicans who opposed the colonial administration to get rid of 'feudalism' and the caste system (Robinson 1995, 16). As Robinson (1995, 16) observes, such division did not disappear after independence but in fact continually appeared in different forms, especially in political affiliations and struggles to capture the local state.[5] Such sharp division partly informed by their positions to the land reform policy gave a local context to the 1965–1966 mass killings, the bloodiest moment in Bali's history facilitated by military forces that had brought an end to the most politically active and modern mass organisations (peasants, labour, women as well as artists) ever occurred in early 1960s. In the aftermath, the Balinese then were involved in 'a conspiracy of silence', which then helped to shape the trajectory of the island under Suharto's New Order Regime for decades to come.

In spite of the authoritarian rule, a small scale of conflicts and resistance was far from absence. During the Green Revolution project, for instance, in contrast to Spiertz (2000) and Parker's (2003) claim that the acceptance of this modernisation of agriculture ran smoothly, resistance towards the project also emerged. As Birkelbach (1973) notes, the chief of *subak* (*kelian* or *pekaseh subak*) responded slowly to the imposed project from above due to their reluctance to change the old practices. She observes that "[o]ne example of this is in the slow introduction of the

[5] The political affiliations were divided into three major political parties in Bali, which were the Indonesian Nationalist Party (PNI), the Indonesian Communist Party (PKI), and the Indonesian Socialist Party (PSI). For further discussion, see Robinson (1995).

IR-5, IR-8, and IR-21 strains of high yield rices to Bali. Close to 9 percent of Java's fields have been planted with the new strains, but has only about 5 percent though the availability to both is substantially the same" (Birkelbach 1973, 160). A similar observation can also be found in Jatiluwih, in which local farmers refused to follow the state's directive to plant *padi bibit unggul* (high yield seeds). Given that every planting year is divided into two planting seasons, they adapted the directive by planting different rice varieties in each season. In the first season (January–June) farmers planted a local rice variety, *beras merah cendana,* known as red-rice of Jatiluwih. Meanwhile, in the second season, prior to the Green Revolution, they used to plant secondary crops (*palawija*), especially onion; later, they replaced them with high-yielding varieties (*mansur, serang*, etc.), as directed by the government. The adjustment that has been retained to date should be seen as a strategy of *subak* to navigate the state project by minimising the political risks derived from a direct confrontation with the state, considering that this took place in the period when *subak* and farmer organisations were systematically de-politicised following the 1965–1966 event.

A rather massive scale of resistance to the New Order eventually emerged in the early 1990s, at a moment when massive tourism investments flocked to the island, brought by Jakarta conglomerates. Such a big amount of capital investment was made possible by the oil boom in 1980s in seeking non-oil sectors for capital investments and the neoliberal policy of deregulation of the banking systems (Warren 1998). The most notorious project was the Bakrie Nirwana Resort (BNR), a luxury resort complex with its facilities, including an 18-hole golf course, in Tabanan, around 1991. Local farmers were forced to sell their agricultural land and those who refused to sell it were intimidated by the state officials and military forces or were labelled as an anti-development or a communist.

Finding difficulty in arguing based on the material interests to protect their land—an argument that would be closely associated with the Indonesian Peasant Front (*Barisan Tani Indonesia*/BTI), an Indonesian Communist Party's bow—made them to use different repertoires for expressing their refusal against the project. As the project was closely situated to the Temple of Pura Tanah Lot, one of the holiest temples for

Balinese Hindus, the local community, supported by student and civil society organisations, found a cultural argument, especially *adat* and religious rules on the sacred radius of the temple or sacred space, to enhance their stance against the state-backed project. In this argument lay a collective understanding that there should be no buildings or activities that might 'pollute' the sanctity of the temple. The argument at that time should be interpreted at least in two senses. First, it served as a borderline on what is culturally acceptable and what is not cultural acceptable according to local values. Those values have become the instrument through which the local community judge whether a tourism project is consistent or inconsistent to 'cultural tourism'—a concept in which Bali's tourism industry should be rooted in Balinese culture in order to ensure local control over the industry. Second, the argument served as a claim that cannot be easily neutralised by the state as it is rooted in Balinese cosmologies. Through this conflict, as discussed earlier, the 1994 *Bhisama* of PHDI concerning the sanctity radius of temples was enacted. Ever since, a similar set of cultural arguments has been used repeatedly in many mega-development projects across the island, including the reclamation of Serangan Island, the Garuda Wisnu Kencana (GWK), and even more recently in the Benoa Bay reclamation project.

Structural Conditions and Forms of Resistance

In social movement literature, the political opportunity theory embraces that the emergence of social movement is influenced by four main elements. They are: "(1) the relative openness or closures of the institutionalised political systems; (2) the stability or instability of that broad set of elites alignments that typically undergird a polity; (3) the presence or absence of elite allies; and (4) the state's capacity and propensity of repression" (Giugni 2009, 361). However, it should not be assumed that in a highly repressive structural condition, resistance and political dissents are absent. Very often, they are expressed in different ways. In this regard, social forces attempt creatively to navigate the structure to articulate their dissent with minimal political and legal risks. As discussed above, under the authoritarian regime of the New Order where open, material-based interests, political dissents would have been neutralised by state repressions, 'culture' was used strategically to be a repertoire of dissent, for example, in the case of Bakrie Nirwana Resort (BNR). On the one side, Balinese 'culture' in terms of artefacts since the colonial period has been regarded as the main competitiveness of Bali in the global tourism market. Hence, the degradation of Balinese culture would also mean a degradation of the island's competitive advantage, which in turn would affect the flow of revenues from the tourism sectors. On the other side, the Balinese whose cultural resources were a currency for negotiations employ 'culture' in terms of value to challenge state projects that may have implications on their livelihood.

The use of culture in contestations over space, people, and resources has been relatively persistent even after the fall of the authoritarian regime. In this regard, the collective identity in contemporary Bali's social movement has been built surrounding the notion of *masyarakat adat* (*adat* community). As we have learnt from the Benoa Bay Case, this form of collective identity is not essentially formed in the first place as a pre-given identity. But rather, resorting to *adat* as an identity for the movement is in fact a last resort for the local opponent groups in finding the next playing field in which they are more comfortable to play in order to pursue their collective interests once the formal venues have been navigated by powerful businesses and state interests. There are at least three conditions shaping this decision, which are history, structural settings, and strategic/tactical choices. Historically, '*adat*' provides a safer identifier for the local communities when strong political messages appear to be constrained due to the traumatic events of 1965–1966, in which Suharto's authoritarian regime built hegemony for at least three decades. Under this repressive condition, *adat* resistance, in fact, emerged when there were limited and restricted political opportunities to channel their voices of dissent against mass tourism development, except to cover up their materially rooted interests using the symbolic narrative of culture and *adat* identity.

Structurally, we know that Bali is a popular tourism destination in the world, in which tourism has been the overriding economic sector on the island. The tourism industry is very sensitive towards open political struggles and dissent. Tourists would be afraid to see a mass demonstration within the Balinese society, which they assumed to be a harmonious and peaceful society, as promoted in the travel brochures. Local communities are also very conscious that tourism is economically significant for their economy but at the same time they have to find a seemingly apolitical message to raise their concerns when the tourism industry crosses the border on what is socially and culturally accepted and not accepted. Strategically, resorting to *adat* serves two things. First, it is to draw boundaries between the locally rooted struggle from the urban middle-class struggle led by NGO and student activists. The boundary has to be made in order to avoid the submission of the local struggle under the NGO movement that is not necessarily having similar strategy and tactics and interests in opposing the project. Secondly and internally, the narrative of *adat* could suspend all social and political differences in the community to focus on what is conceived to be the most important common concern to be addressed.

Channelling collective identity of resistance to *adat* identity leads to the use of cultural forms of resistance, such as religious or *adat* rituals or ceremonies. In scholarly writing, the political role of religious/cultural rituals in Balinese society has been a subject of longstanding debate (see Geertz 1980; Schulte Nordholt 1991; MacRae 2005; Pedersen 2006). Balinese religious/cultural rituals in Western academic literature tend to be regarded as attributes of the state as charismatic spectacles that conjure imitation or a mechanism for concentration of power or a combination of both. None of them sees that rituals may also serve as a resource in social conflicts. Around the mid-2000s, a religious/cultural ritual was conducted as an expression of the refusal of the local communities towards a previous Tomy Winata project. The project planned to reclaim an estuary that is regarded as a sacred space by the local *adat* community in Berawa Beach of Tibubeneng, Badung, to build tourism accommodation. Eventually, the ritual managed to make the company exclude the estuary from its master plan. In the case of Benoa Bay, for instance, the form of cultural resistance was articulated by conducting an *adat* ritual of *Jagat Laknat Upadrawa*—aiming to curse the power holders who have committed religious and customary wrongdoing by facilitating the TWBI project—conducted by the opponents of Winata's project in Tanjung Benoa Village. In fact, this use of ritual was criticised by ForBali, because it was considered 'apolitical' and very likely to be imitated by the proponents of the project.[6]

---

[6] Interview with Luh Kartini, the director of the Bali Organic Association, on 10 August 2014; personal communication with Catur Haryani, the director of the Environmental Education Centre (Pusat Pendidikan Lingkungan Hidup/PPLH) Bali and member of ForBali, on 11 July 2014.

Observing the ritual closely reveals how they became a symbolic occupation of space aimed at building a sense of place and opening unmediated interaction and discussion on the risks of reclamation towards local livelihood. The ritual proves to be a political medium for disseminating information and analysing the internal strengths as it enables the local opponent group to map out their constituencies within the village since those who were supportive of the project were very unlikely to attend such rituals. It also widens the participation of the villagers to declare their refusal towards the project by involving women, elderly, children, priests, and other segments of the society who are not comfortable joining urban middle class forms of resistance, such as demonstrations, rallies, and campaigning through music concerts. To underestimate the potential of this cultural form of resistance, ForBali fails to take advantage of the potential for connecting environmental and cultural concerns through which environmental activism in Bali since the 1990s has engaged the general public (see Warren 1998; Strauss 2015).

Furthermore, the forms of resistance are also informed by the ways in which a society are socially organised. Like other societies, the Balinese is also stratified. The structures of stratification may be different from one locality to the other, based on status, precedence, or even class, showing Balinese is not a homogenous form of society. In the case of the Subak Landscape of Catur Angga Batukaru, and highland of Bali in general, the structure of precedence has been dominant to inform access over resources and power at the local level. As discussed in the Chap. 5, the first attendance of Pasek Badak to build a settlement in Jatiluwih Village has continually been understood as the relative privilege of Pasak Badak sub-clan's descendants to be appointed in leadership positions, either for traditional social organisations or for more modern state institutions. In addition, villagers are also strongly tied with a sense of family deriving from their ancestors as well as through cross-sub-clan marriages. Meanwhile in Pecatu Village, social status especially derived from the relative positions from the centre of power, the noble families, Jakarta conglomerates, foreign investors, or more recently local bureaucrats would be an essential resource to be heard in the community. The figures who manage to accumulate their economic and social resources may possibly dominate public discourse in the community. In Tanjung Benoa Village, however, a class relation is relatively apparent. Someone's stance toward the project is partly informed by the stance held by his/her employer. Those who work for a water sport company owned by an opponent figure against Winata's project tend to join the local opponent group while those who work for a company whose owner is supportive to the project tend to be more appreciative toward the project. Hence, the divided stances towards the TWBI Project in the village are intertwined with local political and economic contestations among the water sport owners as the local capitalist class.

As shown in the case studies, social structures in society define how conflicts should be expressed to be socially acceptable. The Case of Subak Landscape demonstrates how in Jatiluwih Village where social cohesion is relatively strong *pekaseh* and *subak* members are very reluctant to openly express their disagreement and disappointment towards the district government's established management regime. Avoidance has been one of the forms of resistance. It was not only exercised by farmers in Jatiluwih but also by Pecatu villagers whose interests were not implicated by the designation of Uluwatu Temple's sacred radius in the Provincial Spatial Planning Regulation. In addition, *subak* members of Subak Jatiluwih also have challenged the conditions by hitting back at dominant power interests using someone else's hand, especially the provincial and national governments whose positions are relatively contested with that of the district. What is clear from the experience of the Subak Landscape and Pecatu is that a frontal articulation of dissent will often have negative impacts on those who express it due to the imbalance in relations of power (Scott 1985) or legal and institutional constraints (Bal 2014), and the pressure to maintain social 'cohesion'. Many forms of resistance come to the surface with different degrees of success, but at the very least demonstrating that the overarching hegemony of economic and political elites in such a system should never be assumed.

Media, Civil Society, and Fragmentation

As suggested by the political opportunity theory, the post-authoritarian era of Indonesia, the fall of Suharto regime, has opened wider political opportunities to express political dissent in a more articulated manner. Civil society organisations have flourished rapidly, which then become the channel of public concerns and inform social dynamics in society. Bali is not an exception in this regard. The rapid growth of civil society organisations in the island has influenced local political dynamics and has become the vocal points of political mobilisations. Aspinall (2013a) regards Indonesia in the post-authoritarian era as a 'nation in fragments'. For him, fragmentation does not only occur within the state structures, but also in the spheres of civil society. The growth of civil society organisations following the fall of Suharto could not be assumed to be monolithic, as they have different values, objectives, or even tactical strategies to achieve their objectives. Although they technically are outside the state structures and the private enterprises, in their existence, they may also serve the interests of the state and businesses.

Their relative positions to a particular issue may also be informed by their donors, patrons, political affiliations, or elites captured. Among the three case studies, the case of Benoa Bay has clearly shown the fragmentation of civil society organisations between the pros and cons of TWBI's reclamation project. In this case, the scale of mobilisations is partly influenced by the presence of elite allies. Contestations among elites to access power and resources have been essential for them to ally with civil society activists in particular causes to challenge their competitors. There are a number of non-governmental organisations supportive of the project; to mention a few: Devisi Pemantau Pembangunan Bali (DPPB/Division on Bali's Development Monitoring), Gasos Bali, SKPPLH Bali, and Pospera Bali. Gerakan Solidaritas Sosial (Gasos/Social Solidarity Movement) Bali is a non-governmental organisation established by Lanang Sudira, a local politician. The Sekretariat Kerja Penyelamatan dan Pelestarian Lingkungan Hidup (SKPPLH/Working Secretariat on the Protection and Preservation of the Environment) Bali is an environmental organisation led by Made Mangku, a recipient of the Kalpataru environmental award from the Ministry of the Environment and previously an outspoken opponent of BTID's Serangan Island Reclamation Project. The Devisi Pemantau Pembangunan Bali (Bali Development Monitoring Division) was established around the time the controversy of the TWBI project emerged. The key person is Ngurah Mudita, a figure from the Kesiman noble family, who later was known to be one of architects of the project. Last but not least is the Pospera (*Posko Perjuangan Rakyat*)—an association of the 1998 student activists led by Adrian Napitupulu, the former leader of Forkot student movement and recently serving as a member of the National People's Representative Council (DPR) from PDI Perjuangan. Pospera Bali itself is led by Kadek Agus Ekanata, who happens to be TWBI's director of Human Resource Department.

Arguments and counter-arguments have been taking place in the media among the competing leaders of NGOs and other civil society organisations. Made Mangku of the SKPPLH Bali, who recently was persuaded to support the TWBI project, challenges the opponents of the TWBI project, especially ForBali, as having no scientific basis for their claims (*Koran Sindo*, 09/03/2015). Made Mangku is a water sports entrepreneur without scientific training, who argues that when the debate is moved towards a scientific basis, the outcome will be determined by which arguments are empirically and scientifically justified. On the one hand, civil society organisations supportive of the project have the advantage of simply echoing the studies conducted by the TWBI backed by the company's money, expertise, and networks, to underpin their position; on the other hand, civil society organisations opposed to the project have faced difficulty for want of resources to conduct the technical work required to establish the environmental and social risks of the project.

With regard to the role of the media in Balinese struggles, Warren (1998) notes how in many environmental cases in Bali, mass media has played a decisive role in widening the reach of constituents for mobilisations. The media, especially the *Bali Post*, as the oldest and biggest media company in Bali, has been an important source of information through which the wider public responds to it. A relatively supportive and optimistic viewpoint of the media towards the inscription of the *Subak* Landscape of Catur Angga Batukaru to the World Heritage Site served to create a conducive climate for the government to advance the agenda and to make the agenda almost free from criticism, although fears and sceptical positions were also expressed by subak members at the village level. Compared with the previous attempt to list the Temple of Besakih to the WHC, partly due to the role of the media, especially the *Bali Post*, public opinion managed to cease the government from undertaking such an attempt (see Darma Putra and Hitchcock 2005). In the successive nomination, the media played its role to build a national pride if the *subak* system as a Balinese heritage under threats was recognised by the international community. In doing so, it took a position by 'silencing' the other side of the story, especially with regards to the concerns and fears expressed by *subak* members on the impacts of the listing on their livelihood.

The role of media in advancing political dissent could be seen in the case of Benoa Bay. The TWBI project was publicly exposed by the *Bali Post* in the end of June 2013 and ever since the *Bali Post* covered the project critically as its editorial priority for at least three years by openly promoting its political stance almost every day in the front page. A study conducted by Indira and Birowo (2013) to examine the objectivity and proportionality of news on the Benoa Bay Project found that from 49 news contents during the early period of coverage (27 June–18 August 2013), the coverage did not meet the objective criteria of news, as it consisted of a mix of facts, opinions, and imbalances achieved by highlighting the opponents of the project. However, such allegation has no significance, as the *Bali Post* has been devoted to be a conservative campaign media in preserving Balinese culture.

As a result of persistent headlines, the *Bali Post* has managed to dominate public opinion and in turn opened up possibilities for an unprecedented scale of mobilisation against the project. Politically, the *Bali Post*'s opposing position was informed by the rivalry of its owner, Satria Naradha, and the newly elected governor of Bali, Made Mangku Pastika, in the 2013 Gubernatorial Elections. Such a sharp conflict came about after Mangku Pastika filed a lawsuit against the *Bali Post*, its owner and managing editor, concerning flawed news about the governor in response to the Budaga-Kemoning conflict.[7] The Civil Court of Denpasar decided in its verdict that the *Bali Post* was involved in civil wrongdoing and ruled it to ask for apologies publicly.[8] Hence, in the following election,

[7] The conflict was concerning boundaries between Desa Pakraman Budaga and Desa Pakraman Kemoning in Klungkung District, leaving one villager dead. Responding to the conflict, Mangku Pastika was interviewed by journalists and commented emotionally that both *adat* villages would be terminated if they could not stop the conflict. The day after that, the *Bali Post* put out a headline stating that Pastika seeks to terminate the *adat* village, which might be interpreted to apply for all *adat* villages in Bali.

[8] Case Number 723/Pdt.G/2011/PN.Dps.

the *Bali Post* openly endorsed the other candidate, Puspayoga, a noble figure from Puri Satria who once was the vice-governor for Pastika. Losing the election has made the *Bali Post* take an oppositional position *vis-a-vis* the re-elected Governor Pastika and found its interests aligned with NGO activists, in the context of the Benoa Bay project. Gendo Suardana, the leading figure of ForBali and a well-known critic of Pastika, was given an exclusive program named the Merah Putih Talkshow to be aired on Bali TV, a TV channel owned by the *Bali Post* Media Group. Meanwhile, in the other camp, the competitors of the *Bali Post* tended to be the 'mouthpiece' for the governor to counter allegations from the *Bali Post* and the opponent groups.[9] In brief, the crack among elites has influenced the dynamics of alliances in opposing and proposing Winata's project.

The advanced development of information technology, especially the Internet and smartphones, has also shaped the ways through which public opinion is built. Social media, such as *Facebook*, *Twitter*, and others, are channels where news and information from conventional media are circulated and commented upon openly. Hence, social media does not replace the role of conventional media, as it just complements it by widening its reach and enabling dramatisation through uncensored commentaries. As a result, debates on social media, and the Internet in general, on particular issues were unavoidable, especially in the case of Benoa Bay, as both proponents and opponents of the reclamation project mobilise their cyber armies respectively.

However, in the case of the Subak Landscape of Catur Angga Batukaru, the use of social media predominantly tends to be in line with the government's interests to 'promote' tourism in the landscape. Meanwhile, the World Heritage sceptics have not been able to use social media to express their concerns towards the listing since they are not tech savvy, given their economic conditions and ages. In fact, their disappointments are disseminated through local assemblies (*sangkepan*), gossip, as well as encounters with outsiders. Through these, the messages are expected to circulate further in reaching a wider audience and those who have the authority to

---

[9] The most notorious in this media group has been the *Pos Bali*, whose editor-in-chief happened to be Made Nariana, a former journalist for the *Bali Post*.

respond to the messages. For the case of Uluwatu, conventional media, especially the *Bali Post*, played a vital role in depicting Pecatu Village as being co-opted by vested interests in its battle against the newly enacted spatial planning regulation. However, social media was not really a significant instrument to influence the dynamics of alliances and contestations in the case of Uluwatu Temple, as it was not yet popular at that time. Dissemination of local information to enhance solidarity within the village was pursued through the production of alternative media of Majalah Catu, where local issues are discussed and disseminated.

Ambiguity and Ambivalence

The tourism industry indeed keeps pushing its social and ecological limits in the island. Many players of Bali's tourism industry are not in fact unaware of this. They do express their concerns. For example, Cok Ace, a noble figure from Ubud Palace, a tourism entrepreneur, and the former chairman of the Association of the Indonesian Tours and Travel Agencies (ASITA) Bali, and the Bali Tourism Board (BTB), articulates his concerns with the trends of tourism leading to self-destruction. He observes that Bali's tourism industry which has been dominated by global capitalist players has moved away from its original concept of cultural tourism grounded in Balinese culture and managed by Balinese.[10] The ASITA and the BTB have demanded the government to control tourism expansion on the island and returned it to the tract of cultural tourism. Similar concern is also expressed by Anak Agung Ngurah Alit, the chairman of the Indonesian Chamber of Commerce (Kadin) Bali Chapter, on the heavy control of foreign capital over Bali's economy (Chap. 3). This instance shows how the capitalist class itself is not monolithic and does not embrace the iron law of competition blindly. Once their profit-making activities that are embedded in particular social and cultural configurations are threatened by 'outside' global and more powerful capitalist players as a consequence of economic globalisation, they may turn into ethnocentric or nationalistic arguments to maintain their privileges in the name of preserving cultural tourism. Paradoxically,

[10] Interview with Tjokorda Oka Artha Ardhana Sukawati (Tjok Ace) on 24 January 2014.

while demanding the government to control the expansion of global capitalist players in Bali's tourism industry, the local capitalist class encourages the government to intensify the promotion of Bali's tourism abroad in order to attract more global tourism markets.

In the Subak Landscape of Catur Angga Batukaru, the failure of the agricultural sector to adapt to rapid tourism development has been treated by policymakers as the main cause for the impoverishment of Balinese farmers who are, in turn, argued to be responsible for land conversion (see Chap. 5) and the parlous state of the environment. With this in mind, the integration of the agricultural sector into tourism markets through its designation as a World Heritage Site was seen as offering a favourable solution. Besides being cultural agents for preserving the cultural landscape of rice terraces, farmers within the sites are also directed to become entrepreneurs in the heritage tourism business. Not only should individual farmers compete with other farmers to gain benefits from tourism, but also villages within the World Heritage Site should compete with other villages to attract tourist visits. According to Article 51 (4) of Tabanan District Spatial Planning Regulation (Perda RTRW Tabanan No. 11/2012), almost all administrative villages within the Subak Landscape of Catur Angga Batukaru have been designated as *desa wisata* (village tourism) following the success of Jatiluwih, the core zone of the *Subak* Landscape, to extract more revenues from tourist visits.

Although it is logical to assume that the terraced rice landscape of Jatiluwih could be preserved with new value added from tourism for farmers who own the land, the reality is more complex. The technocratic and market-based solution underestimates the political economic causes of the marginalisation of smallholder agricultural sectors in Bali, and indeed globally. The crisis of the agricultural sector has proven the failure of current public policies to address agricultural problems that have their roots in previous state policies, including the imposition of the Green Revolution during the New Order period, and also the current globalisation of deregulation and structural adjustment policies. Rather than blaming the inability of the individual farmers themselves to adapt to economic changes as the source of its problems, the decline of Bali's agrarian eco-system has been due to the expansion of the tourism industry itself. Tourism and real estate development are supported by government policies because of the opportunities these industries present for rent-seeking through the granting of permits and disregard of legal enforcement obligations. In many cases, public officials themselves are part of the tourism business, as shareholders, brokers, and so forth (see Chap. 3).

In the Uluwatu Case, rapid changes in the social-economic, physical, and cultural conditions of Pecatu Village have informed the ways in which villagers perceive space, especially land. They face rapid increases in land taxes and the cost of living as a result of the dramatic growth of tourism, the property market, and associated land transactions. Indeed, the case shows how spatial planning, assumed by planners to be a technocratic exercise, is in fact a very political means for distributing power and resources by privileging particular interests in the designation of space. In the West Java case, Moeliono (2011) has also shown how spatial planning has been captured by private interests. As in the Bali case, this capture has also been attributed to competing interests among different tiers of government in the decentralisation era of Indonesia, where spatial planning policies are used strategically as their instrument. The accommodation of local customary rules to govern sacred spaces in the spatial planning regulations has been seen by planners as a 'win-win' solution to moderate the command-based spatial governance system by providing room for customary rules as an expression of local interests, on the one hand, while recruiting local villagers to the cause of commercial expansion in that space.

Hence, evolving spatial governance surrounding the holiest temples in Bali has moved towards a more complex system based on a 'nested' institutional structure. This structure provides more institutional choices for social actors to advance their interests in accessing a given space and simultaneously opens up the potential to constrain such interests that may compromise other values and interests. Undoubtedly, it shows how the recognition of legal pluralism in development practices has made local *adat* institutions difficult to overlook if a development project expects to avoid local opposition. In the Pecatu case, it appears that from the investors' point of view, engaging with local institutions may provide a valuable instrument for securing their assets and property rights within the village, when doing business under Bali's decentralised complex institutional structures and uncertain government policies.

The Benoa Bay Case, on the other hand, shows that although Winata's project has engaged with local institutions and local elites, popular support is not necessarily to be bought. In fact, in both cases, efforts to co-opt local institutions and elites went hand in hand with paying off higher-level officials within the state apparatus. Rather than making the development process more efficient, as assumed by neoliberal policymakers, costs became even greater. The fragmentation of state institutions is used by state actors to justify the need for private company involvement in managing the bay and simultaneously enabling expanded capital penetration in the province. While rhetorically a neoliberal state is presumed to be a neutral regulator that encourages competition between private enterprises in order to find the most efficient and profitable project for managing the bay's development, the informal interests of state officials have played a central role in advancing one project over others. State support for the TWBI project, perpetuates a model of politico-business alliance that has dominated development planning in Indonesia since the Suharto era.

The construction of new resorts in Benoa Bay by Winata's TWBI may well advantage the well-equipped corporation over traditional fishing communities in accessing the bay areas for their different and often conflicting purposes. However, the obvious outcomes of such 'competition' will be treated as a matter of individual virtue for the winner and a wrong choice made by the loser, not as having underlying structural causes (Rottenberg 2013; Blalock 2014). Empirically, however, the tendencies to construct rational subjects ignores the complex personal and communal experience and towards the current model of tourism development. This equivocality, as Warren (1993, 298) argues, is not new in Balinese cultural arrangements, but has characterised historical struggles over the relationship between private interests and collective goods, and between accommodating and contesting what are often considered external forces affecting development and conservation.

In the case of Uluwatu Temple, for instance, this ambivalence is indicated by the opinions of Putu Yusa, Ibu Marni, and Ibu Oka who seek economic opportunities to fulfil their basic needs, but at the same time support legal protection against infringements of the symbolic meaning of Uluwatu Temple's sacred space. Similar tendencies arise in the case of the Subak Landscape of Catur Angga Batukaru where local farmers, like Pan Suka and Ketut Duita, are proud of their identity as farmers within a landscape with global recognition for its 'outstanding universal value', but at the same time are very concerned about what such recognition may entail for their landscape and livelihood. In the Benoa Bay case, on the grounds of its status as a sacred area and associated *adat* obligations, and despite project proponent claims for rehabilitating the bay and protecting Pulau Pudut from degradation, one after another customary community rejected the project out of social, ecological, and cultural concerns.

Even during the process of enacting the controversial provincial spatial planning law (Perda RTRW Bali No. 16/2009), NGO representatives involved in the drafting team, were similarly ambivalent towards the designation of 'provincial strategic areas'. On the one hand, they saw that power exercised by district elites had to be constrained in order to pursue equity and sustainability for the whole island. On the other hand, the designation of 'provincial strategic areas' would also concentrate power for governing space in the hands of a provincial government that potentially ignored local aspirations, not to mention the fact that it was no less immune from elite capture, corruption, and rent-seeking practices. Overlooking these equivocal and contentious tendencies, the 'economisation' project aims at constructing subjectivity at one pole predicated on self-interest, at the expense of the collective interests that animate many of the struggles and conflicts over locating the 'commonweal', those social domains through which collective goods may be pursued—in contemporary Bali (McCarthy and Warren 2009).

Conclusion

The attempts to establish new modes of spatial and environmental governance are not located in a social vacuum. By design or by default, they will have implications for and from pre-existing social structures. As shown above, the fragmented and pluralistic legal and institutional setting is a historical product of longstanding institutional contests and accommodations in Balinese society. These have been intensified by the rescaling of spatial governance in contemporary Bali, which has opened up new opportunities for engaging in contestations over the meanings and uses of space. Hence, the scale(s) at which these new modes of governance are established or negotiated will shape the outcome of social conflict through defining its modes of participation, the resources to be mobilised, and even the framing or channelling of actors' subjectivities and perceived interests in a given social-spatial field.

Although law, both formal and informal, here may become a resource to be mobilised, parties involved in conflicts do not necessarily resolve their conflicts through legal forums. For social actors who defend their interests based on non-state or informal normative orders, resorting to formal legal instruments would mean giving up their own legal basis and playing within their rival's rules of the game. Rather, they are more likely to engage in 'forum shopping' and 'idiom shopping' to justify their positions (K. von Benda-Beckmann 1981; Spiertz 1991). At the end of the day, once the conflicts are escalated into a zero-sum game, the winners and the losers would partly be defined by the extent to which actors involved in the conflict manage to mobilise their resources and networks in winning the contests of power.

In the contemporary state of social conflict, social actors involved are not tidily demarcated between those who are against tourism industry and those who support the industry. In fact, their stances in the conflict appear to be ambivalent and ambiguous, informed by their relative dependence upon the tourism industry and their positions within social, institutional, and geographical configurations. Above all, they retain their hopes to navigate the tourism industry to pursue their economic interests, but at the same time they fear that the industry may reversely take control over their livelihood. As Bali has deeply integrated into global tourism markets, such ambiguity and ambivalence towards the tourism industry within Balinese society will not be easily resolved. The Balinese attitude towards the industry will continually be a love-hate relationship, except they realise who are actually benefiting the most from the industry on the island, and who in fact have to compete for accessing the trickle-down residual.

8

Conclusion

This book starts from a proposition that Bali is moving towards socio-ecological crisis. Many scholars as well as mass media have argued that Bali has reached its 'tipping point' and is leading to 'self-destruction' (Reuter 2003; *Bali Post*, 11/01/2009; Lewis and Lewis 2009; Fox 2012, 13). The crisis of agriculture, the backbone of Bali's culture, is indicated by the acceleration of land conversion (Warren 2012) as well as the long-standing marginalisation of farmer households (MacRae 2003; Lorenzen and Lorenzen 2005). Environmental degradation has become a serious concern among the Balinese public. Waste and pollution have been chronic issues (Dharma Putra 2009; Marshall 2011). Forest cover that is well below the 30% of the total land area threshold has been under pressure from development (*Okezone*, 20/03/2008), which in turn has affected the flow of water table. Accordingly, by 2025, it is estimated that Bali will be facing a water crisis (Cole 2012; Cole and Browne 2015; Sunarta et al. 2015), worsening water conflicts between the *subaks*, traditional irrigation society, government, and the tourism industry (Strauss 2011; Trisnawati n.d.; Kurnianingsih n.d.; see also *Bali Post* 26/3/2007; 10/1/2011). Conflicts over common spaces, including beaches, forests, and lakes, have occurred more frequently across the island (Suartika 2005; Strauss 2015; see *Bali Post* 20/9/11). Sacred areas that are important

A. Wardana, *Contemporary Bali*, https://doi.org/10.1007/978-981-13-2478-9_8

for religion and culture and also for conservation have been encroached (Wardana 2014b; Strauss 2015).

The ways in which crisis is conceived in contemporary Bali are dominated by three perspectives. The first one is the rational-choice approach that considers that crisis occurred due to the economic calculation of rational agents in the transformation of agrarian society into industrialised society through the tourism industry. The second perspective is the conservative approach which embraces the notion that such crisis is a result of the change in the Balinese identity and values, affected by globalisation and other external forces. The third perspective is the institutionalist approach, which attributes the crisis to the fragmentation of the planning and decentralisation of political power to district governments. In policy discourse and practices, these approaches do not stand in isolation, as they may be blended in particular public policies because they are expected to tackle their underlying root causes respectively. One notable solution to the crisis Bali faces today is advocated through the reorganisation of space and governance to better suit the island's geographical, political, ecological, and cultural contexts. This is derived from the assumption of district competitions as in the post-authoritarian era, Bali has been divided into eight powerful districts and a municipality that compete to extract revenues from tourism development while disregarding impacts for Bali as a whole (Pansus Otsus Bali 2007; Suharyo 2011).

However, those three understandings have at least three flaws. The first one is that they do not examine the political economy questions of the crisis. The second flaw is that they appear to be ahistorical by confining their analyses only within the current phenomenon. Thirdly, they seem uncritical towards tourism as the overriding economic force that conditions Bali's development trajectories for decades. As we see in Chap. 2, the historical conjunctures have shaped the contemporary social, ecological, cultural, and institutional conditions of the island. These conjunctures have been shaped by the relations of power in Balinese society. Thus, as Bali's contemporary socio-ecological crisis should be seen as the product of these conjunctures, it is in fact deeply embedded in the existing relation of power. Without interrogating the relation of power, the historical accounts and the complex legal and institutional configurations, the understanding of the crisis is misconceived, and solutions derived from it will be rather artificial, if not advancing the tourism industry further, as new opportunities for expansion are opened up by the crisis.

In this book, I propose a critical approach to examine the conditions of contemporary Bali. This approach is derived from insights in the anthropology of law and critical geography by reconceptualising the notions of law and space. Following the legal anthropology tradition, law is taken beyond narrow conventional legal centralism—law as a state legal embodiment—to encompass any social phenomena with legal character (Griffiths 1986; F. von Benda-Beckmann 2002) through what is commonly referred to as 'legal pluralism'. Reconceptualising the law through this anthropological lens also means to embrace the idea that a legal order and its underpinning institutions do not stand in isolation from other legal orders and institutions since, as a 'semi-autonomous social field' (Moore 1973), they interact and are shaped by their relationships with each other. Equally, space here is not merely a grounded physical setting, but is reconceptualised as a product of interrelationship, and ongoing processes of social construction and reconstruction (Massey 2005). Accordingly, this opens possibilities for recognising how space is conceived and utilised by social actors deploying different or conflicting legal frameworks governing space, resources, and people (see Lefebvre 1991; Massey 2005; von Benda-Beckmann et al. 2009). In its operation, this approach interrogates the social embeddedness of spatial and legal-institutional reconfiguration and the dynamics of power that shape it.

By employing such an approach, the book finds that the reorganisation of space and governance in the island of Bali has been pursued through different strategies. Ramstedt (2013) notes that the main responses to the problems of decentralisation at the district level have been attempts to push institutional authority 'upward' and 'downward' from the current attention. The upward strategy is engaged through attempts to advocate special autonomy for Bali, with greater authority in the hands of the provincial, instead of district-level government, in order to provide an integral approach to island-wide environmental and cultural issues under the banner of 'one island one management' (Suharyo 2011; Ramstedt 2013; see also Wardana 2015). The downward strategy entails the recognition of customary (*adat*) institutional (banjar/*desa pakraman, subak*) autonomy (Ramstedt 2013; see also Warren 2007). Ramstedt (2013), however, overlooks that decentralisation has also been pushed 'outward' by transferring certain state authorities to private enterprises or hybrid forms of governance involving government, private entities, civil society organisations, as well as local communities. What is certain in this regard is how the boundaries of decentralisation are under constant negotiation. Due to internal dynamics and external forces, the state structure is constantly being transformed and the state-society-market relations are continually reconfigured, as neoliberal rationality has come to dominate state agendas.

Given the long stalled and contentious special autonomy proposal, the provincial government has turned to spatial planning to reorganise spatial and institutional configurations. Through spatial planning, the governance of space is being reconfigured in a way that enables decentralisation policies to accommodate 'upward', 'downward', and 'outward' pressures without compromising the national structure. Indeed, spatial planning serves also as an instrument of both national and provincial governments, to secure access and control over certain designated strategic areas within district territories (see Hudallah and Woltjer 2007; Wardana 2015). These areas, known as 'strategic areas' (*kawasan strategis*), may be designated as having strategic functions on the basis of economic, environmental, or World Heritage values, as well as for national security and defence.

The Provincial Government of Bali has used the Provincial Spatial Planning Regulation to advance its 'special autonomy' aspirations. Here, the role of spatial planning is to rearrange the regional autonomy regime by designating provincial strategic areas over lucrative spaces in district territories to achieve power over development approvals in these areas. Before the Spatial Planning Regulation was enacted, the Provincial Government of Bali and all district/municipal governments across Bali had agreed to a Memorandum of Understanding (MoU) for transferring responsibility for managing several significant areas to the provincial level. These areas include the localities where the case studies were conducted: the Sacred Space of Uluwatu Temple; the Subak Landscape of Catur Angga Batukaru; and Benoa Bay, all of which became contentious and contested development sites. This MoU was then adopted in the new Provincial Regulation on Spatial Planning for Bali (Perda RTRW Bali No. 16/2009) to have legal binding effects.

Moreover, examining spatial governance in contemporary Bali should not overlook the condition of legal and institutional pluralism as an important feature of the decentralised Bali. On the one side, spatial planning as a state instrument for governing space is shaped by such a condition. On the other side, following Jayasuriya's (2012) observation, the pluralistic legal and institutional structure did not emerge naturally, but is shaped by social conflicts. In the context of spatial governance, different interests over—and visions of social world towards—space have shaped how space should be defined, organised, and regulated, and by which institutions. As we have seen, the governance of space by multiple tiers of government is further complicated by claims based on the rights of *adat* villages to govern local space under autonomous customary (*adat*) authority. This has exacerbated already fragmented and pluralistic spatial practices, which in turn impact upon how alliances and contestations over the governance of space, resources, and people are implicated. The consequent reduction of the diverse meanings, uses of space, and institutional configurations to a market-economy logic advocated by the current spatial planning regime has brought controversial outcomes and unintended consequences. The case of Bali also shows how the complex legal and institutional structure provides more arenas for vested interests to manoeuvre, but at the same time provides different forms of legitimacy for social forces to challenge the dominant process.

Among the many lessons to be taken from the Bali cases analysed in this book are the multiple ways in which decentralisation has been contested, negotiated, and pushed in different directions by social actors mobilising the complex legal and institutional configuration of contemporary Bali (Warren 2005b; Lorenzen and Roth 2015). This book shows that space in Bali, as a limited and fundamentally important resource, is highly contested by different actors from local communities, governing bodies, private enterprises, and civil society organisations. These contestations occur because different perceptions among those actors of what institution at what scale is to be given priority for managing a specific spatial unit (Lorenzen and Roth 2015). More importantly, it is also because the meanings tied to space are continually reconstructed as social actors utilise different sets of right claims, grounded in different legal frameworks and social relationships.

Reorganisation of space in Bali also demonstrates how the island is far from harmonious as it has been characterised since the Dutch Colonial. Conflicts and resistance are never absent in Balinese society, despite changes in structural conditions that inform the ways in which struggles are expressed and supressed. In a community in which social cohesion is relatively strong, the dissatisfied groups tend to articulate their dissatisfaction through everyday forms of resistance. In this regard, avoidance, gossiping, as well as scaling up dissent to the scales beyond the locality have been among other choices employed by the dissatisfied group. Meanwhile, in a community where local elites are involved in open contestations with other elites, conflicts may be escalated through the mobilisation of the elites' constituencies based on the patron-client relationship. Hence, such conflicts necessarily involved a contest of power through the mobilisation of political and social institutions available in society and their legal embodiments to justify their antagonistic stances.

Hence, it can be argued that contemporary Bali has been shaped by fragmented and pluralistic spatial and legal-institutional configurations that intertwine with struggles over the meanings and uses of space and resources involving a range of actors and competing values. In these struggles, the notion of scale is an important spatial feature because it establishes the framework within which power can be exercised effectively; scale also informs the ways in which such power can be mediated or challenged by social forces (Robertson et al. 2002; McCarthy and Prudham 2004). F. von Benda-Beckmann et al. (2009, 3) correctly make the point that the organisation of power is informed by how spatial configurations are organised and reorganised because "[a]ll social and legal institutions, relations and practices [as the source of power] are located and distributed in space" (see also Lefebvre 1991).

Conceptually, the reconfiguration of spatial organisation pursued by policymakers has predominantly been informed by the neoliberal ideology. Accordingly, space is rescaled by the state upward, downward, and outward in order to foster competition between spatial units and institutions, facilitate investment, and expand tourism markets. Tourism expansion is expected to provide financial incentives for the local agricultural economy by providing a 'tourist gaze' through heritage tourism, as in the case of the Subak Landscape of Catur Angga Batukaru. In such a case, neoliberalisation has involved scaling up formerly economically insignificant village tourism to the global tourist market through the World Heritage 'brand' and has directed local farmers to develop their entrepreneurial skills in engaging with the tourism industry to survive. The hyper penetration of the tourism industry in Pecatu Village, for instance, has increased the economic and cultural dependency towards the industry. In the extreme case of the Benoa Bay reclamation proposal, the neoliberalisation of space is pursued through the construction of artificial islands for new luxury resort complexes that will be governed by Winata's company through the 'right of management' (*hak pengelolaan*) regime. In all cases, spatial planning has been used to facilitate and legally justify the manufacturing of commercial space, transforming the value of space predominantly in terms of touristic exchange value at the expense of agricultural use value.

However, such spatial reconfiguration is far from realising what is expected to be a neoliberal promise, efficient and rational governance of space, as well as secured property rights. This is exactly because governing space is power-laden as space is embedded in the relations of power in society. This means that reorganising space and governance through spatial planning would necessarily affect the existing power relations. Such reorganisation necessarily involved contestations to maintain or to gain control over space, people, and resources. These contestations occur not only within the state institutional structures, but also between the state structure and non-state local institutions, of which different or antagonistic interests over space are expressed. The case of Bali demonstrates how district governments who became aware of the economic implications of transferring spatial governance to the provincial level have resisted these attempts by designating 'district strategic areas' (*kawasan strategis kabupaten*). At the same time, both the Subak Landscape of Catur Angga Batukaru and Benoa Bay are also designated as 'provincial strategic areas' (*kawasan strategis provinsi*) as well as 'national strategic areas' (*kawasan strategis nasional*).

The neoliberal 'economisation' of space as an attempt to reduce the meanings of space to an object of economic calculation would have significant implications for society. These implications are not only economic, but also socio-cultural in defining whose 'commonweal'—the societal domains where collective good is pursued (McCarthy and Warren

2009, 1)—is to be grounded in the existing spatial configuration. This is exactly why the reorganising of space for economic purposes would very often be contested by social actors whose values and interests are implicated, either through open power struggles or 'everyday forms of resistance' (Scott 1985). Such contestations in Bali are also complicated by the fact that local communities are often ambivalent towards development in their search for a balance between short-term individual and long-term collective interests (Warren 1993, 2016). This shows the impossibility of constructing a neoliberal subject in which individuals can be treated solely as *homo economicus*—a self-interested and profit-making being—by overlooking their complex and multidimensional social positions and subjectivities.

The Framework and Its Implication to Literature

The current wave of the Law and Development Movement has turned to incorporating the long neglected non-state legal orders, including customary law, in developing countries' legal reform projects in pursuit of the rule of law and economic development (see World Bank 2006; Sage and Woolcock 2005; Tamanaha et al. 2012). Unlike the previous waves that embraced a narrow conception of law, the current discourse and practices have broadened this conception to consider that 'law' is interchangeably allied to 'governance', implying a more inclusive mode of governing society beyond the narrow institutional structure of 'government' to include a range of 'stakeholders', be they private enterprises or non-governmental organisations. Hence, the plurality of rules and normative orderings, the central theme of legal pluralism, is inevitable and even celebrated by the current wave, especially in providing a range of legal mechanisms for accessing justice, enforcing contracts, as well as protecting property rights. It embraces the view that law and orderliness in society may not only be achieved through state law alone. Rather, existing social norms, especially in developing countries, also play an important role in governing the lives of the majority.

In this light, Tamanaha (2012) notes that legal pluralism is not necessarily a constraint on development goals, especially the rule of law. Rather, for him, the conception of the rule of law itself should be redefined more broadly so that it is not necessarily limited to the state legal system, but also accommodates other systems of rules beyond or outside it. Accordingly, the rule of law is composed of two different dimensions, 'vertical' (dealing with the operation of state institutions based on law and respecting human rights) and 'horizontal' (dealing with people-to-people interactions based on law and other social norms) in which the 'horizontal dimension' could be served by either state or non-state legal orders (Tamanaha 2012). This is based on the assumption that state law and non-state law are complementary and aim to achieve similar objectives (Fitzpatrick 1992; Vanberg 1996; Crowe 2014). Hence, an ideal free-market society will necessarily have legal plural features that allow "innovation and competition in legal regimes. This might lead to more predictable and stable legal rules in the long run" through which "[i]neffective and unfair legal rules are likely to be modified or abandoned, especially if they are subject to competition from more effective and equitable approaches" (Crowe 2014, 10–11). In the context of spatial planning, Moroni (2007) argues that flexible, open, and pluralistic planning frameworks could be useful to achieve the rule of law and efficient spatial governance.

However, this characterisation of the state and non-state legal orders as complementary is incomplete and simplified. As shown in the study cases, rather than enhance the functions of state law, non-state rules, be they customary practice or *adat* law, religious or personal law, may equip social actors with a range of repertoires to challenge, negotiate with, mediate, or adjust the operations of the formal order within social fields with sharply different and competing interests (see also Roth 2003; Biezeveld 2007; Bakker 2009; von Benda-Beckmann and von Benda-Beckmann 2011). In Bali, specifically, the dichotomy between 'formal/informal laws' does not exist, since customary law that is referred to above as a form of 'informal rules' is in fact more or less recognised and registered formally under the state legal framework. In Indonesia, in general, *adat* law, despite attempts to standardise it, commonly provides different spaces for settling disputes by enabling a 'forum shopping' or 'discourse shopping' strategy (K. von Benda-Beckmann 1981; Biezeveld 2002). The result of this strategy may or may not be compatible with state law. The case studies clearly demonstrate that *adat* law has become a legal resort for challenging state law in the contemporary period. Thus, the relationship between state law and customary law, should not be assumed to be coherent or mutually supportive.

Unlike the assumptions reflected in the current wave of law and development research, which embrace neoliberal concepts aimed at efficiency and security of property rights in spatial governance, the case of Bali clearly shows that the current mode of spatial governance is hardly 'efficient' and 'secure'. In fact, accessing space for development and securing property rights in this complex legal and institutional setting requires even more pay off and collusion with power holders at every institutional tier that may have a legitimate claim over the space concerned. Even if power holders are captured and all institutional tiers are aligned, it should not be assumed that the local populace would submit to unwelcome development or restriction passively.

This book contributes to the literature on law and spatial practices in Asian development. It does so by broadening the definitions of law and space, and applying these within the complex legal-institutional configurations of decentralised Indonesia. In examining three case studies of local contestation over spatial planning in Bali—at Pecatu, Jatiluwih, and Benoa—the book places the power struggles over governance of space, people, and resources within these complex configurations at the centre of analysis. The book demonstrates the mechanisms through which social actors mobilise legal-institutional arrangements to advance their interests. It also shows the extent to which multiple and often conflicting spatial constructions, arising from diverse interests and identities at different governance scales, reflect back on the existing political-legal constellation, with significant social, cultural, and ecological implications.

There are at least two main implications of the reconceptualisaton of concepts of law and space in the context of Asian development proposed by this book. Firstly, by reconceptualising law, this book challenges the common characterisation of the relationship between legal orders in society. Mamdani (1996) and Chanock (1985), for example, argue that the condition of complex legal configuration in developing countries is a product of colonial indirect rule. In post-colonial periods, this configuration is considered as continuing to play a role in a legal division of labour between the formal state legal order and the customary rules. For them, although both systems of rule operate in different spheres—the state legal order operates within the sphere of law and order while customary rules operate within disciplinary spheres—they work in a complementary way to enhance each other (Fitzpatrick 1992; Norrie 1996). Secondly, the reconceptualisation of space reveals that space should not be seen as a fixed, grounded physical setting, but as a configuration that is 'conceived' and 'practiced' (Lefebvre 1991) differently by social actors. The Bali case shows how the 'economisation' of space—as an object of commercialisation, commodification, and privatisation—pursued by policymakers is far from the neoliberal promise to govern space in an economically efficient manner. In fact, these neoliberal promises are used strategically by policymakers as 'ideological deflections' to conceal their collusion with vested interests in accessing and controlling space, people, and resources for their pursuit of short-term interests.

The framework also adds an overlooked element in the literature on the political economy of Indonesia, that is law. In the debate on this theme (Robison and Hadiz 2004; Hadiz and Robison 2013; Pepinsky 2013; Aspinall 2013b; Winters 2013), questions of law tend to be treated in passing. Without the adequate problematisation of social meanings and cognitive significance of law, scholars of political economy tend to characterise the law as merely an instrument of the elites (van Klinken 2007; Bourchier 2007; Hadiz 2010). Winters (2013), for instance, touches on the relationship between the legal system and oligarchies' wealth defence strategies. He argues that legal uncertainty in terms of "conflicting laws across multiple jurisdictions" is the legacy of Dutch Colonial rule and a product of decentralisation that has played "a vital role in the constant game of extortion and forced-sharing that redistributes wealth among Indonesia's oligarchs and elites" (Winters 2013, 29). Robison and Hadiz (2004, 7), examining the ability of oligarchies to reorganise themselves in a changing institutional context, note that "[u]nconstrained by law and regulation, [institutional] reform simply meant that public monopoly became private monopoly in the hands of powerful politico-business families and well-connected corporate interests" (Robison and Hadiz 2004, 7).

It appears that the structural political economists seek to assert the centrality of oligarchy in Indonesia's political and legal life. Their insights are illuminating, indeed, but unfortunately, they stop there. Their analysis on the relation between oligarchy and law in Indonesia, which is predominantly based on the legal instrumentalist approach, risks falling into a circular argument: the 'appropriation of public authority for private interests' or 'wealth defence' mechanisms are advanced as caused by 'legal uncertainty' (in the case of Winters), or because they are 'unconstrained by law and regulation' (in the case of Robison and Hadiz). Yet, the law and regulatory institutions themselves are strongly shaped by and a product of the oligarchic power structure. A basic question struggles to be answered by the legal instrumentalist analysis of the law: if the power of ruling elites or oligarchies was so hegemonic and overarching, why would they need law to justify their class interests in the first place?

Given its central focus on oligarchy, the structural political economist very often overlooks the concrete struggles over how law is produced, mediated, and contested, which may take place beyond the state as the centre of power, in spheres that remain open for other possibilities in the future. As I argue elsewhere, the ability of oligarchies to capture the state and its legal embodiment, the state law, to advance a particular development project is not the end of history; in fact, social forces whose interests would be implicated turned into a 'legal engineering' strategy to challenge such a project (Wardana 2018). The struggles utilising *adat* law in the case of Benoa Bay, for instance, have managed to frustrate Tomy Winata's project in developing luxury resort complexes through reclamation on local *adat* communities' sacred space. As a result, the project has been stopped albeit temporarily due to the expiration of its location permit after having a hard time to deal with the social-cultural impacts. Without the local struggles, the project would have been developed in the bay.

Furthermore, the state structure recently has been reconfigured further through the enactment of a new Village Law No. 6/2014 and Regional Government Law No. 23/2014. Village institutions now become another centre for local development bypassing district governments which used to be the key institution in previous decentralisation policies. It remains to be seen what implications this new legal act of rescaling will have on the constellation of forces contesting the trajectory of development in the three cases considered in this book. What is apparent is that multiple sources of power and legal authority will continue to assert themselves through existing and newly fashioned instruments that represent the plural interests and identities at stake.

Hence, the framework employed in this book complicates this notion to include legal and institutional pluralism in the power struggles to govern space in contemporary Indonesia. In this context, the application of a critical approach will be a valuable tool for examining the ways in which fragmented and pluralistic legal and institutional configurations shape and are shaped by the relations of power in governing space, people, and resources in Bali and beyond. The question that needs to be asked in future research is to what extent and in what ways recent institutional changes through the new Village and Regional Government Laws reframe the complex legal and institutional configurations that have emerged to date and with what implications for the pursuit of the 'commonweal' in society.

References

Books and Article

Adams, Kathleen. 2018. Revisiting 'Wonderful Indonesia': Tourism, Economy, and Society. In *Routledge Handbook of Contemporary Indonesia*, ed. R.W. Hefner. New York and London: Routledge.

Adhika, I Made. 2011a. *Komodifikasi Kawasan Suci Pura Uluwatu di Kuta Selatan, Kabupaten Badung, Dalam Era Globalisasi*. PhD diss., Udayana University.

———. 2011b. Dampak Komodifikasi Daya Tarik Wisata di Desa Pecatu, Kuta Selatan, Bali. In *Penelitian Masalah Lingkungan di Indonesia 2011*, ed. Sudjono, 219–232. Jakarta: ITS and IATPI.

———. 2012. *Komodifikasi Kawasan Suci Pura Uluwatu*. Denpasar: Udayana University Press.

Aditjondro, George J. 1995. *Bali, Jakarta's Colony: Social and Ecological Impacts of Jakarta-Based Conglomerates in Bali's Tourism Industry*. Asia Research Centre, Murdoch University, Working Paper No. 58. Perth: Murdoch University.

Agrawal, Arun. 2003. Sustainable Governance of Common-Pool Resources: Context, Methods, and Politics. *Annual Review of Anthropology* 32: 243–262.

A. Wardana, *Contemporary Bali*, https://doi.org/10.1007/978-981-13-2478-9

Agung, Anak Agung Gde. 2005. *Bali Endangered Paradise?: Tri Hita Karana and the Conservation of the Island's Biocultural Diversity*. Leiden: Leiden Ethnosystems and Development Program.

Alit, Agung. 2012. 'De Raka': Sebuah Tutut untuk Rekonsiliasi. In *Melawan Lupa: Narasi-Narasi Komunitas Taman 65 Bali*, ed. A. Wardana and R. Hutabarat, 13–30. Denpasar: Taman65 Press.

Allmendinger, Philip, and Graham Haughton. 2013. The Evolution and Trajectories of English Spatial Governance: 'Neoliberal' Episodes in Planning. *Planning Practice and Research* 28 (1): 6–26.

Allmendinger, Philip, and Mark Tewdwr-Jones. 2006. Territory, Identity and Spatial Planning. In *Territory, Identity and Spatial Planning: Spatial Governance in a Fragmented Nation*, ed. M. Tewdwr-Jones and P. Allmendinger, 3–21. London and New York: Routledge.

Anders, Gerhard. 2009. The New Global Legal Order as Local Phenomenon: The Special Court for Sierra Leone. In *Spatializing Law: Anthropological Geography of Law in Society*, ed. F. von Benda-Beckmann, K. von Benda-Beckmann, and A. Griffiths, 137–156. Surrey: Ashgate.

Antons, Christoph, ed. 2003. *Law and Development in East and Southeast Asia*. London and New York: RoutledgeCurzon.

Apriando, Tommy. 2014. Jerinx SID: Pembangunan Yang Benar Tidak Melukai Struktur Sosial & Ekologi Bali. *Mongabay*, April 11. http://www.mongabay.co.id/2014/04/11/jerinx-sid-pembangunan-yang-benar-tidak-melukai-struktur-sosial-ekologi-bali/.

Ardika, I Wayan, I Gde Parimartha, and Anak Agung Bagus Wirawan. 2013. *Sejarah Bali: Dari Pra-Sejarah Hingga Modern*. Denpasar: Udayana University Press.

Arida, Sukma. 2008. Krisis Lingkungan Bali dan Peluang Ekowisata. *Jurnal Ekonomi dan Sosial* 1 (2): 118–122.

Arnscheidt, Julia. 2009. *'Debating' Nature Conservation: Policy, Law and Practice in Indonesia*. Leiden: Leiden University Press.

Arya Utama, I Made, and I Ketut Sudiarta. 2011. *Kajian Normatif terhadap Efektifitas Perda Bali No. 16 Tahun 2009 tentang Rencana Tata Ruang Wilayah Provinsi Bali Tahun 2009–2029 serta Strategi Implementasinya*. Paper presented at the *National Seminar on Developing Bali in the Frame of Spatial Planning for Bali*, Udayana University, Denpasar, 6 May 2011.

Aspinall, Edward. 2013a. A Nation in Fragments: Patronage and Neoliberalism in Contemporary Indonesia. *Critical Asian Studies* 45 (1): 27–54. https://doi.org/10.1080/14672715.2013.758820.

———. 2013b. Popular Agency and Interests in Indonesia's Democratic Transition and Consolidation. *Indonesia* 96: 101–121. https://doi.org/10.5728/indonesia.96.0011.

Assegaf, Rifqi. 2007. Judicial Reform in Indonesia, 1998–2006. In *Reforming Laws and Institutions in Indonesia: An Assessment*, ed. N. Sakumoto and H. Juwana, 11–44. Jakarta: Faculty of Law Press, University of Indonesia.

Astarini, Ni Nyoman Dwi. 2015. Tipu-Tipu. *Media Indonesia*, March 15. http://www.mediaindonesia.com/mipagi/read/9311/Tipu-Tipu/2015/03/15.

Atmadja, Bawa. 2010a. *Ajeg Bali: Gerakan, Identitas Kultural dan Globalisasi.* Yogyakarta: LKis.

———. 2010b. *Genealogi Keruntuhan Majapahit: Islamisasi, Toleransi dan Pemertahanan Agama Hindu di Bali.* Yogyakarta: Pustaka Pelajar.

Badan Pengendali Dampak Lingkungan Hidup Daerah (Bapedalda) Bali. 2006. *Status Lingkungan Hidup Provinsi Bali Tahun 2006.* Denpasar: Pemerintah Provinsi Bali.

———. 2010. *Status Lingkungan Hidup Daerah Provinsi Bali Tahun 2010.* Denpasar: Pemerintah Provinsi Bali.

Badan Perencanaan Pembangunan Daerah (Bappeda). 2009. *Materi Teknis Rencana Tata Ruang Wilayah Provinsi Bali 2009–2029.* Denpasar: Pemerintah Provinsi Bali.

Badan Perencanaan Pembangunan Nasional (Bappenas). 2013a. *Laporan Akhir Tahun 2013.* Jakarta: Direktorat Penataan Ruang dan Pertanahan.

———. 2013b. *Laporan Kegiatan Direktorat Tata Ruang dan Pertanahan November 2013.* Jakarta: Direktorat Penataan Ruang dan Pertanahan.

———. 2013c. *Laporan Kegiatan Direktorat Tata Ruang dan Pertanahan Desember 2013.* Jakarta: Direktorat Penataan Ruang dan Pertanahan.

———. 2014a. *Laporan Kegiatan Direktorat Penataan Ruang dan Pertanahan Maret 2014.* Jakarta: Direktorat Penataan Ruang dan Pertanahan.

———. 2014b. *Laporan Kegiatan Direktorat Penataan Ruang dan Pertanahan April 2014.* Jakarta: Direktorat Penataan Ruang dan Pertanahan.

Bakker, Karen. 2005. Neoliberalizing Nature? Market Environmentalism in Water Supply in England and Wales. In *Neoliberal Environments: False Promises and Unnatural Consequences*, ed. N. Heynen, J. McCarthy, S. Prudham, and P. Robbins, 101–113. London and New York: Routledge.

Bakker, Laurens. 2009. The Sultan's Map: Arguing One's Land in Pasir. In *Spatializing Law: Anthropological Geography of Law in Society*, ed. F. von Benda-Beckmann, K. von Benda-Beckmann, and A. Griffiths, 95–113. Surrey: Ashgate.

Bal, Charanpal. 2014. Production Politics and Migrant Labour Advocacy in Singapore. *Journal of Contemporary Asia*: 1–24. https://doi.org/10.1080/00472336.2014.960880.

Baudrillard, Jean. 1975. *The Mirror of Production*. Trans. Mark Poster. St Louis: Telos Press.

Beard, Victoria. 2002. Covert Planning for Social Transformation in Indonesia. *Journal of Planning Education and Research* 22: 15–25. https://doi.org/10.1177/0739456X0202200102.

Bedner, Adriaan. 2008. Amalgamating Environmental Law in Indonesia. In *Lawmaking for Development: Explorations into the Theory and Practice of International Legislative Projects*, ed. J. Arnscheidt, B. van Rooij, and J.M. Otto, 171–198. Leiden: Leiden University Press.

———. 2010. Consequences of Decentralization: Environmental Impact Assessment and Water Pollution Control in Indonesia. *Law and Policy* 32 (1): 38–60. https://doi.org/10.1111/j.1467-9930.2009.00313.x.

Bevir, Mark. 2011. Governance as Theory, Practice, and Dilemma. In *The Sage Handbook of Governance*, ed. Mark Bevir, 1–16. Los Angeles: Sage.

Bianchi, Raoul. 2009. The 'Cultural Turn' in Tourism Studies: A Radical Critique. *Tourism Geographies: An International Journal of Tourism Space, Place, and Environment* 11 (4): 485–504.

Biezeveld, Renske. 2002. Discourse Shopping in a Dispute over Land in Rural Indonesia. *Ethnology* 43 (2): 137–154.

———. 2007. The Many Roles of Adat in West Sumatera. In *The Revival of Tradition in Indonesian Politics: The Deployment of Adat from Colonialism to Indigenism*, ed. J. Davidson and D. Henley, 203–223. London and New York: Routledge.

Birkelbach, Aubrey. 1973. The Subak Association. *Indonesia* 16: 153–169. https://doi.org/10.2307/3350651.

Blackstock, Kirsty. 2005. A Critical Look at Community Base Tourism. *Community Development Journal* 40: 39–49. https://doi.org/10.1093/cdj/bsi005.

Blalock, Corinne. 2014. Neoliberalism and the Crisis of Legal Theory. *Law and Contemporary Problems* 77 (4): 71–103.

Blank, Y., and I Rosen-Zvi. 2010. The Spatial Turn in Legal Theory. *HAGAR Studies in Culture, Polity and Identities* 10 (1): 37–60.

Blomley, Nicholas. 1994. *Law, Space and the Geographies of Power*. New York: Guilford Press.

Blomley, Nicholas, and Gordon Clark. 1990. Law, Theory and Geography. *Urban Geography* 11 (5): 433–446. https://doi.org/10.2747/0272-3638.11.5.433.
Blomley, Nicholas, David Delaney, and Richard Ford, eds. 2001. *The Legal Geographies Reader: Law, Power and Space*. Malden, MA: Wiley-Blackwell.
Bourchier, David. 2007. The Romance of Adat in the Indonesian Political Imagination and the Current Revival. In *The Revival of Tradition in Indonesian Politics: The Deployment of Adat from Colonialism to Indigenism*, ed. J. Davidson and D. Henley, 113–129. London and New York: Routledge.
Bowman, Michael. 2002. *The Ramsar Convention on Wetlands: Has It Made a Difference?* Yearbook of International Co-operation on Environment and Development 2002/2003.
BPS (Badan Pusat Statistik) Badung. 1996. *Kecamatan Kuta Selatan Dalam Angka 1996*. Badung: BPS Badung.
———. 2002. *Kecamatan Kuta Selatan Dalam Angka 2002*. Badung: BPS Badung.
———. 2010. *Kecamatan Kuta Selatan Dalam Angka 2010*. Badung: BPS Badung.
———. 2012. *Kecamatan Kuta Selatan Dalam Angka 2012*. Badung: BPS Badung.
———. 2013. *Kecamatan Kuta Selatan Dalam Angka 2013*. Badung: BPS Badung.
———. 2014. *Badung Dalam Angka 2013*. Badung: Badan Pusat Statistik.
BPS (Badan Pusat Statistik) Bali. 1997. *Bali Dalam Angka 1997*. Denpasar: Badan Pusat Statistik Provinsi Bali.
———. 2001. *Bali Dalam Angka 2001*. Denpasar: Badan Pusat Statistik Provinsi Bali.
———. 2003. *Bali Dalam Angka 2003*. Denpasar: Badan Pusat Statistik Provinsi Bali.
———. 2005. *Bali Dalam Angka 2005*. Denpasar: Badan Pusat Statistik Provinsi Bali.
———. 2011. *Bali Dalam Angka 2011*. Denpasar: Badan Pusat Statistik Provinsi Bali.
———. 2013. *Bali Dalam Angka 2013*. Denpasar: Badan Pusat Statistik Provinsi Bali.
———. 2014a. *Bali Dalam Angka 2014*. Denpasar: Badan Pusat Statistik Provinsi Bali.
———. 2014b. *Luas Lahan Menurut Penggunaannya di Provinsi Bali 2013*. Denpasar: BPS Provinsi Bali.

———. 2015. *Bali Dalam Angka 2015*. Denpasar: Badan Pusat Statistik Provinsi Bali.

BPS (Badan Pusat Statistik) Denpasar. 2014. *Denpasar Dalam Angka 2013*. Denpasar: Badan Pusat Statistik.

BPS (Badan Pusat Statistik) Tabanan. 2014. *Kecamatan Penebel Dalam Angka 2014*. Tabanan: Kantor Badan Pusat Statistik Kabupaten Tabanan.

Brenner, Neil. 1999. Globalisation as Reterritorialisation: The Re-scaling of Urban Governance in the European Union. *Urban Studies* 36: 431–451. https://doi.org/10.1080/0042098993466.

———. 2004. *New State Space: Urban Governance and the Rescaling of Statehood*. Oxford: Oxford University Press.

Brenner, Neil, Jamie Peck, and Nik Theodore. 2010. After Neoliberalization? *Globalization* 7 (3): 327–345. https://doi.org/10.1080/14747731003669669.

Brown, Wendy. 2015. *Undoing the Demos: Neoliberalism's Stealth Revolution*. New York: Zone Books.

Butler, Chris. 2003. *Law and Social Production of Space*. Griffith University. https://www120.secure.griffith.edu.au/rch/file/6e262ab2-3509-3354-9079-f0a16c85949c/1/02Whole.pdf.

———. 2009. Critical Legal Studies and the Politics of Space. *Social Legal Studies* 18 (2): 313–332. https://doi.org/10.1177/0964663909339084.

Butt, Simon, and Nicholas Parsons. 2014. Judicial Review and the Supreme Court in Indonesia: A New Space for Law. *Indonesia* 97: 55–85.

Cassrels, Deborah. 2014. Bali Crime Wave Leaves Expats Bruised and Wary. *The Australian*, May 16. http://www.theaustralian.com.au/news/nation/bali-crime-wave-leaves-expats-bruised-and-wary/story-e6frg6nf-1226919371507.

Chanock, Martin. 1985. *Law, Custom and Social Order: The Colonial Experience in Malawi and Zambia*. Cambridge: Cambridge University Press.

Chidester, David, and Edward T. Linenthal. 1995. *American Sacred Space*. Bloomington and Indianapolis: Indiana University Press.

Cohen, Alice. 2012. Rescaling Environmental Governance: Watersheds as Boundary Objects at the Intersection of Science, Neoliberalism, and Participation. *Environment and Planning A* 44: 2207–2224. https://doi.org/10.1068/a44265.

Cohen, Alice, and Karen Bakker. 2014. The Eco-Scalar Fix: Rescaling Environmental Governance and the Politics of Ecological Boundaries in Alberta, Canada. *Environment and Planning D: Society and Space* 32: 128–146. https://doi.org/10.1068/d0813.

Colchester, M., and M. Farhan Ferrari. 2007. *Making FPIC Work: Challenges and Prospects for Indigenous Peoples*. Moreton-in-Marsh: Forest Peoples Programme.

Cole, Stroma. 2012. A Political Ecology of Water Equity and Tourism: A Case Study from Bali. *Annals of Tourism Research* 39: 1221–1241. https://doi.org/10.1016/j.annals.2012.01.003.

Cole, Stroma, and Mia Browne. 2015. Tourism and Water Inequity in Bali: A Social-Ecological Systems Analysis. *Human Ecology* 43: 439–450. https://doi.org/10.1007/s10745-015-9739-z.

Cooney, Sean, Tim Lindsey, Richard Mitchell, and Ying Zhu, eds. 2002. *Law and Labour Market Regulation in East Asia*. London and New York: Routledge.

Creese, Helen. 2009. Judicial Processes and Legal Authority in Pre-Colonial Bali. *Bijdragen tot de Taal-, Land- en Volkenkunde* 165 (4): 515–550. https://doi.org/10.1163/22134379-90003631.

———. 2016. The Legal Status of Widows and Divorcees (*Janda*) in Colonial Bali. *Indonesia and the Malay World* 44: 84–103.

Cribb, Robert, ed. 1990. *The Indonesian Killings 1965–1966: Studies from Java and Bali*. Clayton, VIC: Centre of Southeast Asian Studies Monash University.

Crowe, Jonathan. 2014. Law Without the State. *Policy* 30 (2): 7–11.

Darma Putra, I Nyoman. 2003. Reflections on Literature and Politics in Bali: The Development of Lekra, 1950–1966. In *Inequality, Crisis and Social Change in Indonesia: The Muted Worlds of Bali*, ed. T. Reuter, 55–86. London: Routledge Curzon.

———. 2011. *A Literary Mirror: Balinese Reflections on Modernity and Identity in the Twentieth Century*. Leiden: KITLV Press.

Darma Putra, I Nyoman, and Michael Hitchcock. 2005. Pura Besakih: A World Heritage Contested. *Indonesia and the Malay World* 33: 1–9. https://doi.org/10.1080/13639810500284116.

De Soto, Hernando. 2000. *The Mystery of Capital: Why Capitalism Triumphs in the West and Fails Everywhere Else*. New York: Basic Books.

Delaney, David. 2005. *Territory: A Short Introduction*. Oxford: Blackwell Publishing.

Desa Pecatu. 2007. *Profil Desa Pecatu, Kecamatan Kuta Selatan, Kabupaten Badung, Provinsi Bali, Tahun 2008*. Jakarta: Departemen Dalam Negeri, Dirjen Pemberdayaan Masyarakat dan Desa.

Dharma Putra, Ketut Gede. 2009. *Pencemaran Lingkungan Hidup di Kawasan Teluk Benoa Bali: Perspektif Kajian Budaya*. PhD diss., Udayana University.

Dharmiasih, DA Wiwik, and Steve Lansing. 2014. Can World Heritage Status Save Bali from Destruction? *Strategic Review – Indonesia* 360. http://www.sr-indonesia.com/in_the_journal/view/can-world-heritage-status-save-bali-from-destruction?pg=all.

Elkington, John. 1997. *Cannibals with Forks: The Triple Bottom Line of 21st Century Business*. Oxford: Capstone.

Erawan, Nyoman. 1994. *Pariwisata dan Pembangunan Ekonomi: Bali Sebagai Studi Kasus*. Denpasar: Upada Sastra.

Erviani, Ni Komang. 2012. Mangrove Tahura Ngurah Rai Bali, Nasibmu Kini…. *Mongabay Indonesia*, December 4. http://www.mongabay.co.id/2012/12/04/mangrove-tahura-ngurah-rai-bali-nasibmu-kini/.

Fagertun, Anette. 2017a. Labour in Paradise: Gender, Class and Social Mobility in the Informal Tourism Economy of Urban Bali, Indonesia. *The Journal of Development Studies* 53 (3): 331–345. https://doi.org/10.1080/00220388.2016.1184248.

———. 2017b. Waves of Dispossession: The Conversion of Land and Labor in Bali's Recent History. *Social Analysis* 61 (3): 108–125.

Faludi, Andreas. 2010. *Cohesion, Coherence, Cooperation: European Spatial Planning Coming of Age?* London and New York: Routledge.

Farid, Hilmar. 2005. Indonesia's Original Sin: Mass Killings and Capitalist Expansion, 1965–1966. *Inter-Asia Cultural Studies* 6 (1): 3–16. https://doi.org/10.1080/1462394042000326879.

Fauzi, Noer. 2009. Land Titles Do Not Equal Agrarian Reform. *Inside Indonesia*, October–December. http://www.insideindonesia.org/land-titles-do-not-equal-agrarian-reform.

Fitzpatrick, Peter. 1992. The Impossibility of Popular Justice. *Social and Legal Studies* 1: 199–215.

Fitzpatrick, Daniel. 2008. Beyond Dualism: Land Acquisition and Law in Indonesia. In *Indonesia: Law and Society*, ed. T. Lindsey, 2nd ed., 224–226. Leichhardt, NSW: The Federation Press.

Fletcher, Robert. 2011. Sustaining Tourism, Sustaining Capitalism? The Tourism Industry's Role in Global Capitalist Expansion. *Tourism Geographies* 13 (3): 443–461.

Fox, James. 2009. The Discourse and Practice of Precedence. In *Precedence: Social Differentiation in the Austronesian World*, ed. M. Vischer, 91–109. Canberra: ANU E Press.

Fox, Karyn M. 2012. *Resilience in Action: Adaptive Governance for Subak, Rice Terrace, and Water Temples in Bali, Indonesia*. University of Arizona Repository. http://arizona.openrepository.com/arizona/handle/10150/242455.

Friedrich, R. 1959 [1849–1850]. *The Civilization and Culture of Bali*. Calcutta: Sisil Gupta (India) Private Ltd.

Galland, Daniel. 2012. Is Regional Planning Dead or Just Coping? The Transformation of a State Sociospatial Project into Growth-Oriented Strategies. *Environment and Planning C: Government and Policy* 30 (3): 536–552. https://doi.org/10.1068/c11150.

Geertz, Clifford. 1959. Form and Variation in Balinese Village Structure. *American Anthropologist* 61: 991–1012.

———. 1973. *The Interpretation of Cultures*. New York: Basic Books, Inc.

———. 1980. *Negara: The Theatre State in Nineteenth-Century Bali*. New Jersey: Princeton University Press.

Geertz, Hildred, and Clifford Geertz. 1975. *Kinship in Bali*. Chicago: Chicago University Press.

Gerard, Kelly. 2014. *ASEAN's Engagement of Civil Society: Regulating Dissent*. New York: Palgrave Macmillan.

Giugni, Marco. 2009. Political Opportunities: From Tilly to Tilly. *Swiss Political Science Review* 15 (2): 361–368.

Goodwin, Edward. 2008. World Heritage Convention, the Environment, Compliance. *Colorado Journal of International Environmental Law and Policy* 20: 157–198.

Google Earth. 2014. Tanjung Benoa, Bali, Indonesia. *Google*. https://www.google.com/maps/@-8.7585119,115.2137007,11348m/data=!3m1!1e3. Accessed Aug 2014.

Goris, R. 1954. *Prasasti Bali*. Badung: Masa Baru.

Grahn-Farley, Maria. 2008. Race and Class: More than a Liberal Paradox. *Buffalo Law Review* 56: 935–952.

Grenfell, Michael, ed. 2008. *Pierre Bourdieu: Key Concepts*. Durham: Acumen Publishing.

Griffiths, John. 1986. What Is Legal Pluralism? *Journal of Legal Pluralism and Unofficial Law* 24: 1–55.

Griffiths, Anne, and Randy Kandel. 2009. The Myth of the Transparent Table: Reconstructing Space and Legal Interventions in Scottish Children's Hearing. In *Spatializing Law: Anthropological Geography of Law in Society*, ed. F. von Benda-Beckmann, K. von Benda-Beckmann, and A. Griffiths, 157–175. Surrey: Ashgate.

Gruchalla-Wesierski, Tadensz. 1984. A Framework for Understanding 'Soft-Law'. *McGill Law Journal* 30: 37–88.

Hadiz, Vedi R. 2010. *Localising Power in Post-Authoritarian Indonesia: A Southeast Asia Perspective*. Stanford: Stanford University Press.

———. 2014. The Organizational Vehicles of Islamic Political Dissent: Social Bases, Genealogies and Strategies. In *Between Dissent and Power: The Transformation of Islamic Politics in the Middle East and Asia*, ed. Khoo Boo Teik, Vedi Hadiz, and Yoshihiro Nakanishi, 42–65. London: Palgrave Macmillan.

Hadiz, Vedi R., and Richard Robison. 2012. Political Economy and Islamic Politics: Insights from Indonesian Case. *New Political Economy* 17 (2): 137–156.

———. 2013. The Political Economy of Oligarchy and the Reorganization of Power in Indonesia. *Indonesia* 96: 35–58. https://doi.org/10.5728/indonesia.96.0033.

Hall, C. Michael. 2007. Tourism, Governance and the (Mis-)Location of Power. In *Tourism, Power and Space*, ed. A. Church and T. Coles, 247–268. London: Routledge.

Hameiri, Shahar, and Lee Jones. 2014. Regulatory Regionalism and Anti-Money Laundering Governance in Asia. *Australian Journal of International Affairs* 69 (2): 144–163. https://doi.org/10.1080/10357718.2014.978737.

Hardin, Garrett. 1968. The Tragedy of the Commons. *Science* 162: 1243–1248.

Harding, Andrew. 2012. The Politics of Law and Development in Thailand: Seeking Rousseau, Finding Hobbes. In *Law and Development in Asia*, ed. G.P. McAlinn and C. Pejovic, 109–136. Oxford: Routledge.

Harley, J. Brian. 1988. Maps, Knowledge, and Power. In *The Iconography of Landscape: Essays on the Symbolic Representation, Design and Use of Past Environments*, ed. D. Cosgrove and S. Daniels, 227–312. New York: Cambridge University Press.

Harman, Benny K. 2007. The Role of the Constitutional Court in Indonesian Legal Reform. In *Reforming Laws and Institutions in Indonesia: An Assessment*, ed. N. Sakumoto and H. Juwana, 47–81. Jakarta: Faculty of Law Press, University of Indonesia.

Harnish, David. 2005. Teletubbies in Paradise: Tourism, Indonesianisation and Modernisation in Balinese Music. *Yearbook of Traditional Music* 37: 103–123.

Haruya, Kagami. 2005. Regional Autonomy in Process: A Case Study in Bali 2001–2003. *Asian and African Area Studies* 5 (1): 46–71.

Harvey, David. 2003. *The New Imperialism*. Oxford: Oxford University Press.

———. 2005a. *A Brief History of Neoliberalism*. Oxford: Oxford University Press.

———. 2005b. *Spaces of Neoliberalization: Towards a Theory of Uneven Geographical Development*. Munchen: Franz Steiner Verlag.

Hasan, Rofiqi. 1998. *Tommy Suharto Versus Warga Pecatu: Warga Dijebak Menandatangani Tanah Turun Temurun Sebagai Milik Pemerintah*. SiaR News Service, APCHR, Murdoch University. https://www.mail-archive.com/siarlist@minipostgresql.org/msg00257.html.

Hassall and Associate. 1992. *Comprehensive Tourism Development Plan for Bali*. Denpasar: Directorate General of Tourism.

Hauser-Schaublin, Brigitta. 2003. The Precolonial Balinese State Reconsidered: A Critical Evaluation of Theory Construction on the Relationship Between Irrigation, the State, and Ritual. *Current Anthropology* 44 (2): 153–182. https://doi.org/10.1086/345824.

———. 2004. The Politics of Sacred Space: Using Conceptual Models of Space for Social-Political Transformation in Bali. *Bijdragen tot de Taal-, Land- en Volkenkunde* 160 (2/3): 283–314.

Hawkins, Donald E., and Shaun Mann. 2007. The World Bank's Role in Tourism Development. *Annals of Tourism Research* 34 (2): 348–363. https://doi.org/10.1016/j.annals.2006.10.004.

Healey, Patsy. 1997. *Collaborative Planning: Shaping Places in Fragmented Societies*. London: Macmillan.

Heath, Christopher. 2003. Industrial Policy and Intellectual Property in Japan and Beyond. In *Law and Development in East and Southeast Asia*, ed. C. Antons, 151–165. London and New York: RoutledgeCurzon.

Hendrawan, G., I.W. Nuarsa, W. Sandi, A.F. Koropitan, and Y. Sugimori. 2005. Numerical Calculation for the Residual Tidal Current in Benoa Bay-Bali Island. *International Journal of Remote Sensing and Earth Sciences* 2: 86–93.

Hermann, S., and E. Osinski. 1999. Planning Sustainable Land Use in Rural Areas at Different Spatial Levels Using GIS and Modelling Tools. *Landscape and Urban Planning* 46 (1–3): 93–101. https://doi.org/10.1016/S0169-2046(99)00050-X.

Heryanto, Ariel, and Vedi R. Hadiz. 2005. Post-Authoritarian Indonesia: A Comparative Southeast Asian Perspective. *Critical Asian Studies* 37 (2): 251–275.

Heynen, Nik, James McCarthy, Scott Prudham, and Paul Robbins, eds. 2007a. *Neoliberal Environments: False Promises and Unnatural Consequences*. London and New York: Routledge.

———. 2007b. Introduction: False Promises. In *Neoliberal Environments: False Promises and Unnatural Consequences*, ed. N. Hyenen, J. McCarthy, S. Prudham, and P. Robbins, 1–21. London and New York: Routledge.

Hirsch, Phillip. 2011. *Titling Against Grabbing? Critiques and Conundrums Around Land Formalisation in Southeast Asia*. Paper presented at the *International Conference on Global Land Grabbing*, University of Sussex, Brighton, UK, 6–8 April 2011.

Hitchcock, Michael, and I Nyoman Darma Putra. 2007. *Tourism, Development and Terrorism in Bali*. Hampshire: Ashgate.

Hobart, Mark. 2011. Bali as a Brand: A Critical Approach. *Journal of Bali Studies* 1 (1): 1–26.

Hobsbawn, Eric. 1983. Introduction: Inventing Traditions. In *The Invention of Tradition*, ed. E. Hobsbawn and T. Ranger, 1–14. Cambridge: Cambridge University Press.

Hofman, Bert, and Kai Kaiser. 2002. *The Making of the Big Bang and Its Aftermath: A Political Economy Perspective*. Paper presented at the conference *Can Decentralization Help Rebuild Indonesia?* Georgia State University, Atlanta, Georgia, May 1–3. http://www1.worldbank.org/publicsector/LearningProgram/Decentralization/Hofman2.pdf.

Howe, Leo. 2005. *The Changing World of Bali: Religion, Society and Tourism*. London and New York: Routledge.

Hudallah, Delik. 2010. *Peri-Urban Planning: Context, Approaches and Institutional Capacity*. PhD diss., University of Groningen.

Hudallah, Delik, and Johan Woltjer. 2007. Spatial Planning System in Transitional Indonesia. *International Planning Studies* 12 (8): 291–303. https://doi.org/10.1080/13563470701640176.

ICOMOS (International Council on Monuments and Sites). 2012. *Advisory Body Evaluation Concerning Cultural Landscape of Bali Province (Indonesia) No. 1194rev*. Paris: UNESCO World Heritage Centre.

Igoe, Jim, and Dan Brockington. 2007. Neoliberal Conservation: A Brief Introduction. *Conservation and Society* 5 (4): 432–449.

Indira, Made, and Mario Antonius Birowo. 2013. Obyektifitas Berita Lingkungan Hidup di Surat Kabar: Analisis Isi pada Berita Lingkungan dalam Pemberitaan Kasus Reklamasi Teluk Benoa Bali di Surat Kabar Periode 27 Juni 2013–18 Agustus 2013. *E-Journal UAJY*. http://e-journal.uajy.ac.id/5377/1/jurnal%20skripsi.pdf.

Indonesia. Coordinating Ministry of Economic Affairs (CMEA). 2011. *Master Plan Acceleration and Expansion of Indonesia Economic Development 2011–2025*. Jakarta: Republic of Indonesia.

Indonesia. Ministry of Culture and Tourism (MCT). 2011. *Nomination for Inscription on the UNESCO World Heritage List: Cultural Landscape of Bali Province*. Dossier Submitted to the Secretariat of World Heritage Committee, UNESCO.

Ionescu-Heroiu, M., M. Neagu, N. Taralunga, P. Ortiz, N. Pertovici, C. Moldovan, and E. Panescu. 2013. *Enhanced Spatial Planning: As a Precondition for Sustainable Urban Development*. Bucharest: World Bank/EU/ The Government of Romania.

Jayasuriya, Kanishka, ed. 1999. *Law, Capitalism and Power in Asia: The Rule of Law and Legal Institutions*. London and New York: Routledge.

———. 2012. Institutional Hybrids and the Rule of Law as a Regulatory Project. In *Legal Pluralism and Development: Scholars and Practitioners in Dialogue*, ed. B. Tamanaha, C. Sage, and M. Woolcock, 145–161. Cambridge: Cambridge University Press.

Jayasuriya, Kanishka, and Garry Rodan. 2007. Beyond Hybrid Regimes: More Participation, Less Contestation in Southeast Asia. *Democratization* 14 (5): 773–749. https://doi.org/10.1080/13510340701635647.

Jessop, Bob. 1998. The Rise of Governance and the Risks of Failure: The Case of Economic Development. *International Social Science Journal* 155: 29–45. https://doi.org/10.1111/1468-2451.00107.

———. 2004. *Spatial Fixes, Temporal Fixes, and Spatio-Temporal Fixes*. Published by the Department of Sociology, Lancaster University, Lancaster LA1 4YL, UK. http://www.comp.lancs.ac.uk/sociology/papers/jessop-spatio-temporal-fixes.pdf.

Juwana, Hikmahanto. 2004. Law and Development Under Globalization: The Introduction and Implementation of Competition Law in Indonesia. *Forum of International Development Studies* 27: 1–16.

———. 2005. Reform of Economic Laws and Its Effect on the Post-Crisis Indonesian Economy. *Developing Economies* XLIII (1): 72–90. https://doi.org/10.1111/j.1746-1049.2005.tb00253.x.

———. 2007. Human Rights Practice in the Post-Soeharto Era: 1998–2006. In *Reforming Laws and Institutions in Indonesia: An Assessment*, ed. N. Sakumoto and H. Juwana, 113–143. Jakarta: Faculty of Law Press, University of Indonesia.

Kam, Garrett. 1993. *Perception of Paradise: Images of Bali in the Arts*. Ubud: Yayasan Dharma Seni Museum Neka.

Karazija, Vyt. 2012. Stingy Bali Tourists, or Bali Government? *The Bali Times*, May 9. http://www.thebalitimes.com/2012/05/09/stingy-bali-tourists-or-bali-government/.

Kawakami, Mitsuhiko, Zhen-jiang Shen, Xiao-Shan Gao, and Ming Zhang, eds. 2013. *Spatial Planning and Sustainable Development: Approaches for Achieving Sustainable Urban Form in Asian Cities*. Dordrecht: Springer.

Kedar, Alexandre. 2003. On the Legal Geography of Ethnocratic Settler States: Notes Towards a Research Agenda. *Current Legal Issues* 5: 401–441.

Kelurahan Tanjung Benoa. 2014. *Profil Kelurahan Tanjung Benoa Tahun 2014*. Badung: Kelurahan Tanjung Benoa.

Kidd, Sue, and Dave Shaw. 2007. Integrated Water Resource Management and Institutional Integration: Realising the Potential of Spatial Planning in England. *Geographical Journal* 173 (4): 312–329. https://doi.org/10.1111/j.1475-4959.2007.00260.x.

Kong, Lily. 2001. Mapping 'New' Geographies of Religion: Politics and Poetics in Modernity. *Progress in Human Geography* 25 (2): 211–233. https://doi.org/10.1191/030913201678580485.

Korn, V.E. 1984 [1926]. The Village Republic of Tenganan Pegeringsingan. In *Bali Studies in Life, Thought and Ritual*. Dordrecht: Foris Publications.

Kough, Elizabeth. 2011. Heritage in Peril: A Critique of UNESCO's World Heritage Program. *Washington University Global Studies Law Review* 10: 593–615.

Kurnianingsih, Atiek. n.d. *Ketika 5000 Ha Lahan Sawah Bersaing Air dengan 4000 Kamar Hotel Berbintang*. http://wisnu.or.id/v2/ID/pdf/5000Ha%20Sawah_4000%20Kamar.pdf.

Lansing, Steve J. 2006. *Perfect Order: Recognizing Complexity in Bali*. New Jersey: Princeton University Press.

———. 2007 [1991]. *Priests and Programmers: Technologies of Power in the Engineered Landscape of Bali*. 2nd ed. Princeton: Princeton University Press.

Lanus, Sugi. 2014. *Ironi Bali Abad 21: Dari Tawan Karang Sampai Karang Ketawan (Reklamasi)*. https://budaya.wordpress.com/2014/10/03/ironi-bali-abad-21-dari-tawan-karang-sampai-karang-katawan-reklamasi/.

Lees, Susan H. 2001. Kicking Off the Kaiko: Instability, Opportunism, and Crisis in Ecological Anthropology. In *Ecology and the Sacred: Engaging the Anthropology of Roy A. Rappaport*, ed. E. Messer and M. Lambek, 49–63. Michigan: University of Michigan Press.

Lefebvre, Henri. 1991. *Production of Space*. Oxford: Blackwell.

Lewis, Jeff. 2006. Paradise Defiled the Bali Bombings and the Terror of National Identity. *European Journal of Cultural Studies* 9 (2): 223–242. https://doi.org/10.1177/1367549406063165.

Lewis, Jeff, and Belinda Lewis. 2009. *Bali's Silent Crisis: Desire, Tragedy, and Transition*. Lanham and Plymouth: Lexington Books.

Li, Mimi, Bihu Wu, and Liping Cai. 2008. Tourism Development of World Heritage Sites in China: A Geographic Perspective. *Tourism Management* 29: 308–319. https://doi.org/10.1016/j.tourman.2007.03.013.

Liefrinck, F.A. 1969 [1886–1887]. Rice Cultivation in Northern Bali. In *Bali: Further Studies in Life, Thought, and Ritual*, 3–4. The Hague: W. Van Hoeve.

Lindsey, Tim. 2004. Indonesia: Devaluing Asian Values, Rewriting Rule of Law. In *Asian Discourses of Rule of Law: Theories and Implementation of Rule of Law in Twelve Asian Countries, France and the U.S.*, ed. R. Peerenboom, 281–317. London and New York: Routledge.

Lisdiyono, Edy. 2008. *Legislasi Penataan Ruang: Studi tentang Pergeseran Kebijakan Hukum Tata Ruang dalam Regulasi Daerah di Kota Semarang*. PhD diss., Diponegoro University.

Lorenzen, Rachel. 2015. Disintegration, Formalisation or Reinvention? Contemplating the Future of Balinese Irrigated Rice Societies. *The Asia Pacific Journal of Anthropology* 16 (2): 176–193. https://doi.org/10.1080/14442213.2014.1000953.

Lorenzen, Rachel, and Stephan Lorenzen. 2005. *A Case Study of Balinese Irrigation Management: Institutional Dynamics and Challenges*. Paper presented at the *2nd Southeast Asian Water Forum*, Bali, Indonesia, 29 August–3 September 2005.

Lorenzen, Rachel, and Dik Roth. 2015. Paradise Contested: Culture, Politics and Changing Land and Water Use in Bali. *The Asia Pacific Journal of Anthropology* 16 (2): 99–105. https://doi.org/10.1080/14442213.2015.1006667.

LPPM (Lembaga Penelitian dan Pengabdian Masyarakat) Unud. 2013. *Ringkasan Laporan Akhir: Studi Kelayakan Revitalisasi Teluk Benoa*. Denpasar: Universitas Udayana.

Lucas, Anton, and Carol Warren, eds. 2013. *Land for the People: The State and Agrarian Conflict in Indonesia*. Athens: Ohio University Press.

MacCannell, Dean. 1992. *Empty Meeting Grounds: The Tourist Papers*. London: Routledge.

MacRae, Graeme. 2003. The Value of Land in Bali: Land Tenure, Land Reform and Commodification. In *Inequality, Crisis and Social Change in Indonesia: The Muted Worlds of Bali*, ed. T. Reuter, 145–167. London and New York: Routledge.

———. 2005. Negara Ubud: The Theatre-State in Twenty-First-Century Bali. *History and Anthropology* 16 (4): 393–413. https://doi.org/10.1080/02757200500344616.

———. 2010. If Indonesia Is Too Hard to Understand, Let's Start with Bali. *Journal of Indonesian Social Sciences and Humanities* 3: 11–36.

———. 2016. Good Intentions, Mixed Realities. *Inside Indonesia*, edition 125, July–September. http://www.insideindonesia.org/good-intentions-mixed-realities.

MacRae, Graeme, and I.W. Alit Arthawiguna. 2011. Sustainable Agricultural Development in Bali: Is the Subak an Obstacle, an Agent or Subject? *Human Ecology* 39 (1): 11–20. https://doi.org/10.1007/s10745-011-9386-y.

Mahmud, Tayyab. 2011. Law of Geography and the Geography of Law: A Post-Colonial Mapping. *Washington University Jurisprudence Review* 3 (1): 64–106.

Mamdani, Mahmood. 1996. *Citizen and Subject: Contemporary Africa and the Legacy of Late Colonialism*. New Jersey: Princeton University Press.

Marshall, Andrew. 2011. Holidays in Hell: Bali's Ongoing Woes. *Time*, April 9. http://content.time.com/time/world/article/0,8599,2062604,00.html.

Marx, Karl. 1990 [1867]. *Capital: A Critique of Political Economy Volume I*. London: Penguin Classics.

Massey, Doreen. 1994. *Space, Place, and Gender*. Minneapolis: University of Minnesota Press.

———. 2005. *For Space*. London: Sage Publications.

McCarthy, John. 1994. *Are Sweet Dreams Made of This? Tourism in Bali and Eastern Indonesia*. Northcote, Australia: Indonesia Resources and Information.

McCarthy, James, and Scott Prudham. 2004. Neoliberal Nature and the Nature of Neoliberalism. *Geoforum* 35: 275–283. https://doi.org/10.1016/j.geoforum.2003.07.003.

McCarthy, John, and Carol Warren. 2009. Communities, Environment and Local Governance in Reform Era Indonesia. In *Community, Environment and Local Governance in Indonesia: Locating the Commonweal*, ed. C. Warren and J.F. McCarthy, 1–25. London and New York: Routledge.

McEwon, Susie. 2011. Buying Property and Business in Bali. *Informer Magazine*, No. 64, November 2011.

Merry, Sally E. 2012. Legal Pluralism and Legal Culture: Mapping the Terrain. In *Legal Pluralism and Development: Scholars and Practitioners in Dialogue*, ed. B. Tamahana, C. Sage, and M. Woolcock, 66–82. Cambridge: Cambridge University Press.

Minca, Claudio. 2000. 'The Bali Syndrome': The Explosion and Implosion of Exotic Tourist Spaces. *Tourism Geographies* 2 (4): 389–403. https://doi.org/10.1080/146166800750035503.

Moeliono, Tristam Pascal. 2011. *Spatial Management in Indonesia: From Planning to Implementation – Cases from West Java and Bandung, A Socio-Legal Study*. Leiden University Open Access. https://openaccess.leidenuniv.nl/bitstream/handle/1887/18242/Proefschrift%20Tristam%20Moeliono%2021%20november%202011.pdf?sequence=.

Moore, Sally F. 1973. Law and Social Change: The Semi-Autonomous Social Field as an Appropriate Subject of Study. *Journal of Law and Society* 7 (4): 719–746.

Moroni, Stefano. 2007. Planning, Liberty and the Rule of Law. *Planning Theory* 6: 146–163. https://doi.org/10.1177/1473095207077586.

Mosse, David. 1997. The Symbolic Making of a Common Property Resource: History, Ecology and Locality in a Tank-Irrigated Landscape in South India. *Development and Change* 28: 467–504. https://doi.org/10.1111/1467-7660.00051.

MUDP (Majelis Utama Desa Pakraman) Bali. 2014. *Analisis UU Desa*. Denpasar: Majelis Utama Desa Pakraman Bali.

Muhajir, Anton. 2013. Wedakarna: Saya Pengennya Jadi Raja di Hati Rakyat. Balebengong, January 19. https://balebengong.id/uncategorized-id/wedakarna-saya-pengennya-jadi-raja-di-hati-rakyat.html.

———. 2014. Soal Reklamasi Teluk Benoa, Berikut Pesan ForBali untuk Jokowi. *Mongabay Indonesia*, September 28. http://www.mongabay.co.id/2014/09/28/soal-reklamasi-teluk-benoa-berikut-pesan-forbaii-untuk-jokowi/.

Mulyanto. 2015. Keberlakuan UU No. 6 Tahun 2014 Tentang Desa di Bali Dalam Perspektif Sosiologi Hukum. *Mimbar Hukum* 27 (3): 418–431.

Noronha, Raymond. 1979. Paradise Reviewed: Tourism in Bali. In *Tourism: Passport to Development? Perspectives on the Social and Cultural Effects of Tourism in Developing Countries*, ed. E. de Kadt, 177–204. Oxford: Oxford University Press.

Norrie, Alan. 1996. From Law to Popular Justice: Beyond Antinomialism. *Social & Legal Studies* 5 (3): 383–404.

North, Douglass C. 1990. *Institutions, Institutional Change and Economic Performance*. Cambridge: Cambridge University Press.

Oliphant, Roland. 2017. Bali Declares Rubbish Emergency as Rising Tide of Plastic Buries Beaches. *The Telegraph*, December 26. http://www.telegraph.co.uk/news/2017/12/28/bali-declares-rubbish-emergency-rising-tide-plastic-buries-beaches/. Accessed 30 Dec 2017.

Onishi, Norimitsu. 2010. Trying to Save Wild Tigers by Rehabilitating Them. *New York Times*, April 21. http://www.nytimes.com/2010/04/22/world/asia/22tigers.html?pagewanted=all&_r=1.

Operational Management Committee of Jatiluwih. 2014. *Laporan Keuangan Managemen Operasional Bulan Juli 2014*. Tabanan: Badan Pengelola Daya Tarik Wisata Desa Jatiluwih.

Pansus Otonomi Khusus (Otsus) Bali. 2007. *Talenta Bali Menuju Otonomi Khusus*. Denpasar: Bali Media.

Parimartha, I G. 2013. *Silang Pandang Desa Adat dan Desa Dinas di Bali*. Denpasar: Udayana University Press.

Parker, Lynn. 1989. *Village and State in 'New Order' Bali*. PhD diss., Australian National University.

———. 2003. *From Subjects to Citizens: Balinese Villagers in the Indonesian Nation-State*. Copenhagen: Nordic Institute of Asian Studies.

Pastika, I M. Mangku. 2013. Reklamasi Teluk Benoa untuk Masa Depan Bali. *Metro Bali: Opinion*, August 5. http://metrobali.com/2013/08/05/reklamasi-teluk-benoa-untuk-masa-depan-bali/.

Peck, Jamie, and Adam Tickell. 2002. Neoliberalizing Space. In *Spaces of Neoliberalism: Urban Restructuring in North America and Western Europe*, ed. N. Brenner and N. Theodore, 33–57. Malden, Oxford, and Carlton: Blackwell.

Pedersen, Lene. 2006. *Ritual and World Change in Balinese Princedom*. Durham, NC: Carolina Academic Press.

———. 2007. Responding to Decentralisation in the Aftermath of the Bali Bombing. *The Asia Pacific Journal of Anthropology* 8 (3): 197–215. https://doi.org/10.1080/14442210701519805.

Pedersen, Lene, and Wiwik Dharmiasih. 2015. The Enchantment of Agriculture: State Decentring and Irrigated Rice Production in Bali. *The Asia Pacific Journal of Anthropology* 16 (2): 141–156. https://doi.org/10.1080/14442213.2014.992458.

Peerenboom, Randall, ed. 2004. *Asian Discourses of Rule of Law: Theories and Implementation of Rule of Law in Twelve Asian Countries, France and the U.S.* London and New York: Routledge.

PEMSEA (Partnership in Environmental Management for the Seas of East Asia) and Bali PMO (Project Management Office). 2004. *Southeastern Coast of Bali: Initial Risk Assessment*. Quezon City, Philippines: GEF/UNDP/IMO and Bali National ICM Demonstration Project.

Pepinsky, Thomas. 2013. Pluralism and Political Conflict in Indonesia. *Indonesia* 96: 81–100. https://doi.org/10.5728/indonesia.96.0079.

Peters, Paul A. 2009. *Spatial Segregation in Complex Urban Systems: Housing and Public Policy in Santiago, Chile*. The University of Texas at Austin Repositories. https://repositories.lib.utexas.edu/handle/2152/18450.

Philippopoulos-Mihalopoulos, Andreas. 2010a. Spatial Justice: Law and the Geography of Withdrawal. *International Journal of Law in Context* 6 (3): 201–216. https://doi.org/10.1017/s174455231000011x.

———. 2010b. Law's Spatial Turn: Geography, Justice and a Certain Fear of Space. *Law, Culture and Humanities* 7 (2): 187–202. https://doi.org/10.1177/1743872109355578.

———. 2012. Mapping the Lawscape: Spatial Law and the Body. In *Beyond Text in Legal Education*, ed. M.D. Bonkowski and P. Maharg, 1–26. Edinburg: Edinburg University Press.

Picard, Michael. 1996. *Bali: Cultural Tourism and Touristic Culture*. Trans. Diana Darling. Singapore: Archipelago Press.

———. 2003. Touristification and Balinization in a Time of Reformasi. *Indonesia and the Malay World* 31 (89): 108–118. https://doi.org/10.1080/13639810304435.

———. 2011. Balinese Religion in Search of Recognition: From Agama Hindu Bali to Agama Hindu (1945–1965). *Bijdragen tot de Taal-, Land- en Volkenkunde (BKI)* 167 (4): 482–510. https://doi.org/10.1163/22134379-90003581.

Pitana, I Gde, and I.G. Setiawan Adi Putra. 2013. *Pariwisata Sebagai Wahana Pelestarian Subak dan Budaya Subak sebagai Modal Dasar Dalam Pariwisata*. Paper presented at *Bali Culture Congress Pengantar Budaya Subak sebagai Warisan Budaya Dunia*, Denpasar, 24–25 September 2013.

Platt, Rutherford. 2004. *Land Use and Society: Geography, Law, and Public Policy*. Rev. ed. Washington and London: Island Press.

Prasiasa, Dewa. 2010. *Pengembangan Pariwisata dan Keterlibatan Masyarakat di Desa Wisata Jatiluwih Kabupaten Tabanan*. PhD diss., Udayana University.

Pratiwi, Wiwik D. 2004. *Tourism and Built Environment Changes in Traditional Communities: Kuta and Nusa Dua, Bali, Indonesia as the Case Studies*. Sheffield: The University of Sheffield. http://etheses.whiterose.ac.uk/12845/1/419575.pdf.

Priemus, Hugo. 1997. Spatial Planning and Housing Policy: On the Ties and That Bind. *Netherlands Journal of Housing and the Built Environment* 12 (1): 77–90. https://doi.org/10.1007/BF02502624.

Pringle, Robert. 2004. *A Short History of Bali: Indonesia's Hindu Realm*. Crows Nest, Australia: Allen & Unwin.

Pusat Pengendalian Pembangunan Ekoregion (PPPE) Bali & Nusa Tenggara. 2015. *Buku Saku Data Kehutanan Provinsi Bali*. Denpasar: Kementerian Lingkungan Hidup dan Kehutanan.

Ramstedt, Martin. 2009. Regional Autonomy and Its Discontents: The Case of Post-New Order Bali. In *Decentralization and Regional Autonomy in Indonesia: Implementation and Challenges*, ed. C. Holtzappel and M. Ramstedt, 329–379. Leiden and Singapore: IIAS and ISEAS Press.

———. 2013. Religion and Disputes in Bali's New Village Jurisdiction. In *Religion in Disputes: Pervasiveness of Religious Normativity in Disputing Processes*, ed. F. von Benda-Beckmann, K. von Benda-Beckmann, M. Ramstedt, and B. Turner, 111–128. New York: Palgrave Macmillan.

Razzaque, Jona. 2013. *Environmental Governance in Europe and Asia: A Comparative Study of Institutional and Legislative Frameworks*. London and New York: Routledge.

Reed, Maureen, and Shannon Bruyneel. 2010. Rescaling Environmental Governance, Rethinking the State: A Three Dimensional Review. *Progress in Human Geography* 34: 646–653. https://doi.org/10.1177/0309132509354836.

Reuter, Thomas, ed. 2003. *Inequality, Crisis and Social Change in Indonesia: The Muted Worlds of Bali*. London and New York: Routledge.

———. 2009. Origin and Precedence: The Construction and Distribution of Status in the Highlands of Bali. In *Precedence: Social Differentiation in the Austronesian World*, ed. M. Vischer, 13–49. Canberra: ANU E-Press.

Rideng, I W., I N. Nurjaya, I M. Subawa, and P. Djatmika. 2015. Assembly of Desa Pakraman Role as Resolver of Dispute Between Desa Pakraman in Bali. *International Journal of Applied Sociology* 5 (3): 131–138.

Rijadi, Prasetijo. 2004. Pembangunan Kebijakan Penataan Ruang dalam Konteks Konsep Kota Berkelanjutan: Studi Kebijakan Penataan Ruang di Kota Surabaya. *Dialogue JIAKP* 1 (2): 231–244.

Robertson, Susan, Xavier Bonal, and Roger Dale. 2002. GATS and the Education Service Industry: The Politics of Scale and Global Reterritorialization. *Comparative Education Review* 46 (4): 472–495. https://doi.org/10.1086/343122.

Robinson, Geoffrey. 1995. *The Dark Side of Paradise: Political Violence in Bali*. Ithaca and London: Cornell University Press.

Robison, Richard. 1986. *Indonesia: The Rise of Capital*. Jakarta and Kuala Lumpur: Equinox Publishing.

———. 2014. Political Economy and the Explanation of the Islamic Politics in the Contemporary World. In *Between Dissent and Power: The Transformation of Islamic Politics in the Middle East and Asia*, ed. Khoo Boo Teik, Vedi Hadiz, and Yoshihiro Nakanishi, 19–41. London: Palgrave Macmillan.

Robison, Richard, and Vedi R. Hadiz. 2004. *Reorganising Power in Indonesia: The Politics of Oligarchy in an Age of Markets*. London and New York: RoutledgeCurzon.

Rodan, Garry, Kevin Hewison, and Richard Robison. 2006. Theorising Markets in Southeast Asia: Power and Contestation. In *The Political Economy of Southeast Asia: Markets, Power and Contestation*, ed. G. Rodan, K. Hewison, and R. Robison, 1–38. Oxford: Oxford University Press.

Roosa, John. 2006. *Pretext for Mass Murder: The September 30th Movement and Suharto's Coup d'Etat in Indonesia*. Madison: University of Wisconsin Press.

Roth, Dik. 2003. *Ambition, Regulation and Reality: Complex Use of Land and Water Resources in Luwu, South Sulawesi, Indonesia*. Library of Wageningen University. http://library.wur.nl/WebQuery/wurpubs/fulltext/19978.

———. 2009. Property and Authority in a Migrant Society: Balinese Irrigators in Sulawesi, Indonesia. *Development and Change* 40 (1): 195–217. https://doi.org/10.1111/j.1467-7660.2009.01511.x.

Roth, Dik, and Gede Sedana. 2015. Reframing Tri Hita Karana: From 'Balinese Culture' to Politics. *The Asia Pacific Journal of Anthropology* 16 (2): 157–175. https://doi.org/10.1080/14442213.2014.994674.

Rottenberg, Catherine. 2013. The Rise of Neoliberal Feminism. *Cultural Studies*: 1–20. https://doi.org/10.1080/09502386.2013.857361.

Rukmana, Deden. 2015. The Change and Transformation of Indonesian Spatial Planning After Suharto's New Order Regime: The Case of the Jakarta Metropolitan Area. *International Planning Studies* 20 (4): 350–370. https://doi.org/10.1080/13563475.2015.1008723.

Sage, Caroline, and Michael Woolcock. 2005. *Breaking Legal Inequality Traps: New Approaches to Building Justice System for the Poor in Developing Countries.* Paper presented at the *World Bank Conference, New Frontiers of Social Policy: Developing in a Globalizing World*, Arusha, Tanzania, December 12–14.

———. 2012. Introduction: Legal Pluralism and Development Policy, Scholars and Practitioners in Dialogue. In *Legal Pluralism and Development: Scholars and Practitioners in Dialogue*, ed. B. Tamanaha, C. Sage, and M. Woolcock, 1–17. Cambridge: Cambridge University Press.

Sahlins, Marshall. 1974. *Stone Age Economies*. Chicago and New York: Aldine-Atherton, Inc.

Santos, Boaventura de Sousa. 1987. Law: A Map of Misreading. Toward a Postmodern Conception of Law. *Journal of Law and Society* 14 (3): 279–302. https://doi.org/10.2307/1410186.

———. 2005. Beyond Neoliberal Governance: The World Social Forum as Subaltern Cosmopolitan Politics and Legality. In *Law and Globalisation from Below: Towards a Cosmopolitan Legality*, ed. B.d.S. Santos and C.A. Redriguez-Garavito, 29–63. Cambridge: Cambridge University Press.

Sardjono, Agus. 2007. The Development of Indonesian Intellectual Property Laws in the Legal Reform Era: Between Need and Reality. In *Reforming Laws and Institutions in Indonesia: An Assessment*, ed. N. Sakumoto and H. Juwana, 145–186. Jakarta: Faculty of Law Press, University of Indonesia.

Sawita, Roro. 2012. Tanah, Landreform dan Kemelut 1965. In *Melawan Lupa: Narasi-Narasi Komunitas Taman 65 Bali*, ed. A. Wardana and R. Hutabarat, 1–12. Denpasar: Taman65 Press.

Schroll, Henning, Jan Andersen, and Bente Kjargard. 2012. Carrying Capacity: An Approach to Local Spatial Planning in Indonesia. *The Journal of Transdisciplinary Environmental Studies* 11 (1): 27–39.

Schulte Nordholt, Henk. 1991. *State, Village, and Ritual in Bali: A Historical Perspective*. Amsterdam: VU University Press.

———. 2000. Localizing Modernity in Colonial Bali During the 1930s. *Journal of Southeast Asian Studies* 31 (1): 101–114.

———. 2007. *Bali, An Open Fortress 1995–2005: Regional Autonomy, Electoral Democracy and Entrenched Identities*. Singapore: NUS University Press.

———. 2010. *Spell of Power: A History of Balinese Politics, 1650–1940*. Leiden: KITLV Press.

———. 2011. Dams and Dynasty, and the Colonial Transformation of Balinese Irrigation Management. *Human Ecology* 39: 21–27. https://doi.org/10.1007/s10745-010-9330-6.

Schulte Nordholt, Henk, and Garry van Klinken, eds. 2007. *Renegotiating Boundaries: Local Politics in Post-Soeharto Indonesia*. Leiden: KITLV Press.

Scott, James C. 1985. *Weapon of the Weak: Everyday Forms of Peasant Resistance*. New Haven and London: Yale University Press.

———. 1990. *Domination and the Art of Resistance: Hidden Transcripts*. New Haven: Yale University Press.

———. 1998. *Seeing Like a State: How Certain Schemes to Improve the Human Condition Have Failed*. New Haven and London: Yale University Press.

Shibata, Kuniko. 2008. Neoliberalism, Risk, and Spatial Governance in the Developmental State: Japanese Planning in the Global Economy. *Critical Planning* 15: 92–118.

Silanawa, Nyoman. 2008. *Pengaturan Perlindungan Kawasan Lindung Dalam Pengaturan Daerah Provinsi Bali Nomor 3 Tahun 2005 Tentang Recana Tata Ruang Wilayah Provinsi Bali*. Master diss., Udayana University.

Smith, Neil. 1995. Remarking Scale: Competition and Cooperation in Prenational and Postnational Europe. In *Competitive European Peripheries*, ed. H. Eskelin and F. Snickars, 59–75. Berlin: Springer.

Smith, Laurajane. 2006. *Uses of Heritage*. London: Routledge.

Sorensen, Eva, and Peter Triantafillou. 2009. The Politics of Self-Governance: An Introduction. In *The Politics of Self-Governance*, ed. E. Sorensen and P. Triantafillou, 1–22. Surrey and Burlington: Ashgate.

Spiertz, H.L. 1991. The Transformation of Traditional Law: A Tale of People's Participation in Irrigation Management on Bali. *Landscape and Urban Planning* 20: 189–196.

———. 2000. Water Rights and Legal Pluralism: Some Basic of a Legal Anthropological Approach. In *Negotiating Water Rights*, ed. B.R. Bruns and R.S. Meinzen-Dick, 162–199. New Delhi: Vistaar Publications.

Springer, Simon. 2010. *Cambodia's Neoliberal Order: Violence, Authoritarianism, and the Contestation of Public Space*. Oxford: Routledge.

Strauss, Sophie. 2011. Water Conflicts Among Different User Groups in South Bali, Indonesia. *Human Ecology* 29: 69–79. https://doi.org/10.1007/s10745-011-9381-3.

———. 2015. Alliances Across Ideologies: Networking with NGOs in a Tourism Dispute in Northern Bali. *The Asia Pacific Journal of Anthropology* 16 (2): 123–140. https://doi.org/10.1080/14442213.2014.1001996.

Suartika, G.A.M. 2005. *Vanishing Paradise: Planning and Conflict in Bali*. PhD diss., University of New South Wales.

Suasta, Putu, and Linda Connor. 1999. Democratic Mobilization and Political Authoritarianism: Tourism Developments in Bali. In *Staying Local in the Global Village: Bali in the Twentieth Century*, ed. R. Rubinstein and L.H. Connor, 91–122. Honolulu: University of Hawai'i Press.

Subadra, I.N., and N.M. Nadra. 2006. Dampak Ekonomi, Social-Budaya, dan Lingkungan Pengembangan Desa Wisata di Jatiluwih-Tabanan. *Jurnal Manajemen Pariwisata* 5: 46–64.

Sudhiatmika, I Dewa Nyoman Ketha. 2010. *Orang Bali Yang Lain: Proses Saling Me-'Liyan'-kan Antara Orang Nusa Penida dan Bali Daratan*. Master Thesis. Yogyakarta: Universitas Sanata Dharma.

Sudiarta, Ketut, I Gede Hendrawan, Ketut Sarjana Putra, and I Made Iwan Dewantama. 2013. *Kajian Modeling Dampak Fungsi Teluk Benoa Untuk Sistem Pendukung Keputusan (Decision Support System) Dalam Jejaring KKP Bali*. Denpasar: Conservation International Indonesia.

Suharyo. 2011. *Laporan Penelitian tentang Pembentukan Otonomi Khusus di Bali dan Pengaruhnya Bagi Keutuhan NKRI*. Jakarta: Badan Pembinaan Hukum Nasional, Kementerian Hukum dan HAM RI.

Sukada and Mentra. 2010. *Selayang Pandang Kelurahan Tanjung Benoa*. Badung: Kelurahan Tanjung Benoa.

Suksma, K. 2015. Antara Tambling Lampung dan Benoa Bali. *Kompasiana*, September 27. http://www.kompasiana.com/kadeksuksma/antara-tambling-lampung-dan-benoa-bali_5606ef380e93739607bfaeee.

Sumiya, Sukhbaatar. 2012. Law and Development, FDI, and the Rule of Law in Post-Soviet Central Asia: The Case of Mongolia. In *Law and Development in Asia*, ed. G.P. McAlinn and C. Pejovic, 137–163. Oxford: Routledge.

Sunarta, I Nyoman, and Abd Rahman As-syakur. 2015. Study on the Development of Water Crisis in Bali Island in 2009 and 2013. *E-Journal of Tourism Udayana University* 2 (1): 45–57.

Sunarta, N., M.S. Mahendra, A.A.S. Wiranatha, and S.A. Paturusi. 2015. Study of Land-Use Change on Tourism Area Using High Spatial Resolution of Remote Sensing Imagery. *International Journal of Multidisciplinary Educational Research* 8 (1): 17–31.

Suryani, Luh De. 2014. Investor Yakinkan Reklamasi Benoa Tak Rusak Lingkungan. Benarkah? *Mongabay*, December 8. http://www.mongabay.co.id/2014/12/08/investor-yakinkan-reklamasi-benoa-tak-rusak-lingkungan-benarkah/.

Suryani, L., A. Page, C.B.J. Lesmana, I.D.G. Basudewa, and R. Taylor. 2009. Suicide in Paradise: Aftermath of the Bali Bombings. *Psychological Medicine* 39 (8): 1317–1323. https://doi.org/10.1017/s0033291708004893.

Sutawan, Nyoman. 2001. Eksistensi Subak di Bali: Mampukah Bertahan Menghadapi Berbagai Tantangan. *SOCA: Socio-Economic of Agriculture and Agribusiness* 1 (2): 1–10.

Suweda, I Wayan. 2013. *Analisis Dampak Bangkitan Lalu Lintas Terhadap Rencana Kawasan Reklamasi Teluk Benoa Bali*. Paper presented at *Konferensi Nasional Teknik Sipil 7*, Sebelas Maret University, Solo, Central Java, 24–26 October 2013.

Tamanaha, Brian. 2012. The Rule of Law and Legal Pluralism in Development. In *Legal Pluralism and Development: Scholars and Practitioners in Dialogue*, ed. B. Tamanaha, C. Sage, and M. Woolcock, 34–49. Cambridge: Cambridge University Press.

Tamanaha, Brian, Caroline Sage, and Michael Woolcock, eds. 2012. *Legal Pluralism and Development: Scholars and Practitioners in Dialogue*. Cambridge: Cambridge University Press.

Taylor, William M. 2006. *The Geography of Law: Landscape, Identity and Regulation*. Oxford and Portland: Hart Pub Limited.

Thanadsillapakul, Lawan. 2012. Thailand and Legal Development. In *Law and Development in Asia*, ed. G.P. McAlinn and C. Pejovic, 305–328. Oxford: Routledge.

Timothy, Dallen. 2007. Empowerment and Stakeholder Participation in Tourism Destination Communities. In *Tourism, Power and Space*, ed. A. Church and T. Coles, 199–216. London: Routledge.

Topsfield, Jewel. 2017. 'Bali is Safe': Indonesian President Urges Tourists to Holiday in Bali. *Sidney Morning Herald*, December 23. https://www.smh.com.au/world/bali-is-safe-indonesian-president-urges-tourists-to-holiday-in-bali-20171223-h09n8f.html.

Tourtellot, Jonathan B. 2007. 111 Islands. *National Geographic Traveler*. http://sanibelislandvacations.com/img/reviews/National-Geographic-Sanibel-Island.pdf.

Trisnawati, H. n.d. Dampak Perkembangan Infrastruktur Pariwisata terhadap Konflik Air di Kabupaten Badung dan Tabanan. *E-Journal UNUD*. http://ojs.unud.ac.id/index.php/jip/article/view/3671/2699.

Turk, Austin T. 1976. Law as a Weapon in Social Conflict. *Social Problems* 23 (3): 276–291.

TWBI (Tirta Wahana Bali Internasional). 2014a. *Proposal Reklamasi: Revitalisasi Teluk Benoa Bali*. Jakarta: PT Tirta Wahana Bali Internasional.

———. 2014b. *Kerangka Acuan Analisis Dampak Lingkungan Hidup (KA-ANDAL) Revitalisasi Teluk Benoa di Kabupaten Badung dan Kota Denpasar Bali dan Kegiatan Tambang (dalam Menunjang Kegiatan Reklamasi Teluk Benoa) di Kabupaten Lombok Timur, Provinsi Nusa Tenggara Barat*. Jakarta: PT Tirta Wahana Bali Internasional.

TWBI and Dinamika Atria Raya. 2016. *Analisis Dampak Lingkungan Hidup (ANDAL) Rencana Kegiatan Revitalisasi Teluk Benoa dan Penambangan Pasir Laut (Dalam Menunjang Kegiatan Revitalisasi Teluk Benoa)*. Jakarta: PT TWBI and PT Dinamika Atria Raya.

UNDP/USAID/World Bank. 2006. *Bali Beyond the Tragedy: Impact and Challenges for Tourism-led Development in Indonesia*. Washington, DC: World Bank.

UNECE (United Nations Economic Commission for Europe). 2008. *Spatial Planning: Key Instrument for Development and Effective Governance with Special Reference to Countries in Transition*. New York and Geneva: United Nations.

Urry, John. 1985. Social Relations, Space and Time. In *Social Relations and Spatial Structures*, ed. D. Gregory and J. Urry, 20–48. Hong Kong: Macmillan Publishers Ltd.

———. 2002. *The Tourist Gaze*. 2nd ed. London: Sage.

Utting, Peter, and Ann Zammit. 2009. United Nations-Business Partnership: Good Intentions and Contradictory Agendas. *Journal of Business Ethics* 90: 39–56. https://doi.org/10.1007/s10551-008-9917-7.

Uwiyono, Aloysius. 2007. Indonesian Labor Law Reform Since 1998. In *Reforming Laws and Institutions in Indonesia: An Assessment*, ed. N. Sakumoto and H. Juwana, 187–203. Jakarta: Faculty of Law Press, University of Indonesia.

van Klinken, Gerry. 2007. Return of the Sultans: The Communitarian Turn in Local Politics. In *The Revival of Tradition in Indonesian Politics: The Deployment of Adat from Colonialism to Indigenism*, ed. J. Davidson and D. Henley, 149–169. London and New York: Routledge.

van Rossum, Wibo, and Sanne Taekema. 2013. Introduction to Law as Plural Phenomenon: Confrontations of Legal Pluralism. *Erasmus Law Review* 6 (3/4): 155–157.

Van Uytsel, Steven. 2012. China's Antimonopoly Law and Recurrence to Standards. In *Law and Development in Asia*, ed. G.P. McAlinn and C. Pejovic, 241–275. Oxford: Routledge.

Vanberg, Viktor. 1996. Hayek's Theory of Rules and the Modern State. In *Jurisprudence of Liberty*, ed. S. Ratnapala and G.A. Moens, 47–66. Sydney: Butterworths.

Vel, Jacqueline A.C., and Adriaan W. Bedner. 2015. Decentralisation and Village Governance in Indonesia: The Return to the Nagari and the 2014 Village Law. *The Journal of Legal Pluralism and Unofficial Law* 47 (3): 493–507. https://doi.org/10.1080/07329113.2015.1109379.

Vickers, Adrian. 2003. A Paradise Bombed. *Griffith Review* 1: 91–98.

———. 2011. Bali Rebuilds Its Tourism Industry. *Bijdragen tot de Taal-, Land- en Volkenkunde* 167 (4): 459–481. https://doi.org/10.1163/22134379-90003580.

———. 2012. *Bali: A Paradise Created.* 2nd ed. Tokyo, Vermont and Singapore: Tuttle Publishing.

Vink, Markus. 2003. 'The World's Oldest Trade': Dutch Slavery and Slave Trade in the Indian Ocean in the Seventeenth Century. *Journal of World History* 14 (2): 131–177.

von Benda-Beckmann, Keebet. 1981. Forum Shopping and Shopping Forums: Dispute Processing in a Minangkabau Village in West Sumatera. *Journal of Legal Pluralism* 19: 117–159. https://doi.org/10.1080/07329113.1981.10756260.

von Benda-Beckmann, Franz. 2002. Who's Afraid of Legal Pluralism. *Legal Pluralism and Unofficial Law* 47: 37–82. https://doi.org/10.1080/07329113.2002.10756563.

von Benda-Beckmann, Keebet. 2009. Anthropological Perspective on Law and Geography. *PoLAR: Political and Legal Anthropology Review* 32 (2): 265–278. https://doi.org/10.1111/j.1555-2934.2009.01043.x.

von Benda-Beckmann, Franz, and Keebet von Benda-Beckmann. 2009. Contested Spaces of Authority in Indonesia. In *Spatializing Law: An Anthropological Geography of Law in Society*, ed. F. von Benda-Beckmann, K. von Benda-Beckmann, and A. Griffiths, 115–135. Surrey: Ashgate.

———. 2011. Myths and Stereotypes About Adat Law: A Reassessment of Van Vallenhoven in the Light of Current Struggles over Adat Law in Indonesia. *Bijdragen tot de Taal-, Land- en Valkenkunde* 167 (2/3): 167–195.

———. 2013. *Political and Legal Transformations of an Indonesian Polity: The Nagari from Colonisation to Decentralisation.* Cambridge: Cambridge University Press.

von Benda-Beckmann, Franz, Keebet von Benda-Beckmann, and Anne Griffiths. 2009. Space and Legal Pluralism: An Introduction. In *Spatializing Law: An Anthropological Geography of Law in Society*, ed. F. von Benda-Beckmann, K. von Benda-Beckmann, and A. Griffiths, 1–27. Surrey: Ashgate.

Wardana, Agung. 2012. Bali: Antara 'Surga' dan 'Neraka'. *Balebengong: Opinion*, June 1. http://balebengong.net/opini/2012/06/01/bali-antara-surga-dan-neraka.html.

———. 2013. Melihat Kembali Merosotnya Wacana 'Ajeg Bali'. *Journal of Bali Studies* 3 (2): 211–216.

———. 2014a. *Adat-Dinas in the Cultural Landscape of Bali Province: Defining the Domain of World Heritage Within a Pluralistic Legal Setting.* Paper presented at the *International Conference on State Policy and the Cultural Politics of Heritage-Making in East and Southeast Asia*, Singapore, January 16–17.

———. 2014b. Alliances and Contestations in the Legal Production of Space: The Case of Bali. *Asian Journal of Comparative Law* 9: 145–171. https://doi.org/10.1017/S2194607800000958.

———. 2015. Debating Spatial Governance in the Pluralistic Institutional and Legal Setting of Bali. *Asia Pacific Journal of Anthropology* 16 (2): 106–122. https://doi.org/10.1080/14442213.2014.997276.

———. 2016. *Conserving Cultural Heritage in the Neoliberal Times of Bali.* Paper presented at the *International Conference on Heritage as Aid and Diplomacy*, Leiden, the Netherlands, May 26–28.

———. 2018. Legal Engineering in a Contest over Space in Bali. *Australian Journal of Asian Law* 19 (1): 1–12. Available at SSRN: https://ssrn.com/abstract=3239776.

Wardana, Agung, and Carol Warren. forthcoming. *Adat and Dinas: Balinese Villages and State-Society Relations Under the 2014 Village Law.* Paper presented at the *International Workshop on New Law, New Villages? Changing Rural Indonesia*, Leiden, the Netherlands, May 19–20.

Warren, Carol. 1990. *The Indonesia.* Working Paper 66 Monash University. Clayton, VIC: Centre of Southeast Asian Studies, Monash University.

———. 1993. *Adat and Dinas: Balinese Communities in the Indonesian State.* Kuala Lumpur and New York: Oxford University Press.

———. 1998. Tanah Lot: The Cultural and Environmental Politics of Resort Development in Bali. In *The Politics of Environment in Southeast Asia: Resources and Resistance*, ed. P. Hirsch and C. Warren, 229–261. London and New York: Routledge.

———. 2005a. Community Mapping, Local Planning and Alternative Land Use Strategies in Bali. *Geografisk Tidsskrift – Danish Journal of Geography* 105 (1): 29–41. https://doi.org/10.1080/00167223.2005.10649524.

———. 2005b. Mapping Common Futures: Customary Communities, NGOs and the State in Indonesia's Reform Era. *Development and Change* 36 (1): 49–73. https://doi.org/10.1111/j.0012-155X.2005.00402.x.

———. 2007. Adat in Balinese Discourse and Practice: Locating Citizenship and the Commonweal. In *The Revival of Tradition in Indonesian Politics: The Deployment of Adat from Colonialism to Indigenism*, ed. J. Davidson and D. Henley, 170–202. London and New York: Routledge.

———. 2009. Off the Market? Elusive Links in Community-Based Sustainable Development Initiatives in Bali. In *Community, Environment and Local Governance in Indonesia: Locating the Commonweal*, ed. C. Warren and J. McCarthy, 197–226. London: Routledge.

———. 2012. Risk and the Sacred: Environment, Media and Public Opinion in Bali. *Oceania* 82: 294–307. https://doi.org/10.1002/j.1834-4461.2012.tb00135.x.

———. 2013. Legal Certainty for Whom? Land Contestation and Value Transformation at Gili Trawangan, Lombok. In *Land for the People: The State and Agrarian Conflict in Indonesia*, ed. A. Lucas and C. Warren, 243–273. Athens: Ohio University Press.

———. 2016. Leadership, Social Capital and Coastal Community Resource Governance: The Case of the Destructive Seaweed Harvest in West Bali. *Human Ecology*. https://doi.org/10.1007/s10745-016-9832-y.

———. n.d. Unfinished Business: Environmental Impact Assessment and Political Legacies in the Bali Turtle [Serangan] Island Development Case. Unpublished.

Warren, Carol, and Anton Lucas. 2013. Indonesia's Land Titling Program (LAP) – The Market Solution? In *Land for the People: The State and Agrarian Conflict in Indonesia*, ed. A. Lucas and C. Warren, 93–113. Athens: Ohio University Press.

Warren, Carol, and John F. McCarthy. 2009. *Community, Environment and Local Governance in Indonesia: Locating the Commonweal*. London and New York: Routledge.

Warren, Carol, and Agung Wardana. 2018. Sustaining the Unsustainable?: Environmental Impact Assessment and Overdevelopment in Bali. *Asia Pacific Journal of Environmental Law* 21 (2): 101–125.

Wartha Bakti Mandala, PT. 2012. *Draft Laporan Akhir Rencana Tata Ruang (RTR) Kawasan Tempat Suci Pura Luhur Uluwatu*. Denpasar: PT. Wartha Bakti Mandala.

Watson, Alan. 1977. *Society and Legal Change*. Edinburgh: Scottish Academic Press.

Wegener, Michael. 2000. New Spatial Planning Models. *International Journal of Applied Earth Observation and Geoinformation* 3 (3): 224–237. https://doi.org/10.1016/s0303-2434(01)85030-2.

Whitecross, Richard. 2009. Migrants, Settlers and Refugees: Law and the Contestation of 'Citizenship' in Bhutan. In *Spatializing Law: Anthropological Geography of Law in Society*, ed. F. von Benda-Beckmann, K. von Benda-Beckmann, and A. Griffiths, 57–74. Surrey: Ashgate.

Wiber, Melanie G. 2009. The Spatial and Temporal Role of Law in Natural Resource Management: The Impact of State Regulation of Fishing Spaces. In *Spatializing Law: Anthropological Geography of Law in Society*, ed. F. von Benda-Beckmann, K. von Benda-Beckmann, and A. Griffiths, 75–94. Surrey: Ashgate.

Wilmsen, Edwin. 2009. The Regulation of Commodity Exchange in Southern Africa During the Eighth to Fifteenth Centuries CE. In *Spatializing Law: Anthropological Geography of Law in Society*, ed. F. von Benda-Beckmann, K. von Benda-Beckmann, and A. Griffiths, 177–193. Surrey: Ashgate.

Windia, Wayan. 2013. Penguatan Budaya Subak Melalui Pemberdayaan Petani. *Journal of Bali Studies* 3 (2): 137–158.

———. 2015. Bali 'Tong Sampah' Kejahatan. *Majalah Bali Post*, Edisi 26 Juni–5 Juli.

Windia, I Wayan P. 2010. *Dari Bali Mawacara Menuju Bali Santi*. Denpasar: Udayana University Press.

Winters, Jeffrey. 2013. Oligarchy and Democracy in Indonesia. *Indonesia* 96: 11–33. https://doi.org/10.5728/indonesia.96.0099.

World Bank. 1974. *Appraisal of Bali Tourism Project Indonesia*. Washington, DC: The International Bank for Reconstruction and Development.

———. 2006. *The World Bank Legal Review Vol 2: Law, Equity, and Development*. Washington, DC: The World Bank and Martinus Nijhoff Publishers.

Yamashita, Shinji. 2003. *Bali and Beyond: Exploration in the Anthropology of Tourism*. Trans. J.S. Eades. New York: Berhahn Books.

Yudasuara, I Ketut. 2015. Pengelolaan Daya Tarik Wisata Berbasis Masyarakat di Desa Pecatu, Kuta Selatan, Kabupaten Badung. *Jurnal Master Kajian Pariwisata* 2 (1): 132–149.

Legislation, Legal Texts and Case

Legislation

1960 National Law No. 5 on Basic Agrarian Law.
1979 National Law No. 5 on Village Government.
1992 National Law No. 24 on Spatial Planning.
1994 National Law No. 12 on Land and Building Tax.
1999 National Law No. 22 on Regional Government.
2004 National Law No. 10 on the Establishment of Legislation.
2004 National Law No. 32 on Regional Government.
2007 National Law No. 25 on Investment.
2007 National Law No. 26 on Spatial Planning.
2007 National Law No. 27 on Coastal Area and Small Island Management.
2009 National Law No. 32 on the Protection and Management of the Environment.
2014 National Law No. 6 on Village.
2014 National Law No. 32 on Regional Government.
1996 National Government Regulation No. 40 on the Right of Management.
1997 National Government Regulation No. 24 on Land Registration.
1999 National Government Regulation No. 27 on Environmental Impacts Assessment.
2012 National Government Regulation No. 27 on the Environmental Permit.
2011 Presidential Decree No. 45 on Spatial Planning for Denpasar, Badung, Gianyar and Tabanan (Sarbagita) Metropolitan Areas.
2012 Presidential Decree No. 122 on Reclamation in Coastal Areas and Small Islands.
2014 Presidential Decree No. 51 on the Amendment of the Presidential Decree No. 45/2011 on Spatial Planning for Denpasar, Badung, Gianyar and Tabanan (Sarbagita) Metropolitan Areas.
2001 Provincial Regional Regulation No. 3 on Desa Pakraman.
2005 Provincial Regulation No. 3 on Spatial Planning for Bali Province.
2009 Provincial Regulation No. 16 on Spatial Planning for Bali Province.
2012 Provincial Regulation No. 9 on Subak.
2011 Badung District Regulation No. 25 on the Management of Tourism in Uluwatu Temple's Complex.
2013 Badung District Regulation No. 26 on Spatial Planning for Badung.

2011 Denpasar Municipal Regulation No. 27 on Spatial Planning for Denpasar.
2012 Tabanan District Regulation No. 11 on Spatial Planning for Tabanan.
2014 Tabanan District Regulation No. 6 on Green Zones.
1988 Governor Regulation No. 15 on Tourism Areas in Bali.
2010 Governor Regulation No. 32 on the Establishment of the Governing Assembly for Bali's Cultural Heritage.
2012 Governor Decision No. 2138/02-C/HK/2012 on the Permit for the Utilisation, Development and Management of Water Areas of Benoa Bay to the TWBI.
2013 Governor Decision No. 1727/01-B/HK/2013 on the Permit for Undertaking Feasibility Studies to the Utilisation, Development and Management of Water Areas of Benoa Bay.
2000 Badung District Head Decision No. 79 on Detailed Plans for the Arrangement of the Uluwatu Temple Complex.
2013 Tabanan District Head Decision No. 84 on the Establishment of the Jatiluwih Tourism Governing Body.

Legal Texts

Bhisama PHDI Pusat No 11/Kep./1/PHDIP/1994 concerning *Bhisama* on Sacred Areas and Temples' Sanctity Radius.
Awig-Awig of Desa Pakraman Pecatu.
Awig-Awig of Subak Jatiluwih.
Perarem of Subak Tempek Kedamaian.
Decision of the Assembly of Sabha Pandita PHDI Pusat No. 1/KEP/SP Parisada/IV/2016 concerning Benoa Bay Sacred Areas.
Decision of the Assembly of Sabha Pandita PHDI Pusat No. 3/Sabha Pandita Parisada/IV/2016 concerning Recommendation on the Besakih National Tourism Strategic Areas and the Benoa Bay Areas.

Case Law

Anak Agung Alit Gede Sardjitha & I Gusti Alit Netra on behalf of Uluwatu Foundation v. Badung District Head [2010] Supreme Court, No. 149 PK/TUN/2010.
Badan Permusyawaratan Desa (BPD/Village Consultative Assembly) v Governor of Bali [2010] Supreme Court, No. 35 P/HUM/2010.

Desa Pakraman Pecatu v. Governor of Bali [2010] Supreme Court of Indonesia, No. 34 P/HUM/2010.

Gubernur Bali I Made Mangku Pastika v. PT Bali Post & Nyoman Wirata [2011] Civil Court of Denpasar, No. 723/Pdt.G/2011/PN.Dps.

I Made Deg v. Governor of Bali [2010] Supreme Court of Indonesia, No. 30 P/HUM/2010.

I Wayan Puja v. Governor Bali [2010] Supreme Court of Indonesia, No. 32 P/HUM/2010.

Uluwatu Foundation v. Badung Office of Land Bureau and Pengempon Pura Luhur Uluwatu Jurit [2011], Denpasar Administrative Court, No. 07/G/2011/PTUN.Dps.

Uluwatu Foundation v. Badung Office of Land Bureau and Pengempon Pura Luhur Uluwatu Jurit [2012], Surabaya Administrative Court of Appeal, No. 03/B/2012/PT.TUN.SBY.

Verdict of the Constitutional Court No. 3/PUU-VIII/2010 on *Adat* Forest.

Wahana Lingkungan Hidup Indonesia (Walhi) v. Governor of Bali [2014], Supreme Court, No. 151 K/TUN/2014.

Newspapers

Antara News
Bali Post
Berita Bali
Bisnis Indonesia
CNN Indonesia
Hukumonline
Jakarta Globe
Jakarta Post
Kabar Nusa
Koran Sindo
Liputan 6 News
Media Indonesia
Merdeka Online
Metro Bali
Mongabay Indonesia
Nusa Bali
Okezone News

Pos Bali
Radar Bali – Jawa Post
Tribun Bali

Websites

www.indonesiainvestment.org
www.lpdpecatu.or.id
www.phdi.or.id

Index[1]

[1] Note: Page numbers followed by 'n' refer to notes.

A. Wardana, *Contemporary Bali*, https://doi.org/10.1007/978-981-13-2478-9

S

T

U